Culturally Proficient
Inclusive Schools

Culturally Proficient Inclusive Schools

All Means ALL!

Delores B. Lindsey

Jacqueline S. Thousand

Cynthia L. Jew

Lori R. Piowlski

CORWIN

A SAGE Publishing Company

FOR INFORMATION:

Corwin

A SAGE Company

2455 Teller Road

Thousand Oaks, California 91320

(800) 233-9936

www.corwin.com

SAGE Publications Ltd.

1 Oliver's Yard

55 City Road

London EC1Y 1SP

United Kingdom

SAGE Publications India Pvt. Ltd.

B 1/I 1 Mohan Cooperative Industrial Area

Mathura Road, New Delhi 110 044

India

SAGE Publications Asia-Pacific Pte. Ltd.

3 Church Street

#10-04 Samsung Hub

Singapore 049483

Program Director: Jessica Allan

Senior Associate Editor: Kimberly Greenberg

Editorial Assistant: Katie Crilley

Production Editor: Amy Schroller

Copy Editor: Karin Rathert

Typesetter: C&M Digitals (P) Ltd.

Proofreader: Dennis W. Webb

Indexer: Sheila Bodell

Cover Designer: Alexa Turner

Marketing Manager: Charline Maher

ISBN 978-1-5063-5624-2

This book is printed on acid-free paper.

MIX
Paper from
responsible sources
FSC
www.fsc.org   FSC® C012947

17 18 19 20 21 10 9 8 7 6 5 4 3 2 1

Contents

Foreword

Douglas Fisher and Nancy Frey

We cannot even begin to count the number of school mission statements that we have seen that include the phrase "All children can learn." Of course they can! We have decades worth of evidence that indicate that all children can learn and how they do so (e.g., Donovan & Bransford, 2005). So, why do schools keep writing what is obvious to so many? Because all children don't, in fact, learn what they were supposed to. Yes, they *can* learn, but there are still so many gaps in students' mastery of content. Perhaps schools would be better served if they revised their mission statements to read, "All children can learn when they are taught well, in an inclusive environment in which the adults around them are culturally proficient." That would actually be more accurate and would point to the responsibilities that educators have for ensuring that the outcomes of schooling are equitable for every student. The simple statement, "all children can learn," could be construed to place responsibility (or blame) on the students. The revised mission statement makes it clear that educators have an essential role to play in students' learning.

We do not suggest that classrooms become teacher-directed, didactic places where teachers tell students information and ask them to regurgitate it later. Rather, we advocate that classrooms be places where responsibility for learning is shared—teachers doing their part, and students doing theirs. There has to be a balance in these responsibilities, with the adults monitoring the impact that instruction has on students learning. To enact the revised mission statement, high quality instruction would have to become the norm. As we have noted, "Every student deserves a great teacher, not by chance, but by design" (Fisher, Frey, & Hattie, 2016, p. 2). This requires identifying "what works" so that effective learning environments can be designed. And it requires that teachers are supported in becoming great. We do not subscribe to the belief that great teachers are born. We know that great teachers work hard to create environments that are conducive to learning.

In this important and timely book, Lindsey, Thousand, Jew, and Piowlski address the need for all truly meaning all within a culturally proficient inclusive education framework. The authors give a straightforward approach for educators to closely examine the vision and mission statements and the actual evidence of who they say they are and who they serve. The alignment of an inclusive vision with inclusive actions is the heart of this book. The authors present concepts and terms, descriptive case stories, and user-friendly tables and figures to guide readers to use and build on the twin concepts of Cultural Proficiency and Inclusive Education to guide educators who are serious about educating all learners to develop and implement an action plan for transformational schooling. The authors provide readers to respond with "Yes, I know!" to the inquiry, "What can work for any learner?"

In support of the approach offered in this book, we are particularly taken with John Hattie's (2009) technique of answering the "what works" question. Using meta-analyses in which he aggregates large numbers of research studies, he has identified a wide range of influences on students' learning that educators can use to make instructional decisions. For example, Hattie showed that ability grouping, tracking, and grade-level retention were not effective approaches for promoting student learning, despite their widespread practice in many schools. These less-than-effective approaches consume valuable professional learning time that could have been spent elsewhere.

In terms of ensuring equity, Hattie showed that teacher and student expectations for learning are a powerful influence, yet many educators do not hold high expectations for all students. He also showed that positive teacher-student relationships foster learning. And he showed that teacher clarity contributed in positive ways to students' learning. We have argued that teacher clarity is critical for students who are at most risk for educational failure (Echevarria, Frey, & Fisher, 2016). We believe that students deserve to know what they are expected to learn and how they will know they have learned it. Again, it's about shared responsibility for learning between teachers and students.

Hattie's synthesis of research, now with over 300 million students represented, helps educators make decisions about their instructional repertories. But that's only part of the equation. Equity requires that students have access to the regular classroom and that they receive the supports they need to excel and that their aspirations are fostered and realized. That's where this book comes in. The authors have developed a framework that integrates cultural proficiency and inclusive education. Both are necessary ingredients that must be added to high quality instruction for students to excel.

Inclusive education demands that all students have access to the general education classroom with the supports and services necessary to be successful. Far too many students are taught in segregated settings, often by teachers who themselves have not demonstrated mastery of the general education curriculum. It's hard to imagine that students who have difficulty learning will have a fair chance when their teacher doesn't actually know the history, science, art, or language development expected of students at a given grade level. Special educators, by and large, excel at providing students with personal supports, differentiating curriculum and instruction, and peer negotiation. They are not, as a group, experts in the general education curriculum standards. Students with disabilities need both—general educators who understand the content expectations and special educators who can increase access to that content.

Cultural proficiency demands that educators understand, value, and respect the unique backgrounds of students' heritage. A lack of Cultural Proficiency telegraphs messages to students that their lives are less important than others or that they have deficits that must be corrected. Culturally proficient educators make connections with their students, celebrate their gifts, and recognize opportunities for learning. Culturally proficient inclusive educators do their work first. They know who they are in relation to the students and communities they serve. Culturally proficient inclusive education is not an add-on program. It is the lens through which all other work is viewed. This approach allows, invites, and expects educators to work together in ways that value all learners and their families for the assets they bring to the classroom and school.

As Mahatma Gandhi noted, "The true measure of any society can be found in how it treats its most vulnerable members." We believe that the same can be said of schools. Ensuring that students who are most vulnerable realize their aspirations should be a measure that we use to determine the impact that schools have within a community. In this book, the authors articulate a system for ensuring that all students, including those who are most vulnerable, achieve their dreams. By taking actions to ensure that every student realizes his or her aspirations, as described in this book, we can tutor the next generations of citizens to not only respect, but deeply value individual differences. As these graduates become leaders within our communities, they will be equipped to act to ensure that equity is not a dream deferred.

Doug Fisher (dfisher@mail.sdsu.edu) and Nancy Frey (nfrey@mail.sdsu .edu) are professors in the Department of Educational Leadership at San Diego State University and teacher leaders at Health Sciences High and Middle College.

Acknowledgments

We are appreciative for the many people who have contributed to the completion of this book: the support of our families, the contributions of many professional colleagues, and the time and input from parents of children and youth with special education needs. This book is written to honor and acknowledge their support for this work.

For me, Delores, cowriting this book has been another path of my personal and professional learning journey. I continue to grow as an educator and a writer. We knew this was the right time to write this book. As educators throughout the United States and Canada continue to strive to deliver for high-level instruction, curriculum, and assessment for all students, we wanted to offer all educators the lens of Cultural Proficiency and the Inclusive Schooling approach as one way to achieve that goal. I thank my co-authors for their expertise, their willingness to share their experiences, and their patience with me as a learner. I greatly appreciate and acknowledge the many general educators and special educators with whom we work (the composite case stories) who continue to confront issues of inequity and injustice on behalf of students and employees. Students, their parents, and educators are the people for whom we do this work. Thanks to Corwin's editorial staff for the professional and personal support you always give us. I give special thanks, always, to my husband, Randy, for being my cowriter and best friend.

For me, Jacque, cowriting this book provided me the opportunity to deeply reflect upon my career and experience gratefulness beyond measure. First, I am so very grateful to Dr. Wayne Fox, my former boss at the University of Vermont's University Affiliated Program, for authoring, in 1981, the federally funded model demonstration project, *Homecoming*. Thank you for hiring me to be on the dream team with Tim Fox, Joanne Godek, and Rich Reid to assist seventeen Vermont schools in five districts to show the world that students with severe disabilities and their teachers could transition from regional segregated classrooms far from their homes and learn, be loved, and thrive in their home school general education classrooms. The *Homecoming* experience was a true professional gift and the springboard for all that I have learned and done since. I also am most grateful to the many individuals in the schools and communities across the country who were the early pioneers, believing we could and would educate all students with disabilities in Inclusive Schools and classrooms. The Barriers you experienced and overcame are described and illustrated through stories in this book. The actions you took and the processes and strategies you invented have endured, been refined, and are included in each chapter. The world is indebted to your courageous willingness to step into the unknown and invent the academic and social support and differentiation that is the hallmark of quality Inclusive Education. Thank you, today, to the cross-disciplinary team members who are rapidly making co-teaching the organizational structure and practice for weaving the knowledge and skills of the "masters of content" (i.e., general educators) with the complementary knowledge and skills of the "masters of access" (i.e., special educators, English language development and other related services personnel and specialists) in order to deliver a Multi-Tiered System of Supports personalized for every child. Thank you to my friends and to the students and colleagues at California State University San Marcos, who make life and teaching and learning a daily joy. And thank you to Dr. Richard Villa, my husband of thirty-five plus years, for being such a brilliant and inspiration leader and "partner in crime" in this journey of life and inclusion. It's been and continues to be a blessed road to travel.

For me, Cindy, being part of this team and cowriting this book has been a chance to merge my professional work with my personal life. Definitely honoring the work of those who have dedicated their lives to living social justice and educating our children has been the focus of this book. Many thanks to Drs. Randy and Delores Lindsey, Dr. Jacqueline Thousand, and Dr. Lori Piorwiski for adding theory and experience to this body of work. I wish to thank Dawn Evenson, Amber Raskin, and the entire team at Santa Clarita Valley International Charter School who created the vision and live each day with the commitment and dedication to educating my child, Jordyn. For me, the face of special education and Cultural Proficiency is the face of my daughter, Jordyn. She is the inspiration and the reason that I do this work and share our story. She is my hero. I dedicate this work to my daughter, Kiera, who with unfailing calmness and daily commitment works tirelessly with her sister. Finally, as a parent, I am part of that "voice of parents who have children with diverse needs" who will "change the world for our children."

For me, Lori, cowriting this book has provided me the opportunity to reflect, dig into, and learn about what educators need to work through concerning Inclusive Education during a time where change is essential to ensuring the success of ALL students in preK–12 schools. Teacher support and professional opportunities are crucial for teachers to be able to grow in their Cultural Proficiency from the inside out. I extend my gratitude to Dr. Marilyn Grady at the University of Nebraska, Lincoln. She has not only been a mentor to me but an inspiration to what it means to lead others through their personal and professional journeys! She lifts up those around her with high expectations and a kind heart. I feel very fortunate to be supported by Minnesota State University, Mankato's College of Education, where I have been encouraged to stretch my wings through extensive national research presentations. I treasure the opportunities to share research and learn from colleagues around the country! The co-authors of this book have given me the gift of writing with them. Thank you for this incredible opportunity to learn from you and provide information for educators about Inclusive Education. Having experience teaching both special educators and general educators, I know that all educators will benefit from this book! Lastly, I thank my husband, John, and my kids, Cole, Nick, and Sydney, for your abundance of moral support—without all of you I would not be where I am now!

Our colleagues at Corwin have been and continue to support our work in deep, authentic ways. Jessica Allen and Dan Alpert, our acquisitions editors, continuously serve as "friends of the work of equity," and both embody the commitment to social justice we associate with Corwin. We greatly appreciate and acknowledge the work of Doug Fisher and Nancy Frey, who graciously agreed to write the foreword for this book. They are our friends, mentors, and heroes, having shaped the landscape of general and special education in the United States and the world through their many books, practical monthly "Show and Tell" column in the Association for Curriculum Development *Education Leadership* journal, and their modeling of truly Inclusive Schooling and community-school partnerships at the Health Science High and Middle College in San Diego. Nancy and Doug were instrumental in establishing the school, and they continue to teach at the school and lead and guide as beacons of caring and effective education for every student.

About the Authors

Delores B. Lindsey, PhD, retired as an associate professor at California State University San Marcos (CSUSM) and continues to serve as an instructor in the Joint Doctoral Program. While a full-time faculty member at CSUSM for nine years, she served as the Education Administration Program coordinator for six and taught in the master's degree program option for Education Administration and Leadership as well as the Joint Doctoral Program. Prior to coming to the CSUSM, she was visiting faculty at Pepperdine University in the master of arts in Education Leadership program and Educational Leadership doctoral program. Dr. Lindsey served as a middle grade and high school teacher, assistant principal, principal, and county office of education administrator. She received her PhD from Claremont Graduate University. Her primary area of research is creating, leading, and sustaining Culturally Proficient teaching and learning environments. She is co-author of numerous articles and books: *Culturally Proficient Instruction: A Guide for People Who Teach, 3rd ed.* (2012), *Culturally Proficient Coaching: Supporting Educators to Create Equitable Schools* (2007), *Culturally Proficient Learning Communities: Confronting Inequities Through Collaborative Inquiry* (2009), and *A Culturally Proficient Response to the Common Core: Ensuring Equity Through Professional Learning* (2015).

Using the lens of Cultural Proficiency, Dr. Lindsey helps educational leaders examine their policies and practices as well as their individual beliefs and values about cross-cultural communication. Her message to her audiences focuses on socially just educational practices and diversity as assets to be nurtured. Dr. Lindsey facilitates educators to develop their own inquiry and action research. Her favorite reflective questions are: *Who are we?* and *Are we who we say we are?* Often, her favorite co-lecturer and co-author, Dr. Randall Lindsey, also her husband, joins her to co-teach.

Jacqueline S. Thousand, PhD, is professore emerita at California State University San Marcos, where she designed and coordinated special education professional preparation and master's degree programs in the College of Education, Health, and Human Services. She previously taught at the University of Vermont, where she directed Inclusion Facilitator and Early Childhood Special Education graduate and postgraduate programs and coordinated federal grants, which, in the early 1980s, pioneered the inclusion of students with moderate and severe disabilities in general education classrooms of their local schools. Prior to working as a university teacher, Dr. Thousand served as a special educator in Chicago area and Atlanta public schools and as the coordinator of early childhood special education services for children ages three through six in the Burlington, Vermont, area. Dr. Thousand is a nationally known teacher, author, systems change consultant, and disability rights and Inclusive Education advocate. She is the author of twenty-one books and numerous research articles and chapters on issues related to Inclusive Education, organizational change strategies, differentiated instruction and universal design for learning, co-teaching and collaborative teaming, cooperative group learning, creative problem solving, positive behavior supports, and now, culturally proficient special education. Dr. Thousand is actively involved in international teacher education and inclusive education endeavors and serves on the editorial boards of several national and international journals.

Cynthia L. Jew, PhD, is a professor at California Lutheran University, where she serves as chair and program director of the Counselor Education Department. Dr. Jew teaches courses in resiliency, school systems, and the foundational course in Cultural Proficiency for candidates receiving their master's degree in Counselor Education. Dr. Jew also consults using the cultural proficiency model in the Educational Leadership Department. Dr. Jew serves as a student support consultant to a public charter school. She received her PhD in school psychology from the University of Denver, and her primary area of research is developing culturally aware counselors and advocates in school and college environments. She is a co-author of the 2008 Corwin publication, *Culturally Proficient Inquiry: A Lens for Identifying and Examining Educational Gaps.* She is also the author of the *Resiliency Skills and Abilities Scale.*

Using the lens of Cultural Proficiency, Dr. Jew prepares school and college counselors. She is a single mother of two adopted daughters from China. Kiera provides the "test" of whether we are living the vision of Cultural Proficiency; Jordyn, who uses cochlear implants, provides the reason for doing this cultural proficiency work. They are teachers, leaders, and the "soul" of the community into which we all hope to grow.

 **Lori R. Piowlski** is an assistant professor in the Elementary Education Department at Minnesota State University, Mankato, and is dedicated to advancing access and equity in teacher education. She received her PhD from the University of Nebraska, Lincoln, in Educational Administration in Higher Education. Dr. Piowlski also consults with New Knowledge United as a subject matter expert in the areas of special education, English language learners, literacy, elementary education, and assessment, by developing, aligning, and optimizing higher education eLearning courses. Her research interests are in the areas of preparation of cultural proficient teachers, the national edTPA teacher performance assessment, parent engagement in schools, partnership development in schools, and mentoring/induction of new teachers. She serves as an edTPA national consultant and presents frequently at national conferences. Prior to her higher education faculty roles, she worked with diverse populations as a preK through Grade 12 elementary and special education teacher, which ignited her passion to study culturally proficient teaching. She continues to empower future teachers to celebrate their ability to execute global cultural competence, allowing them to differentiate their instruction to meet the needs of all twenty-first century students.

This book is lovingly dedicated to school-aged children and youth with the hope that they will have teachers and administrators who find and nurture their strengths and bring joy to learning through the use of the principles and strategies such as those offered in this book.

---◆---

I dedicate this book to Josiah and Jordyn and their families.

Josiah, our great-nephew, is an amazing young man who has cerebral palsy. He has taught me perseverance, tenaciousness, and laughter when confronting challenges.

Jordyn, our granddaughter, is an impressive young lady who is deaf and wears cochlear implants. She inspires others and me with her love for life and learning.

—Delores

---◆---

I dedicate this book to my school-aged grandchildren and great-grandchildren:

Arden Sofia Villa-Nguyen
Amaya Rosalie Villa-Nguyen
Daryn Aeioun Chanan
Alaina Chantrea Reynoso-Yem
Kalven Richard Chheng Rath
Rosalynn Sovanary Phan Rath

—Jacque

---◆---

I dedicate this book to Jordyn and Kiera, who love without conditions or boundaries and bring hope to me when the world seems hopeless.

This book is offered in memory of Mary, my life soul-mate of twenty-nine years, who died too early and whom I miss every day.

—Cindy

---◆---

I dedicate this book to my husband, John;
my children, Nicole, Nick, Ashley, and Sydney;
and my mom and dad.

They all inspire me to create change and make a difference, big and small, remembering that even the smallest stone makes a ripple in the water.

—Lori

Part I

Commitment to ALL!

The *Every Student Succeeds Act* (ESSA, 2016), the reauthorization of No Child Left Behind Act (2002), is the nation's general education law and stands as the opportunity for all students, irrespective of their abilities, to receive support and resources to achieve at high levels. One of the primary goals and requirements of the mandate is to keep students with disabilities on track for success. All students must have access to the general education curriculum. Federal assurances are in place to keep students with disabilities from being denied access to graduation, college required courses, and other high-level curriculum requirements. ESSA identifies that students eligible for special education are general education students first and must receive access to and all of the benefits of participation in the general curriculum and the general education environment. Today, more than ever, general and special educators have opportunities to work in unison to better serve every students to achieve at levels higher than ever before. With the backing of federal and state mandates and state college and career readiness standards, educators can collaborate to provide equitable educational supports and services to all students. In this book we illustrate how *ALL* can mean *ALL*.

Chapter 1 provides the rationale for why we were compelled and needed to write this book. We describe the structure of the book and invite you to join us on the journey of *reflection-on-action* and *reflection-for-action*.

Chapter 2 introduces the four Tools of Cultural Proficiency and describes how they can be used as lenses to examine and implement inclusive educational practices. The tools are intended to inform you about the importance of knowing who you are and the values, beliefs, and assumptions you hold about who learns and how they learn. Inclusive Education is defined and through a vivid classroom snapshot, illustrates how general and special educators can create and sustain a rich and nurturing educational environment through collaborative partnerships, such as co-teaching.

Chapters 3 and 4 introduce the reader to the Barriers to Cultural Proficiency and the most instrumental tool—Overcoming the Barriers to Cultural Proficiency. Barriers to culturally proficient and Inclusive Schooling are identified and described in Chapter 3. Barrier busting principles, assumptions, and actions are offered in Chapter 4.

The tools that energize educators to move forward and transcend Barriers are the Guiding Principles and five Essential Elements defined in Chapter 2. The Guiding Principles are described in greater detail in Chapter 4. The Essential Elements are illustrated in Chapters 5 through 9 of the second part of this text. At the end of each of Chapters 5 through 9, a case story presents an Essential Element in action. The Lakeside Union School District is a composite district from our combined experiences and serves as the setting for educators who use the elements of cultural competency to create and sustain an inclusive educational environment. Chapter 10 guides you to develop a plan of action for Inclusive Schooling using the five Essential Elements.

We provide two resources following Chapter 10. Resource A, "Book Study Guide," is offered for you to use with groups or individually to enhance and deepen knowledge, understanding, and commitment to the concepts and actions of culturally proficient Inclusive Schooling. Resource B, "Cultural Proficiency and Inclusive Schooling Books' Essential Questions," details a list of books about Cultural Proficiency and Inclusive Schooling. Essential questions help you focus on key concepts for each book.

NOTE TO THE READER: YOU AND WE

We use the pronoun *you* to personalize our relationship to the readers of this book. The pronoun *we* refers to the co-authors of the book. The co-authors have combined our years of work as educators, school administrators, parents, and scholar practitioners to bring you our experiences, our research, and our best thinking about the importance of responding to the need for educating all learners, unlike anytime in this nation's history.

THE FORMAT OF THIS BOOK

This book is designed to be used as an individual guide for reflection and action. It is also designed to be used with interdisciplinary colleagues—in small groups or in large groups—as a book study for developing a school or district action plan. The stakeholders of the groups may be parents, administrators, general and special education teachers, higher education faculty, and paraprofessionals. Each chapter has lines for you to compose your responses to prompts about the text and suggestions for reflection and action at the end of each chapter. The reflections and the dialogues with your co-learners will deepen your learning. Your learning community will be enhanced by the diversity of your perspectives, experiences, and expertise. We wish you well and now join you on your life-long journey of creating and sustaining culturally proficient inclusive educational environments for all learners.

1

What Are Equity and Access Gaps? Why Do They Persist?

When school goals are developed from mission statements without shared values and clear vision, then goals and action plans will be nebulous and the mission will, again, not address the needs of all students in the school.

Frattura & Capper (2007, p. 41)

GETTING CENTERED

As an introductory activity for reading this book, examine your school and district's mission and vision statements. In what ways are the statements aligned with your values, beliefs, and assumptions? In what ways are the statements aligned with your day to day actions as a member of the school/district community? In what ways are the values, beliefs, assumptions, and actions of your colleagues aligned with these vision and mission statements? What might be some responses to the Frattura and Capper quote when you share it with your colleagues?

_____

_____

_____

_____

WHEN MANDATES MEET MORALITY

This book focuses on what it takes for all educators to believe they can educate all learners in ways that embrace students' cultures as assets and students' learning differences as just that—differences rather than deficits. Believing we can educate all learners is a powerful belief statement that drives action in classrooms and schools. Not too many years ago, educators would proclaim, _I believe all students can learn!_ The statement became part of nearly every vision and mission statement, slogans in classrooms, posted on banners throughout school buildings, and chanted as mantras across classrooms far and near. Of course, the proclamation was intended as a powerful belief statement to guide teachers' actions in the classroom. One problem was the widely accepted statement developed silent exceptions that were attached to the end. _All students can learn . . . except the students with special needs; All students can learn . . . except those kids who live in the trailer park . . . except those kids who don't speak English . . . except those kids who have an aide with them all the time._ The responsibility for learning seemed to be on the students rather the educators.

This book takes the statement, _"We believe all educators can educate all learners!"_ and places the responsibility with all educators, school and district administrators, support personnel including paraprofessionals, custodians, front office staff members, and school board members. Truly, we are all in this business of educating learners together. And along with us are our partners: parents, community members, health and human services, and other support agencies. As partners, who hold a belief system that is inclusive of educating all learners and educators who possess a skill set that is grounded in culturally relevant and equitable instructional practices, we can create a culturally proficient inclusive educational environment.

We present the four Tools of Cultural Proficiency and the Inclusive Schooling practices and philosophies as a framework for action to facilitate you and other educators to be able to provide equitable educational opportunities to meet the needs of _all_ learners, especially learners who may benefit from special education services. We provide case stories, tables, figures, and reflective and dialogic activities to engage you in applying the four Tools and Inclusive Schooling practices to your current context. This book is written to guide you on your cultural proficiency journey in support of inclusive classrooms and schools.

Certainly, we recognize that an abundance of laws already exist to support our work with children and youth with identified disabilities and other learning challenges. In 1975, Congress passed the Education for All Handicapped Children's Act (Public Law 94-142), which guarantees that all students with disabilities receive a free and appropriate public education in the least restrictive environment. Since then, the law's name has changed, most recently, in 2004, to the Individuals with Disabilities Education Improvement Act (IDEIA). Regardless of name changes, the law has provided the foundation for Inclusive Education and codified advancements in policy and practices that forward Inclusive Education. Bolstering IDEIA is the Every Student Succeeds Act (ESSA), the 2015 reauthorization of the Elementary and Secondary Education Act. ESSA maintains the act's legacy as a civil rights law in at least three ways. First, it ensures that states and districts hold schools accountable for the progress of every student subgroup (e.g., students with disabilities). Second, it dedicates resources and supports so that students with disabilities, English learners, and vulnerable student subgroups (e.g., children of low-income, homeless, or migrant worker families) have equitable access to rigorous curriculum and quality educators. Third, it requires districts to use evidence-based, whole-school interventions in its lowest-performing schools and in schools where subgroups (e.g., students with IEPs, English learners) persistently underperform. In short, ESSA articulates an expectation that schools foster and be held accountable for high educational standards, equality of opportunity to learn, and excellence in student performance for every child.

Even with these mandates in place, students with special educational needs continue to lag behind their counterparts in achievement, according to performance data in today's data-rich environments. As a matter of fact, we emphasize these education gaps persist today, despite an abundance of federal laws and compliance checks. Many of today's schools now describe these achievement gaps as issues of disproportionality (Linn & Hemmer, 2011). Disproportionality may be defined as the "over- or under-representation of a given population group, often defined by racial and ethnic backgrounds, but also defined by socioeconomic status, national origin, English proficiency, gender, and sexual orientation, in a specific population category" (Elementary and Middle School Technical Assistance Center, n.d., para.1). Disproportionality in special education involves the inappropriate over-identification, misidentification, and/or misclassification of certain groups of students as special education eligibility. Sullivan (2011) describes the over-representative identification, and placement of culturally and linguistically diverse students and students of color in special education as a long-standing phenomenon, which "strongly indicates systemic problems in inequity, prejudice, and marginalization within the education system" (p. 318).

General educators and members of the special education community have an ongoing need to learn about and have tools to recognize institutional Barriers, individual beliefs, and deeply held societal or personal assumptions that foster and perpetuate these gaps. We address the need to narrow and close these gaps through the content of this book. Our goal through intentional actions is to support and teach students who require and need differentiated learning and behavior supports to easily access and progress in the general education curriculum to fully participate in their educational lives. We focus the content of this book on what to do when *mandates meet morality.*

REFLECTION

To what extent are you aware of the laws that pertain to students with special educational needs? In what ways do these opening comments resonate with you and your context? What are the moral issues facing educators in preK–12 schools and classrooms today regarding equity and access? What gaps and disproportionality exist in your school/district? What's being done to address these issues?

_____

_____

_____

_____

WHY WE WROTE THIS BOOK

We drew from our personal and professional experiences to write this book. We are parents, grandparents, and active community members. We are teachers, administrators, education consultants, and higher education faculty. We work directly in the field with soon-to-be teachers and administrators, psychologists and counselors, and community organizers. We wanted to use our collective experiences, combined knowledge, collaborative skills, and multiple perspectives to address the often stated and never challenged vision statement: *We believe that all students can learn.* While we do have a strong belief that students can and will learn, the evidence is clear that many educators, in fact, must not believe all students can learn because the education gap still persists. As stated by co-authors Lindsey, Kearney, Estrada, Terrell, and Lindsey (2015), "You are also aware that though the Common Core State

Standards implies through use of phrases such as 'all students,' our reality is that equity can never be assumed—it must be explicitly expressed" (p. 11).

This book is NOT written for special educators, specifically. The book is written for *all* who interact with and support students who have a documented learning need, have educational gaps, and/or who receive special education services. When we say *all*, we refer to anyone in the community where children and youth learn, work, and play. We have written this book to demonstrate a shift in thinking from putting the full responsibility for student's learning on "they, the students" to our responsibility "we, the educators." Certainly, we are advocates for students being engaged in their own learning with parents as partners in the student's educational life. We support the belief that students must take responsibility for their own learning and progress. And more than that, we believe and value the role of educators have in creating conditions for students and parents to be able to their best work and their best thinking. That is why we wrote this book. We are supporting you to use the lens of Cultural Proficiency to create classrooms and schools that are inclusive of all learners.

This book went to press shortly after the inauguration of the 45th president of the United States and following a contentious presidential election season, unlike any the co-authors have experienced over our many years. The issues that many voters faced were grounded in personal values, beliefs, and assumptions about the candidates and the two-party system of our democracy. Social media, false news sites, and hostile candidates' attack ads forced our educators, now more than ever before, to create safe spaces and places for students to think, talk, and learn with each other. We cannot forecast what the next years will bring, but we can provide an inclusive educational environment where students and their families are valued, respected, and appreciated as learners. Our democracy is designed for us to express our rights and freedoms. Our classrooms are the perfect places for our students to express and experience that democracy in action. Let's work together to provide an educational environment where *ALL* truly means *ALL*, irrespective of who our elected officials are. Hopefully, schools and programs will benefit from state and federal programs/funds to support all students. However, we as educators cannot wait on those resources. We must act together and act now!

WHAT IS CULTURALLY PROFICIENT INCLUSIVE EDUCATION?

Throughout the book we will use a variety of terms to support your learning. The following terms are defined as they are used with the context of inclusion and equity using the lens of cultural proficiency.

Access involves opportunities for preK–12 students to fully participate in and benefit from high-quality curricular, instruction, and assessment experiences in school.

Cultural proficiency learning and leading is distinguished from other diversity and equity approaches in that it is anchored in the belief that, in order to be effective in a cross-cultural setting, a person must learn one's own assumptions, beliefs, and values about people and cultures that are different from him or herself.

Culturally proficient inclusive educational environments are created and maintained when educators intentionally use the four Tools of Cultural Proficiency and tenets of Inclusive Schooling for the benefit of all preK–12 students to fully participate in and benefit from high-quality curricular, instruction, and assessment experiences in school.

Equity is fairness and justice in assessing and providing for student academic and social needs.

Inclusive Education (also referred to as Inclusive Schooling) is both the *vision* and *practice* of welcoming, valuing, empowering, and supporting the diverse academic, social/emotional language and communication learning of all students in shared environments and experiences for the purpose of attaining the desired goals of education: belonging, mastery, independence, and generosity.

Multi-Tiered System of Supports (MTSS) is the umbrella term used to describe a comprehensive school-wide and district-wide system of high-quality instruction and interventions for any student, regardless of whether that student is struggling or has advanced learning needs. It is designed to prevent the need for referral for special education services through early detection. The system is conceptualized as a three-tiered approach, with Tier 1 being high quality core instruction in general education and frequent student progress monitoring. Tier 2 involves supplemental, targeted interventions, particularly for students not making adequate progress on expected curriculum benchmarks. Tier 3 involves more intensive (e.g., more frequent and individualized) interventions for students whose response to Tier 1 and 2 instruction is deemed inadequate.

Professional learning is used in this book to reflect the changes required for teachers and administrators as active participants in their learning rather than passive receivers of only workshop presentations. Learning Forward, the national professional learning organization, shifted from using the term *professional development* to *professional learning*. Professional learning calls for educators to focus on knowing and doing in order to meet the needs of all students (Learning Forward, 2011). In support of the new term as continuous improvement, Lois Brown Easton states, "Developing is not enough. Educators must be knowledgeable and wise. They must know enough in order to change. They must change in order to get different results. They must become learners and they must be self-developing" (2008, p. 756).

Student success and achievement is meeting formative and summative performance measures that ensure successful grade completion and high school graduation/completion as per state requirements.

ASSUMPTIONS WE HOLD

The co-authors held these assumptions as we wrote this book:

- Students learn best when they are in schools and classroom with educators, administrators, support personnel (e.g., psychologists, counselors, speech language pathologists, occupational and physical therapists), and paraprofessionals who hold a high value for students' cultures, their learning styles, their abilities and strengths, and their families.
- Students learn best when they are in schools and classroom with educators, administrators, support personnel, and paraprofessionals who hold a high value for inclusion and equity.
- Educators work inclusively and effectively when they value students' parents and guardians as critical resources for students' well-being and achievement during and beyond the school day.
- Professional learning that is intentional, inclusive, continuous, and focused upon system-wide goals and that uses the five Essential Elements for Cultural Competence leads to an expansion of Inclusive Schooling and a narrowing of access and equity gaps.
- The work of leading change toward Inclusive Education is not someone else's work; it is my/our work.
- Changing people's beliefs and perspectives causes emotional turmoil and, therefore, requires compassion and perseverance.

WHO ARE YOU?

As an active participant in this book, who are you? We invite you to engage with us as a reader and a writer as you begin this book. Some of you may have read cultural proficiency books prior to this one. You may already know about inclusive classrooms and schools. Now, you have the opportunity to discover more about yourself by using the lens of Cultural Proficiency to examine your current context and your journey as an educator in creating an inclusive school, where *all* really does mean *all*. If this is your first time to read about the Tools of Cultural Proficiency and/or Inclusive Schooling, you have selected the perfect time to start your journey. We have provided reflective questions and blank spaces for you to write your thoughts and new questions. Welcome to this work. We are delighted to have you join us on our journey of challenges, rewards, reflections, new learning, and action toward creating and sustaining classrooms and schools where all students are welcomed, valued, and experience success because of who they are and the attributes they bring to school each day.

GOING DEEPER

What expectations are you holding as you have read the front matter and this first chapter? In what ways might this book support your learning as an educator?

How might this book help you and your colleagues as you work together on serving more/all students?

_____

_____

_____

_____

Chapter 2 offers an introduction, definitions, and illustrations of the frameworks of Cultural Proficiency and Inclusive Schooling and answers the questions: Why use the Tools of Cultural Proficiency as a lens for examining the current work you are doing to better serve all students? How do inclusive learning environments address educators' questions for better serving students eligible for special education and other support services?

2 Using the Tools of Cultural Proficiency and the Vision and Practices of Inclusive Education as a Conceptual Framework

To meet each student where they are, they need to be understood as persons and learners. This means recognizing the fullness of their gifts; their passions; their race, class, and culture; additional aspects of context and history; their families; their belief and values; and their possibilities.

Gleason & Gerzon (2013, p. 4)

GETTING CENTERED

In what ways does this opening quote resonate for you? Who are your students? What gifts and talents might they bring to your school community? In what ways do you provide for and support their possibilities? What more do you want to know to better serve your students and their families?

_____

_____

_____

_____

The purpose of this chapter is to offer descriptions of Inclusive Education and Cultural Proficiency. We also demonstrate how to use these two conceptual frames as guides for examining the beliefs and assumptions that drive your instructional practice as well as the values and assumptions that ground the policies and procedures of your school and district. Finally, we summarize the chapter with opportunities to merge the two concepts into an educational practice we call culturally proficient Inclusive Classrooms and Schools.

INCLUSIVE EDUCATION: WHAT IT IS AND WHAT IT IS NOT

One of the authors of this book is fond of observing that "half of knowing what something *is* is knowing what it is *not*." So to define Inclusive Education, we examine both what it *is* and what it is *not*.

What Inclusive Education Is NOT

Let's begin with Inclusive Education is *not*. First, Inclusive Education *is not mainstreaming*. Hark back to the 1970s. Most of the decade predated the implementation of Public Law (Pub. L.) 94-142, the federal law (now reauthorized as the Individuals with Disabilities Education Improvement Act of 2004) that stipulates that no child, regardless of disability, can be denied an appropriate public education in the least restrictive environment. Mainstreaming, the prevalent practice of the time, was (and still is, in many places is) the practice of allowing students with disabilities access to general education classrooms when they could do pretty much what everybody else could do. Mainstreaming was primarily applied to students considered to have "mild" disabilities, described as students with learning disabilities, students eligible for speech and language services, and students with physical limitations that did not significantly impact their academic performance or ability to communicate verbally. Rather than schools and classrooms being ready to educate and support student differences, in order to be invited into general education, the onus was on the child to become "ready" to learn and behave in the same way as other students. Norman Kunc describes this practice as "forcing children to earn the right to belong" (2000, p. 88). For many students, mainstreaming resulted in being in general education mainly for related arts classes (e.g., art, music, physical education), lunch and recess, or being placed in class-rooms with younger rather than same-aged peers. In many instances, in the general education classroom this looked like a paraprofessional in the back of the classroom sitting with the students who were supported by an IEP. Very little differentiation of instruction or in-class support was pro-vided by general educators or specialists, so students, parents, and educa-tors alike often experienced mainstreaming as students being "dumped" into classrooms with little support for educators or students.

*Inclusive Education also **is not** integration.* With the initial implementa-tion of Public Law 94-142 in the late 70s, the special education *integration* movement of the 1980s expanded the discussion of who could and should be educated in general education beyond students with mild disabilities to students with more pervasive support needs (i.e., students considered as having moderate and severe disabilities). Integration, however, focused primarily on physical and social access, with limited or no academic expectations for students with more intensive needs.

Inclusive Education **is not** routinely or automatically grouping stu-dents with disabilities and other students perceived as low performing or educationally or behaviorally challenging in *homogeneous-level* groups for instruction, particularly in the high-stakes content and assessment areas of literacy and mathematics. Homogeneous grouping **is** appropriate for tar-geted interventions and short-term remediation, as long as groupings are flexible and fluid, based upon ongoing data collection and analysis char-acteristic of a healthy Multi-Tiered System of Supports (described in Chapter 4). The bottom line is that in Inclusive Education, students spend the vast majority of their instructional time learning in *heterogeneous mixed-ability* groupings.

Inclusive Education IS: Legal

The legal mandate driving Inclusive Education in the United States originated in 1975 with the promulgation of Public Law 94-142. Although the specific term *Inclusive Education* is not found in the law, the law guarantees students with disabilities a free and appropriate public education (FAPE) in the least restrictive environment (LRE). Specifically, the law requires each public agency (including school districts) to ensure the following:

(i) To the maximum extent appropriate, children with disabilities, including children in public or private institutions or other care facilities, are educated with children who are not disabled; and

(ii) Special classes, separate schooling, or other removal of children with disabilities from the regular educational environment occurs only when the nature or severity of the disability is such that education in regular classes with the use of supplementary aids and services cannot be achieved satisfactorily. (34 C.F.R. § 300.114 [a] [2])

Every subsequent reauthorization of the original 1975 legislation has reaffirmed the preference that children with disabilities be educated in general education with similar-aged peers unless a compelling educational justification otherwise exists. The law requires the least restrictive environment (LRE) to be determined based upon each student's strengths and needs by a team comprised of people who have expertise and experience with the student, inclusive of parent(s) and, whenever possible, the student. If the team determines a student can progress toward his or her goals in general education with the use of supplementary aids and services, then general education is the least restrictive environment for that student.

Since the 1975 promulgation of Public Law 94-142, federal court decisions and the LRE mandate have built upon one another to clarify the following:

- School districts must consider placement in general education for any students with a disability, regardless of the severity of the disability.
- Both social and academic benefits of placement in general education must be taken into consideration.
- The above considerations may not be token gestures.
- LRE placement is not "dumping" a student with disabilities in general education without needed supports, but, rather, placing that student and providing the necessary supports, services, and supplementary aids.

In other words, the legal standard for denying a student with disabilities an Inclusive Education is very high.

Inclusive Education IS: A Vision and Pragmatic

We have described what Inclusive Education is *not* and provided the legal foundations for Inclusive Education. So then, what **is** Inclusive Education? Consider this scenario offered by Falvey, Givner, Villa, and Thousand.

It is third period in Mr. Rice's freshman language arts class, and the 32 students have just finished "reading" the final chapter of *To Kill a Mockingbird* by Harper Lee (1960). Some students have listened to the book using text-to-speech software, have read versions of the book at lower readability levels, or have had the chapter in both English and their native language, in order to accommodate their varying literacy levels in English. . . . Several students in Mr. Rice's class qualify for special education services; five qualify for gifted and talented services; a quarter of the students, who are bilingual in Spanish and English, are considered long-term English language learners. Mr. Rice has a team with whom he meets weekly to support the differentiation of materials, instruction, and assessment for his students.

Mr. Gonzales, the 9th and 10th grade English language development educator, is working with Mr. Rice to develop students' academic language in English and plan visual and other scaffolds to make content accessible. Mr. Gonzales co-teaches with Mr. Rice on Mondays and models the explicit academic language development strategies they have planned and will use for the week. Ms. Mikel, Mr. Rice's special education support teacher, co-teaches in the classroom Tuesday through Thursday and is available, as is the classroom teacher, to support . . . any student who may want or need assistance.

Students in the class who are long-term English language learners are partnered with bilingual classmates with stronger English academic language. The pairs have a choice of preparing bilingual presentations with visual aids in both languages or preparing their presentation in English.

Casandra, who has multiple disabilities, uses . . . an electronic communication device to convey her thoughts and responses. Casandra's partner is Jimmy, a classmate who qualifies for gifted and talented services. Jimmy surfs the web for information related to the topic and then decides with Casandra what to include in their presentation. Casandra and Jimmy enter their content into

Casandra's electronic device, which has a voice output that will be activated to deliver their presentation to the class. (Falvey, Givner, Villa, & Thousand, 2017, pp. 7–8).

Mr. Rice's class not only reflects the diversity of 21st century classrooms but embraces the students who otherwise might have been moved to a gifted and talented program, been left to sink or swim in a classroom with little explicit language development or differentiation, or placed in a segregated "special education" language arts class. Mr. Rice's class is a pragmatic snapshot of Inclusive Education in action and the values and vision that underpins it.

So, what *is* Inclusive Education? Villa and Thousand define Inclusive Education as "both the *vision* and *practice* of welcoming, valuing, empowering, and supporting the diverse academic, social/emotional, language and communication learning of all students in shared environments and experiences for the purpose of attaining the desired goals of education" (2016, p. 18). Inclusion is a *belief* that everyone is a valued and contributing member of the school community. Inclusion happens when everyone belongs, regardless of perceived need or ability. Inclusive Education is the assumption that learning together benefits everyone, not just children given a label (e.g., those considered gifted, not yet English-proficient, or having a disability). Inclusive Education is the presumption that general education is the placement option of first choice for every child, including students with pervasive support needs. And it is the presumption that any student with a disability will be educated alongside his or her non-disabled peers through the provision of specially designed instruction (special education services), supplemental aids and services, and related services.

Inclusive Education is also a constellation of *practices* that reflect this vision and presumptions. Students with disabilities attend the home school or school of choice they would attend if they did not have an Individual Education Program (IEP) plan. Students with disabilities are educated with same-aged or similar-aged peers and have access to the same curricular and co-curricular (before and after school) activities as their peers. Inclusive educators practice assessing and using students' strengths (learning styles, interests and personal motivators, Multiple Intelligences) to facilitate their reaching their potential and having their unique needs met. It is the practice of differentiating instruction for any student through collaborative planning and teaching among all members of the school community, including students and families. Inclusive Education provides all students with instruction in and opportunities to learn and practice independence, self-advocacy, and self-determination (choice making) in learning and goal setting. It is the practice of assessing and adjusting curriculum, instruction, and human resources so that students in each subgroup (e.g., students also learning English, students with IEPs, children living in poverty) achieve mastery (e.g., show one month gain with one month of instruction). And Inclusive Education is much more, as described and illustrated in the following chapters that delve into the particular presumptions, dispositions, principles, and practices that allow Inclusive Education to be the schooling paradigm of a learning community.

In *The Inclusive Education Checklist: A Self-Assessment of Best Practices*, Villa and Thousand (2016) offer 15 indicators of what Inclusive Education IS. These best practices were derived from research, model demonstrations, and their over 40 years of supporting school communities to install Inclusive Education for all students. One of these indicators targets at least 90% (rather than the national average of 61%) of students with IEPs having general education as their primary educational placement. Given the relatively low national average, why set a 90% target?

> Because national averages are just that, a central tendency measure representing schools performing both below and above the mean. Averages factor in the fact that there *are* states, districts, and individual schools across the nation that *do* exceed the mean and, in some cases, are known . . . to have approached and hit the suggested targets. Since this is a *best practice* indicator, we chose a target that substantially exceeds the national average, yet is within reach. (p. 22)

Another related indicator suggests that at least 80% of students with IEPs receive instruction in *core academic content* in general education (in the best case scenario with special education support through co-teaching) rather than in segregated content classes. Why set an 80% target? The authors note that, unlike the previous indicator, no federal or state data exist regarding "the proportion of students with IEPs receiving or *not* receiving academic content instruction from credentialed general education content experts in general education content courses (i.e., language arts, mathematics, science, social studies) or classrooms" (Villa & Thousand, 2016, p. 22). They note that a sizable number of secondary students still receive core academic content instruction in replacement classes comprised solely of students with IEPs and that many students with more intensive support needs still "receive little *academic content instruction* and none in general education classrooms" (Villa & Thousand, 2016, p. 22). The 80% standard acknowledges these realities, with a goal being that the target increases as schools do better on these and the other inclusive education indicators.

Inclusive Education IS: Supported by Research

As early as the 1980s, research indicated that providing special education services in segregated settings outside of general education had little to no positive effects for students, regardless of the category or intensity of their disabilities (Lipsky & Gartner, 1989). In fact, Baker, Wang, and Wahlberg's (1994) landmark meta-analysis examining the effectiveness of various special education service delivery models concluded that "special-needs students educated in regular classes do better academically and socially than comparable students in non-inclusive settings" (p. 34). This finding held true regardless of grade level or type of disability.

In 1995, the U.S. Department of Education reported that "across a number of analyses of post-school results, the message was the same: those who spent more time in regular education experienced better results after high school" (p. 87). A decade later, Blackorby and colleagues (2005) studied 11,000 students with disabilities and found that those who spent more time in general education classrooms had fewer absences, performed closer to grade level, and had higher standards-based assessment and achievement test scores than peers served in pull-out settings.

A significant early argument against Inclusive Education offered by some educators and families of children without disabilities was that presence of students with disabilities in general classrooms would adversely impact the other students in the classroom. This argument has been examine and put to rest. Namely, Kalambouga, Farrell, Dyson, and Kaplan, in their 2007 meta-analysis, found that 81% of reported search outcomes showed that the inclusion of students with disabilities resulted in either positive or neutral effects for students without disabilities. As for students with more extensive support needs, researchers have also found that their inclusion not only fails to adversely affect classmates' academic and behavioral success as measured by standardized tests and report card grades but actually enhanced classmates' as well as their own achievement, self-esteem, and school attendance (Kelly, 1992; Straub & Peck, 1994).

Overall, the data clearly show that Inclusive Education facilitates academic and social/emotional mastery and success for student with and without disabilities and confirms what federal legislation acknowledges in the Individuals with Disabilities Education Improvement Act (IDEIA) of 2004:

> Nearly 30 [now over 40] years of research and experience has demonstrated that the education of children with disabilities can be made more effective by having high expectations and ensuring students' access in the general education curriculum to the maximum extent possible . . . [and] providing appropriate special education and related services and aides and supports in the regular classroom to such children, whenever possible. (20 U.S.C. 1400(c)(5))

Inclusive Education IS: A Journey

At the writing of this book, a reported 61% of students with disabilities spend 80% or more of their day in general education settings (U.S. Department of Education, 2015). Where does the "80% or more of the day" statement come from? Annually, states are required to report data to the U.S. Office of Special Education and Rehabilitative Services (OSERS), which then is made public in annual OSERS reports to the U.S Congress (e.g., OSERS, 2016). These data are analyzed to determine the percentage of students ages 6 through 21 who receive their education in general education (a) 80% or more of the day, (b) between 40% and 79% of the day, and (c) less than 40% of the day. Note that "a day" is defined as the *entire* school day, which includes lunch, recess, study periods, physical education, art, music, and other specials.

In an ideal world, the goal of Inclusive Education is for nearly 100% of students with disabilities to be educated within general education nearly 100% of the school day. Current national data (i.e., 61% of students educated in general education classrooms for 80% or more of the day) suggest that many schools have a distance to go in their journey to achieving this ideal. Why? Some school systems have yet to attempt or achieve community consensus for an inclusive *vision*. Some systems are blind to or fail to see an urgency to orchestrate structural supports (e.g., co-teaching, master schedules that allow for collaborative planning) to make it easily happen. Some districts have yet to provide school personnel with professional learning and coaching in how to meet diverse student needs in mixed-ability classrooms. Some district leaders cannot envision how students with more pervasive support needs could be educated in other than separate special classes. And there are those few students for whom general education, 100% of the day, does not best support their momentary needs or goals (e.g., students who are hospitalized, secondary students engaged in job development in the community for part of the school day). Chapter 3 further examines potential Barriers to the journey toward Inclusive Education and then suggests culturally proficient, barrier busting paradigms of special education service delivery. The remaining chapters describe and illustrate additional pathways to achieving Culturally Proficient Inclusive Education.

REFLECTION

As you think about Inclusive Education in your current setting, what's important for you to notice? What questions are surfacing for you about what is and is NOT Inclusive Education? Of what do you want to be mindful about your educational practice given the descriptions of inclusive classrooms and schools?

_____

_____

_____

_____

CULTURAL PROFICIENCY AS A CONCEPTUAL FRAMEWORK

The cultural proficiency model needed on this inclusive journey is one that illustrates the manner in which cultural assets form the basis for core values to guide educators toward inclusive classrooms and schools. Once you recognize and understand the tension that exists for people and schools in terms of Barriers and assets, you are better prepared to serve all students in classrooms, schools, and districts. A crucial first step toward using a cultural proficiency framework is to see students for who they are and capitalize upon the strengths and interests (i.e., assets) they bring to the school community every day.

Table 2.1 displays the *conceptual framework of Cultural Proficiency* and shows the four Tools of Cultural Proficiency and the relationship among the tools. Unlike most "table reading" experiences, begin by reading Table 2.1 from the bottom up.

REFLECTION

What do you notice about the framework? What's emerging for you as a learner? As an educator? What sense are you making from the arrows? As you talk with a fellow educator, what is your learning from their perspective about the relationship of the Four Tools?

_____

_____

_____

_____

Table 2.1 The Cultural Proficiency Framework

The Essential Elements — *Standards for Planning, Assessing, and Transforming Self and Organization*

- **Assessing Culture:** Identifying cultural self and all cultural groups present in the system
- **Valuing Diversity:** Developing and demonstrating an appreciation for the differences among and between groups
- **Managing the Dynamics of Difference:** Learning to respond appropriately and effectively to the issues that arise in a diverse environment
- **Adapting to Diversity:** Changing and adopting new policies and practices that support diversity and inclusion
- **Institutionalizing Cultural Knowledge:** Driving the changes into the systems of the organization

Cultural Proficiency Continuum

Change Mandated for Tolerance			*Change Chosen for Transformation*		
DESTRUCTION	**INCAPACITY**	**BLINDNESS**	**PRECOMPETENCE**	**COMPETENCE**	**PROFICIENCY**
Eliminate differences The elimination of other people's cultures	*Demean differences* Belief in the superiority of one's culture and behavior that disempowers another's culture	*Dismiss differences* Acting as if the cultural differences you see do not matter or not recognizing that there are differences among and between cultures	*Respond inadequately to the dynamics of difference* Awareness of the limitations and potential of one's skills or an organization's policies and practices when interacting with other cultural groups	*Engage with differences using the essential elements as standards* Using the five essential elements of cultural proficiency as the standard for individual behavior and organizational practices	*Esteem and learn from differences as a lifelong practice* Knowing how to learn about and from individual and organizational culture; interacting effectively in a variety of cultural environments. Advocating for others.

Reactive Behaviors, Shaped by the **BARRIERS**

- Systems of oppression
- Unawareness of the need to adapt
- Systems of privilege and entitlement
- Resistance to change

Proactive Behaviors, Shaped by the **PRINCIPLES**

- Culture is a predominant force in people's and school's lives.
- People are served in varying degrees by the dominant culture.
- People have group identities and individual identities.
- Diversity within cultures is vast and significant.
- Each cultural group has unique cultural needs.
- The best of both worlds enhances the capacity of all.
- The family, as defined by each culture, is the primary system of support in the education of children.
- School systems must recognize that marginalized populations have to be at least bicultural and that this status creates a unique set of issues to which the system must be equipped to respond.
- Inherent in cross-cultural interactions are dynamics that must be acknowledged, adjusted to, and accepted.

Using the Four Tools of Cultural Proficiency

The Tools of Cultural Proficiency enable you to

- Describe Barriers to Cultural Proficiency you may have experienced or observed that impede Cultural Proficiency
- Describe how the Guiding Principles of Cultural Proficiency serve as core values for your personal, professional, and organizational values and behavior
- Describe unhealthy and healthy values and behaviors and school policies and practices and plot them on the Cultural Proficiency Continuum.
- Describe and use the five Essential Elements of Cultural Competence as standards for your personal and professional behavior and your school's formal policies and nonformal, prevalent practices (Lindsey, Kearney, Estrada, Terrell, & Lindsey, 2015)

Barriers Versus Cultural Assets: The Tension for Change

The **Barriers to Cultural Proficiency** and the Guiding Principles (e.g., core values) of Cultural Proficiency are the "invisible guiding hands" of the framework. Barriers inform the negative aspects of the Continuum—cultural destructiveness, incapacity and blindness; while the Guiding Principles serve to inform the positive aspects of the Continuum—precompetence, competence, and proficiency. Being able to recognize and acknowledge the Barriers to Cultural Proficiency is basic to understanding how to overcome resistance to change within us and in our schools. From Table 2.1 you learned there are Barriers to culturally proficient attitudes, behaviors, policies, and practices that affect our daily lives and impact educational leaders decisions (Cross, Bazron, Dennis, & Isaacs, 1989; Lindsey, Nuri-Robins, & Terrell, 2009):

- Being unaware of the need to adapt
- Not acknowledging systemic oppression
- Benefitting from a sense of privilege and entitlement
- Being resistant to change

Notice the line between the Barriers and the Guiding Principles. That line extends between cultural blindness and cultural precompetence and represents the paradigmatic shifting point where educators have clearly delineated choices:

- To the left of the line people may be victims of social forces and act on beliefs grounded either in cultural deficit theory applied to marginalized communities or, every bit as damaging, the intractability of systemic oppression visited on marginalized communities; or

- To the right of the line people choose to believe in their capacity to effectively educate all students, irrespective of their racial, ethnic, gender, socio-economic, sexual identity, special needs, or faith communities.

The **Guiding Principles** of Cultural Proficiency function as a counter to the Barriers to Cultural Proficiency by serving as core values in developing our capacity for personal and professional work that results in marginalized students being academically successful and full participants in the extra-curricular programs of the school. Culture is inculcated in the guiding principles and can be readily seen in our behaviors, policies, and practices. Let us be direct and specific: To be effective, the core values must be deeply held beliefs and values. They cannot and must not be lightly agreed to in nodding assent and then, blithely ignored. The Guiding Principles inform our actions for being culturally precompetent, culturally competent, and culturally proficient. The Guiding Principles are the following:

- Culture is a predominant force in people's and school's lives.
- People are served in varying degrees by the dominant culture.
- People have group identities and individual identities.
- Diversity within cultures is vast and significant.
- Each cultural group has unique cultural needs.
- The best of both worlds enhances the capacity of all.
- The family, as defined by each culture, is the primary system of support in the education of children.
- School systems must recognize that marginalized populations have to be at least bicultural and that this status creates a unique set of issues to which the system must be equipped to respond.
- Inherent in cross-cultural interactions are dynamics that must be acknowledged, adjusted to, and accepted.

The Continuum

Six points along the **Cultural Proficiency Continuum** depict the unhealthy and healthy practices of individuals and reflect practices and policies within organizations. The Continuum aligns the six phases of Cultural Proficiency, so you can clearly see that cultural destructiveness, incapacity, and blindness are informed by the Barriers to Cultural Proficiency. These phases are, at best, half-hearted compliance-driven behaviors that rarely result in actions to support the academic and social success of students having different needs and abilities. In marked contrast, the Guiding Principles of Cultural Proficiency serve as core values to support culturally precompetent, competent, and proficient behaviors, policies, and practices for students by assuming all educators can teach all learners and by honoring all students' abilities, gifts, and talents and by esteeming their home cultures and support. The points on the Continuum are the following:

- Cultural destructiveness: The elimination of other people's cultures. (*Those kids don't belong in this school. We can't help them.*)
- Cultural incapacity: Belief in the superiority of one's culture and displaying behaviors that demeans other's. (*There's really no such thing as autism, they just need more discipline and a stronger hand.*)
- Cultural blindness: Acting as if cultural difference doesn't exist or not recognizing any differences among cultures. (*I don't know what the big deal is, I treat them all just alike.*)
- Cultural precompetence: Increasing awareness of what you and others need to know about working with diverse settings; willing to examine and confront assumptions about students with different abilities. (*We need to be more aware of how our general educators are learning from our special educators about to better serve our students.*)
- Cultural competence: Aligning personal values and behaviors and the school's policies and practices in a manner that is inclusive of cultures that are new and different from yours and the school's and enables healthy and productive interactions. Using the five Essential Elements as standards of behavior and organizational practices. (*In what ways might we examine our practices for assessing our student's academic needs with our assumptions about how students learn?*)
- Cultural Proficiency: Knowing how to learn about and from individual and organizational cultures; interacting effectively in a variety of cultural environments; interacting with colleagues, students, their families, and their communities as advocates for life long learners to serve the educational needs of all learners. (*Whom else might we include on this journey?*)

The Five Essential Elements

At the top of the Framework are the **five Essential Elements** of Cultural Competence that are informed by the Guiding Principles and the Barriers. These are the standards for values, behaviors, policies, and practices aligned with the Guiding Principles. These elements are the actions that will move you forward from being stuck in old ways or in the status quo, best described by the Barriers on the left side of the Continuum shown in Table 2.1.

Terry Cross and colleagues (1989) describe the Essential Elements as actions that meet the standard of Cultural Competence on the Continuum (see framework, Table 2.1). These elements give actions to operationalize the Guiding Principles. When educators ask, "Now that I know the Tools of Cultural Proficiency, what do I do?" the Essential Elements shape the behaviors for culturally proficient educational practice and inclusive classrooms and schools. Table 2.2 presents the five Essential Elements—(1) Assessing Cultural Knowledge, (2) Valuing Diversity, (3) Managing the Dynamics of Change, (4) Adapting to Diversity, and (5) Institutionalizing Cultural Knowledge—and behaviors consistent with a culturally proficient member of an inclusive learning community.

The four Tools of Cultural Proficiency act as a framework for doing the work of equity and access for all students. This is not "add on" work or extra work to assign to faculty and staff members for purpose of compliance and conformity. These tools provide you with a lens through which you can examine the current work you are doing. In other words, use the lens to examine the school-wide plan for "equity and access." Is the school discipline plan a culturally proficient plan? Is the plan for serving students considered gifted and talented a culturally proficient plan? Who's being served by that plan? What does the data show about demographic groups represented in special education, in suspensions and expulsions? The Tools of Cultural Proficiency provide a frame for transforming the culture of classrooms and schools from places of exclusion and inequity to spaces of inclusion and equity.

REFLECTION

Review the four Tools of Cultural Proficiency presented in Table 2.1 in the context of our description of Inclusive Education. What is emerging for you as a single framework that integrates Cultural Proficiency and Inclusive Education? Given your current context, what are questions you have about how to use these frameworks to more forward with creating a school where all means all? In what ways might the four Tools of Cultural Proficiency inform your current work?

_____

_____

_____

_____

Table 2.2 Behaviors of a Culturally Proficient Member of an Inclusive Learning Community by Essential Element

5 Essential Elements of Cultural Proficiency	As a culturally proficient member of an inclusive learning community, I will . . .
Assessing Cultural Knowledge Identifying the cultural groups present in the school and system	• Become and be self-aware of my own culture and the effect it may have on the students, families, and others in the school with whom I work • Become and be aware of what I know about others' cultures and about how I react to others' cultures and the diverse communities within my school • Become and be aware of how educators in the school as a whole react to diversity • Extend our knowledge of what constitutes diversity • Become and be aware of what I need to learn, know, and do to be effective in a multicultural classroom and school that includes individuals with perceived disabilities and other learning, behavior, or communication differences
Valuing Diversity Developing an appreciation for the differences among and within groups	• Welcome, value, empower, and support the diverse academic, social/emotional, language, and communication learning of all students in shared environments and experiences for the purpose of attaining the desired goals of education • Appreciate the challenges and gifts that diversity brings and share this appreciation with students in order to develop a collaborative and naturally supportive learning community • Initiate and support formal and informal decision-making groups inclusive of parents/guardians, community members, people whose viewpoints and experiences that are different from mine, and students themselves in order to enrich conversations, decision making, and problem solving
Managing the Dynamics of Change Learning to respond appropriately and effectively to the issues that arise in a diverse environment	• Appreciate conflict as a natural and normal process with cultural contexts that need to and can be understood and that contribute to creative problem solving • Help students understand that what appear to be conflicts may be cultural clashes and teach them how to mediate their own conflicts • Teach students to detect and manage the feelings associated with conflict and develop self-management and conflict resolution strategies to manage unresolved conflict • Learn and use creative problem solving, conflict resolution, and instructional differentiation approaches as natural and routine processes to manage conflict and accommodate differences in student learning, behavior, and interpersonal relations

5 Essential Elements of Cultural Proficiency	As a culturally proficient member of an inclusive learning community, I will . . .
Adapting to Diversity Changing and adopting new policies and practices that support diversity and inclusion	• Actively and continuously learn about marginalized and/or underserved cultural groups different from my own and use their experiences and backgrounds to enhance teaching and learning, student empowerment and self-advocacy, and home-school-community relations • Actively and continuously learn about and implement what is necessary to (a) enhance the relevance of my instruction, (b) differentiate instruction for any student, and (c) deal with issues caused by differences • Actively tap the leadership potential of members of cultural groups (i.e., students with disabilities) • Advocate for changes in school and district policies and practices so that they reflect the guiding principles of Cultural Proficiency and challenge negative stereotypical assumptions and perceptions regarding disability
Institutionalizing Cultural Knowledge Drive the changes into the systems of the organization	• Work to influence the vision, mission, policies, and practices of the school and district to be aligned with the guiding principles of Cultural Proficiency • Make learning about underserved and marginalized cultural groups within the school and community an integral part of my ongoing learning • Advocate for learning about underserved and marginalized cultural groups as a major focus of the school's and district's professional learning • Create opportunities and take advantage of teachable moments for diverse groups to learn about each other and engage in ways that both honor who they are and challenge them to be even better • Be the change that I want to see!

Transforming the Culture of School

Of all the cultural groups that schools serve, the organizational culture of school is the group that most often is the focus of "change, or needs to be changed." Organizational and school culture has been studied extensively even in recent years. Researchers concur that schools as organizations have a culture of their own and need leaders who understand and manage that culture in a positive way (Deal & Kennedy, 1982; Fullan, 2008; 1982; Schein, 1989; Wenger, McDermott, & Snyder, 2002). Both veteran and new educators acknowledge that change is not easy. Within schools abide forces that either block (Barriers) or facilitate (Guiding Principles) student achievement.

Implementing new practices in schools is often difficult and made even more difficult when issues serving special needs students are embedded in change processes. While it may be true that change is not easy, we know also that change is inevitable and natural. When properly understood and implemented, the change process can be led in ways that target the educational needs of special needs students and, at the same time, benefit all learners in our schools.

SUMMARY

Inclusive Education and Cultural Proficiency are educational frameworks grounded in research and belief systems that put the responsibilities of educating all children and youth with the educators in partnership with parents, families, and communities. The intersection of the two frameworks creates the space where students are respected, valued, and included by educators and their peers. Culturally Proficient Inclusive Education practice is an approach that helps all students achieve at levels higher than before. Public education is a national treasure of both the United States and Canada and is ours to nurture and tend. Culturally Proficient Inclusive Education practice helps us guarantee that treasure for future learners.

Chapter 3 provides an in-depth view of the Barriers to Culturally Proficient Inclusive Education. Chapter 4 offers ways to use the nine Guiding Principles of Cultural Proficiency and other barrier busters for creating opportunities to learn new ways of behaving to overcome these Barriers.

3

Barriers to Culturally Proficient Inclusive Education

The significant problems we have cannot be solved at the same level of thinking with which we created them.

Albert Einstein
(as cited at www.quotationspage.com/quote/23588.html)

GETTING CENTERED

Often obstacles get in the way of plans for establishing Culturally Proficient Inclusive Classrooms and Schools. This quote attributed to the famous theoretical physicist, Albert Einstein, highlights how challenging it can be to step out of our comfort zone and tackle serious problems and challenges. What was your reaction when you first read the quote? In what ways might you and your co-learners confront the Barriers illustrated by these words within the quote? What opportunities might evolve from this perceived Barrier?

_____

_____

_____

_____

IDENTIFYING THE BARRIERS

On your journey toward Culturally Proficient Inclusive Classrooms and Schools, you will encounter obstacles, conflicts, and interruptions. We identify these as Barriers, and the tool we use is _Overcoming the Barriers_. The first step to Overcoming the Barriers is to be aware that they even exist and that they serve as a set of deeply held assumptions on which educator behaviors and school/district policies and practices are established. The Barriers are grounded in systems of historical oppression that continue to exist today and are imbedded in actions taken in schools and districts. These barriers have historically and presently obstructed school reform efforts focused on providing appropriate educational access and opportunities to all students, including those who have been underserved and/or marginalized because of their race, ethnicity, language, socio-economics, faith, gender, sexual orientation, or perceived ability. The No Child Left Behind Act (NCLB) of 2001 publically exposed the education gap between white students and their African American counterparts that existed and still exists today in the United States by requiring school districts to dis-aggregate student achievement data by demographic groups. These data have been available to school district officials since 1971 when National Assessment of Education Progress (NAEP) provided evidence of persis-tent disparities among demographic groups of students (Perie, Moran, & Lutkus, 2005).

Nationwide educational reform efforts were most widely present in the federal reauthorization of the Elementary and Secondary Education Act (ESEA), Title I's NCLB, which required school districts and school leaders to set specific performance targets for all demographic groups, including special education students (CampbellJones, CampbellJones & Lindsey, 2010). Since NCLB 2001, Race to the Top, and finally the most recent federal reauthorization of ESEA, in 2015, Every Student Succeeds Act (ESSA) continue to require gap-closing school action plans. New to these expanding ESEA reform efforts, ESSA requires school districts to include an equity plan prior to receiving Title I funds. State reforms have also included academic and performance standards, inclusive of all stu-dents. As a national reform effort focused on closing education gaps, the Common Core State Standards (CCSS) focused on state-wide efforts begun as early as 2009. Once the state-by-state content standards examination process was concluded, individual states began adopting the CCSS based on their existing adoption process. In many states, the state school boards formally adopted the standards. In others, the decision was made or ratified by the state superintendent of education, state legislature, or governor. As of the printing of this book, 42 states, the District of Columbia, four territories, and the Department of Defense Education Activity (DoDEA) have adopted the Common Core and are implementing the standards according to their own timelines (http://www.corestandards.org/).

The United States now has common shared academic and content standards. Educational gaps have been revealed to the general public. However, this progress toward equity has not totally overcome the historical obstacles of (a) systemic practices of oppression that still fail large segments of our population and (b) the accrued benefits within systemic entitlement that continues to serve some students well. By revealing previously ignored or hidden data through the use of the Tools of Cultural Proficiency, these historical obstacles or barriers have been made visible. With this information, action can be taken to close access and equity gaps and install inclusive practices that tear down barriers in ways that benefits all students yet does not impinge upon the education of students historically successful in schools. These Barriers manifest themselves in at least the following four distinct ways described in the next four sections.

Systems of Oppression

Systems of oppression are historical forms of discrimination that are, knowingly and unknowingly, operationalized in schools and organizations. Forms of oppression and marginalization evidenced in schools today include racism, sexism, ableism, ethnocentrism, and homophobia. These "isms" are persistent and prolonged and go unexamined, intentionally and unintentionally, through policies, practices, procedures, and structures. These systems remain in place as permanent fixtures of United States and Canadian schools until educators intentionally examine and reveal the underlying assumptions that serve as barriers to impede and restrict access and equitable outcomes for all students.

Ableism Examined. In the realm of special education, the deeply held assumptions about ability and ableness have come to be known as *ableism*. Ableism is rooted in the devaluing, disregard, and discrimination experienced by many people with disabilities. Smith, Foley, and Chaney (2008) describe ableism and its effects:

Ableism is a form of discrimination or prejudice against individuals with physical, mental, or developmental disabilities that are characterized by the belief that these individuals need to be fixed or cannot function as full members of society . . . As a result of these assumptions, individuals with disabilities are commonly viewed as being abnormal rather than as members of a distinct minority community. (p. 304)

Hehir (2005) effectively argues that ableism is "deeply imbedded in schooling" (p. 22) yet rarely discussed or examined. He asserts that the unexamined devaluing ableist perspective "results in societal attitudes that uncritically assert that it is better for a child to walk than roll, speak than sign, read print than read Braille, spell independently than use a spell-check, and hang out with nondisabled kids as opposed to other disabled kids" (p. 3).

An ableistic bias is manifest in school through special education's historically segregated service delivery model and the special education eligibility process. Since the 1975 promulgation of the Individuals with Disabilities Education Act (IDEA)—the federal law that ensures students with disabilities a free and appropriate public education (FAPE) in the least restrictive environment (LRE)—IDEA has failed to shed a *medical model* approach for determining special education eligibility and delivering special education services. In a medical model approach, disability is treated as an ailment or defect that can be healed and possibly "cured." For a child to become eligible for special education support, a *problem* needs to be identified within the child by professionals who assess to *diagnose* for eligibility in one or more of 13 federal eligibility categories.[1] Then a *treatment* is developed for the problem, which is articulated in an Individualized Educational Program (IEP) plan necessitating specialized personnel (e.g., special educators, speech and language pathologists, occupational and physical therapist, psychologists) and historically, specialized classes separate from general education for part to all of the school day (Cosier & Ashby, 2016). Although educators, particularly special educators, lament the time, procedures, and labeling required in this process. The process has changed little in the over 40 years of IDEA implementation (Wolter, 2016), resulting in the perpetuation of an ableist view of disabled people as incapable and less than.

---

[1] The Individual with Disabilities Educational Act (IDEA) of 2004 identifies 13 different disability categories under which students ages 3 through 21 may be eligible for special education services: autism, deaf-blindness, deafness, emotional disturbance, hearing impairment, intellectual disability, multiple disabilities, orthopedic impairment, other health impairment, specific learning disability, speech or language impairment, traumatic brain injury, and visual impairment.

REFLECTION

Former director of the U.S. Department of Education's Office of Special Education Programs, Thomas Hehir, has observed that "[t]he most damaging ableist assumption is the belief that disabled people are incapable" (2005, p. 27). What might be some assumptions that you have heard about people with disabilities that might serve to restrict their access to an equitable education? Of what are you aware about deeply held assumptions that function as barriers? What's your experience with surfacing assumptions about students with disabilities and how these students are treated and served? How are these assumptions preventing educators from breaking through the Barriers?

_____

_____

_____

_____

Systems of Privilege and Entitlement

Systems of privilege and entitlement are historical benefits that have accrued to certain cultural groups solely by membership in that group. A sense of privilege and entitlement emerges from indifferences based on one group's societal benefits. Although one may acknowledge these benefits may not have come easily, the fact remains that membership in that societal group provided an assumed advantage. This entitled group identity is often referred to as the dominant culture in society or in an organization (Nuri-Robins, Lindsey, Lindsey, & Terrell, 2012: Lindsey, Nuri-Robins, & Terrell, 2009). This dominant group may also acknowledge that schools were not designed historically to serve all students; today's public schools are making monumental efforts to become inclusive and to close gaps caused by segregation and unequal distribution of resources. We can safely say that educators of today did not cause the historical inequities and education gaps that we face, but we must agree that those inequities and gaps still exist for us to address, resolve, and correct. Culturally proficient educators must be aware of the historical implications of segregation and social stratification that impact schools today as we work to educate all learners. All learners have different needs and require a variety of learning supports. If educators can begin to dissect learner needs and plan for providing the supports needed for optimal learning, it is then that teachers can honestly say that they are practitioners of inclusive practices.

Unawareness of Need to Adapt

Unawareness of the need to adapt is evident by educators' lack of attention during planning to make adaptations for assessments, instruction, and curriculum needs of students. The demographics of school communities change from year to year, as do the educators serving those communities. However, as the world around the school changes, including technology, schools seem to stay the same. The expectation that students and families need to assimilate into the culture of the school instead of the school adapting to the culture of the community is a hurdle to be addressed. The Barrier of unawareness of need to adapt to better serving our students goes unnoticed and remains to inform our practice. We often hear comments like, "It worked for me, so it'll work for these kids." They just need to learn how we do things around here. This is our school." Even well intended educators are unaware that students with special needs are changing and they need different responses and supports to their needs this year than the response and supports they received at last year's IEP. As an educator in the twenty-first century, we can no longer use the excuse, "Oh, I didn't know. . . . " We must be able to recognize and adapt to the changing needs of our students and communities around us.

Resistance to Change

Resistance to change occurs when educators are confronted with a new or different way of meeting the needs of students. Resistance to a change initiative is an expression of a perspective that change is someone else's responsibility and actions. While change is a natural and normal part of how people and organizations grow, opposition to any change in the *way we do things around here* is often disconcerting and time consuming. Some educators get comfortable with the status quo and resist new or different ways to respond to student or community needs. People do not function well when they are frightened or angry or threatened. When change initiatives are introduced without first preparing the environment and individuals for success, employees will often rebel, resist, and even refuse to carry out details of the implementation plan (Fullan, 2008). Culturally proficient educators find ways to support change initiatives so that members of the organization are valued and understand that the purpose of the initiative is to address the needs of all learners.

REFLECTION

In what ways have you seen or experienced any of these four Barriers? In what ways might conversations about these Barriers guide actions toward overcoming these Barriers? What are "systems" examples of these Barriers that work against students and their families?

_____

_____

_____

_____

FOCUS ON THE NEED TO ADAPT AND CHANGE

The four Barriers often work in concert to intentionally or unintentionally establish obstacles for students and their parents as they navigate through school. For example, a parent may find her child is not reading well at the end of second grade and is advised by her daughter's teacher to seek tutoring over the summer. The parent also asks if her daughter could possibly benefit from special services in the fall. The teacher responds, "I don't really know about all that special ed stuff. You'll have to check on that when school starts. I don't do any of that in my classroom. You may even have to send her to a different school since she doesn't speak English very well either."

The teacher in this scenario has created obstacles for the parent and her daughter based upon the teacher's unawareness of the need to adapt to the needs of her students and her resistance to changes in her own field.

A Closer Look at Unawareness of the Need to Adapt in a Special Education Context

Unawareness of the need to adapt is a Barrier to Cultural Proficiency, which, in schools, is manifested in statements such as, "I've been very successful when working with 'non-disabled' students." And, "What's wrong with what we're doing? Most students are doing well." We also hear, "Our test scores are just fine, if we don't include the scores of the special education kids."

Unawareness of the need to adapt means failing to see the need to make personal changes or changes in school-wide practices to respond to the increasing diversity of our student body. This unawareness may exist because it never occurs to those in the dominant group—those who do not experience a disability or who do not have to learn English along with learning the curriculum—that there is a problem with how we have traditionally educated children who experience challenges in learning because of their individual learning style, language, communication, social-emotional characteristics, and needs.

People who are unaware of the need to adapt sometimes believe that students who need specialized support or differentiated instruction to benefit from schooling are best educated elsewhere—in a specialized classroom, with a specialized educator. They may believe that these students need "remediation" or to be "rehabilitated" in order to join in and succeed in the general education curriculum or classroom (Van der Klift & Kunc, 2002). Or these educators may find intolerance of human diversity as "politically incorrect," socially unacceptable," or "morally wrong." From these educators you might hear statements of *resignation,* such as "I'll have her in my class; somebody has to." Or you might hear statements of *benevolence,* such as "Of course, Joel can join my class; I know he won't do well, but that's to be expected given his difficulties," or "The paraprofessional will take care of his accommodations, so it doesn't affect my teaching the other students." Van der Klift and Kunc (2002) point out the limitations of such feelings and expressions of tolerance, noting that "simply being tolerated is not the same as being valued. Few have as their life's goal to simply be tolerated" (p. 24). Those not yet aware of the need to adapt likely do not see tolerance and benevolence responses as falling short of an ultimate response of genuine valuing of diversity. Nor do they realize that once the commitment to Cultural Proficiency is made, everyone (including themselves) necessarily will change to envision and create a new school culture.

REFLECTION

What might be some examples of unawareness of the need to adapt to changes in your surroundings or school context? What are some benefits or adaptation? What are some risks or consequences involved in not adapting?

_____

_____

_____

_____

Manifestations of These Barriers

Now that we've defined the four Barriers, let's take a closer look at them in action in schools and organizations. In what ways do these Barriers manifest themselves in the work and lives of educators? The four Barriers are broad categories describing historical and organizational frameworks that get in the way of Culturally Proficient Inclusive

Classrooms and Schools. Within these four Barriers exist examples of blocks and obstructions that shape those Barriers. Let's examine the intersections of where these four Barriers come together.

A Closer Look at Resistance to Change: Internal and External Blocks

Often educators, including those unaware of the need to adapt, experience impending change (e.g., implementation of Common Core and College and Career Readiness standards; the education of students with severe disabilities in general education) as an outside force that deems what they have been doing as inadequate or outright wrong. This outside force is viewed as a threat that must be resisted. Why? Deal and Peterson (1990) years ago observed that the inevitable result of a major change within an organization is the fear of loss of the organization's culture, a loss of the "historically rooted, socially transmitted set of deep patterns of thinking and ways of acting that give meaning to human experiences" (p. 8).

People become emotionally attached to shared meaning that comes from shared experiences, practices, traditions, rituals, and the accompanying history and stories that define for them their culture. And as Deal (1987) notes, "[w]hen attachments to people or objects are broken . . . people experience a deep sense of loss and grief" (p. 7). Consequently, when change threatens the prevailing culture, people have the urge to dig in their heels and resist it with all their might (Villa, Thousand, Paolucci-Whitcomb, & Nevin, 1990). After all, change may mean altering one's practices and, at least temporarily, becoming or feeling less than fully competent while comfortable instructional practices and routines give way to new, challenging, and unpredictable demands and worldviews.

Resistance to change toward culturally proficient schooling also can be the result of blocks or barriers to creative thinking. Some blocks are internal, driven by negative assumptions about others and us. Other blocks are external, reflecting societal values. External blocks are particularly prevalent in public schools, where strong spoken and unspoken social norms and rules, cultural and historical traditions, and habits of mind and behavior prevail.

A new teacher who summed up her first experience of back-to-school night provides an example of blocking creative thinking as well as the external blocking of unspoken social traditional norms:

> I wanted to change the traditional back-to-school night from teacher talk and presentation in my classroom to a celebration of families, with food and conversation. I did not know that changing things up would become such a topic of discussion in my school. Being a new teacher, I wanted

to be closely connected to how my parents felt during back to school night. I was not the same race and religion as most of my students. I wanted to practice what my teacher preparation and best practices had instilled in me—to know my students' families and their stories to build relationships. I couldn't think of a better way than breaking bread with them, so we ate and talked. Then, sitting down, we talked about differences in families, cultures and learning needs. I thought it was amazing and was extremely excited to talk about it! My family and classmates that I keep in touch with shared my excitement, but my fellow colleagues did not. I came back to school and my back to school night was not considered a celebration but was put under a microscope. I have never felt so alone in what I thought was thinking outside the box to expedite the building of relationships with my families.

Perceptual Blocks as Barriers. James Adams, in his well-known book entitled *Conceptual Blockbusting: A Guide to Better Ideas* (2001), identifies several sets of blocks, the first of which are internal and have to do with how a person perceives a situation. Perceptual blocks include adding extra rules that aren't really there and not being able to picture something differently or from another viewpoint. Many examples of these blocks exist from famous and brilliant individuals. For example, consider the following (cited in Goleman, Kaufman, & Ray, 1993, p. 128). The president of the Michigan Saving Bank, advising Henry Ford's lawyer not to invest in the Ford Motor Company, stated, "The horse is here to stay; but the automobile is only a novelty—fad." In 1927, Harry Warner, the president of Warner Brothers at the dawn of the "talkies," asked "Who the he[ck] wants to hear actors talk?" Two decades later, in 1946, Daryl Zanuck, head of 20th Century Fox, commenting on television, stated, "Video won't be able to hold on to any market it captures after the first six months. People will soon get tired of staring at a plywood box every night."

Cultural and Environmental Blocks as Barriers. Other blocks we may face are cultural and environmental in nature. Adults and children alike can experience a variety of *cultural* blocks as barriers in school. Some blocks manifest themselves as unspoken norms that fantasy, playfulness, humor, fun, imagination, and displaying wild and crazy ideas are time wasters or taboos to the serious business of teaching and learning via reason, logic, and seriousness. An example of an *environmental* block is a school structure that builds in little to no time for educators to collaborate in planning and problem solving, so that educators might exercise the "two heads are better than one" phenomenon of synergy. Another environmental block would be a top-down school or school district governance structure that rarely solicits or seriously considers teacher, parent, and student perspectives and input.

Emotional Blocks as Barriers. Emotional blocks are possibly the most common and invisible of the creativity barriers to thinking and acting in different ways. Fear—fear of failure, fear of thinking and being different, fear of looking or sounding foolish or unintelligent—represents an extremely strong emotional block. The preference to judge and negate rather than imagine options and the preference to make quick decisions rather than be relaxed, be tentative, incubate, or "sleep on it" are two additional emotional blocks that can inadvertently be fostered in schools where quick solutions are reinforced over imaginative, fanciful, and reflective thinking.

Language as a Barrier. "We know that language shapes perceptions, so a small word choice can make a big difference in communicating attitudes toward people with disabilities [or any other perceived difference] and assumptions about the quality of their lives" (Research and Training Center on Independent Living, 2013, p. 1). Language can be a powerful block to (or facilitator of) cultural proficient thinking and actions. The language we use to describe others either positively or negatively influences our own thinking and the thinking of others about whom we speak and write. Failing to recognize and use language that communicates valuing, respect, appreciation, belonging, and membership and distinguish it from language that communicates inferiority, undesirability, and nonmembership (e.g., "socially disadvantaged," "culturally deprived," "suffering from a disability") can perpetuate negative stereotypes, offend those being referenced, and bring a change effort to a standstill—all through the power of words.

Fortunately, over the past several years, disability rights organizations and individuals with disabilities have voiced the preference for their portrayals to be objective and neutral, which are more likely to lead to culturally proficient thinking and actions of inclusion, valuing, and advocacy. One fundamental preference is for the use of "people first language," the practice of referring to someone as a person first and making reference to a disability as second (e.g., saying "students eligible for special education" rather than "special education students"; saying "Lori who has a learning disability" rather than "that learning disabled kid"). People first language honors the fact that a person with a disability is first and foremost a person, not a disability or a diagnosis or someone who is defective or a victim (ADA National Network, 2015). Another fundamental preference is the use of language that emphasizes a person's abilities rather than his or her limitations (e.g., "students who use communication devices" rather than "non-verbal student;" "Delores who uses a wheelchair for mobility" rather than "Delores who is wheelchair-bound").

Thomas Armstrong (1987) illustrates how easy it can be to transform a negative reference of a person into a positive characteristic—how to turn *lead* language into *gold* language, if you will. For example, rather than thinking and referring to a child as *hyperactive*, consider the child to be a *kinesthetic* learner. Rather than referring to Jacque as *scattered*, consider her behaviors to represent *divergent thinking*. Rather than describing Rich as *irritable* and *plodding*, think of and refer to him as *sensitive* and *thorough*! *Lead* language offers little more than a stereotyping label. *Gold* language— thinking of and referring to students' or colleague's attributes as talents, gifts, and strengths—gives us a foundation on which to build.

For the most up-to-date guidelines on how to speak and write about people with disabilities, see the ADA National Network (2015) and Research and Training Center on Independent Living (2013) website guidelines. Note that these guidelines can be applied to the prompt, respectful portrayal of and interactions with any student or adult subgroup.

To sum up, perceptual, cultural, environmental, emotional, and language blocks and barriers to creative thinking are subtle and often invisible to creative and culturally proficient thinking. Overcoming these blocks and barriers requires self-examination, intentionality, commitment, reflection, energy, practice, and being mindful of the Guiding Principles of Cultural Proficiency. In fact, a subtle but pervasive block to thinking or acting in a different way is the amount of mental effort and intellectual (and moral) commitment and energy that is used to learn and practice anything new or unfamiliar.

DIALOGIC ACTIVITY

With your grade level team, your department group, and your faculty and paraprofessionals, engage in a dialogue using the following prompts:

What is our shared knowledge about the four major Barriers to creating Culturally Proficient Inclusive Classrooms and Schools? What might be examples of these Barriers that block student access to general education environments, curriculum, and instruction? What do data reveal about over- or under-representation of students in support, intervention, or enrichment experiences and programs by English proficiency, race, ethnicity, special education eligibility, gender, sexual orientation, or socioeconomic status? In what ways has this chapter informed your work?

_____

_____

_____

_____

SUMMARY

The purpose of this chapter was to present an in-depth view of the Barriers to creating and sustaining Culturally Proficient Inclusive Classrooms and Schools. Once educators are aware of the Barriers and the obstacles educators must confront, overcoming those Barriers through intentional behaviors, practices, and policies becomes their work. Chapter 4 offers strategies for Overcoming Barriers to Inclusive Education by using the nine Guiding Principles of Cultural Proficiency and a Barrier-busting paradigm of special education service delivery.

4 Overcoming Barriers and Creating Opportunities for Learning

Society, in agreeing to assign medical meanings to disability, colludes . . . to keep it a personal matter and "treat" the condition and the person with the condition rather than "treating" the social processes and policies that constrict people's lives.

Simi Linton (1998, p. 11)

GETTING CENTERED

What is your reaction to this quote? What might be some educational antidotes to deep seated systems of oppression, privilege, and entitlement; unawareness of the need to adapt; perceptual, cultural, environmental, emotional, and language blocks and barriers to creative thinking and action; and ableist medical model treatments of student learning variability?

COUNTERING THE BARRIERS WITH THE NINE GUIDING PRINCIPLES

The four Tools of Cultural Proficiency introduced in Chapter 2 comprise a frame that offers an antidote to Barriers identified in Chapter 3. Often, educators do not verbalize their values; however, their behaviors and written policies and practices often reflect those deeply held values and assumptions. Behavioral changes that result in policy and procedural changes can occur when protocols like reflection and dialogue are facilitated so educators can confront their values, belief, and assumptions.

Surfacing Our Values, Beliefs, and Assumptions

As indicated in Chapter 2, the Tool of the Guiding Principles of Cultural Proficiency allows educators to focus on students' assets in ways that overcome Barriers. What follows are restatements of the nine Guiding Principles in the form of questions. We invite you to read the nine questions and the brief discussions and employ your skills of reflection and dialogue. First, read each question and the comments and *reflect* on your personal responses. Ask yourself, "What is my truthful, honest response to each question and how do I react to the comments that follow each question?" Educators who are willing to look deeply within to examine the *why* of *how* they developed certain attitudes and values are well prepared to even better serve diverse communities of learners.

Second, in whatever role you have in your educational community, we invite you to engage with your colleagues in *dialogue* to surface deeply held assumptions and reach shared understanding of what "Overcoming Barriers" means to the school community. From these inclusive dialogue sessions carefully crafted statements can emerge to inform everyone in your school community of your shared beliefs and values about all students. At that point, students will be learning, because their culture is embraced as an asset as opposed to being viewed as a deficit that limits their learning.

These nine questions adapted from the Lindsey, Diaz, Nuri-Robins, Kikanza, and Lindsey (2010) **"Focus on Assets, Overcome Barriers"** article are designed as guides for individual educators and school district members to probe and understand their core values in working with communities that have populations with cultural characteristics different from their own.

The Nine Questions for Reflection and Dialogue

1. To what extent do you honor culture as a natural and normal part of the community you serve?

State and federal legislation has brought us face to face with the reality of cultural demographic groups in ways we have never before experienced in this country. Although gaps in learning and access to the general education classroom and curriculum have always been present, we now have the opportunity to discuss student learning and access in terms of race, ethnicity, gender, perceived ability, and language learning. As educators, each of us must recognize the extent to which we regard these and other cultural groupings as asset-rich resources upon which to build our educational programs, not as accountability inconveniences, deficits, or sources of problems.

2. To what extent do you recognize and understand the differential and historical treatment accorded to those least well served in our schools?

The disparities that we now acknowledge as the achievement or learning gaps in many cases have been developed over many generations. Though we may not have been party to intentional practices of segregation, racism, sexism, ethnocentrism, ableism, or any other form of oppression, our collective responsibility is to now recognize and address these educational disparities. Said another way, although we may not have created the problems of today, they're ours to address.

3. When working with people whose culture is different from you, to what extent do you see the person as both an individual and as a member of a cultural group?

We believe most of us like to be seen and valued for who we are. We may enjoy being part of a team that achieves; however, one's group identity does not detract from also wanting to be appreciated for who we are as individuals. Yet, when working in cross-cultural venues, some educators too often revert to use of terms such as *they* and *them* when referencing people from cultural groups different from themselves.

4. To what extent do you recognize and value the differences within the cultural communities you serve?

The cultural groups in our schools are no more single cultures than those of us educators who populate the ranks within our schools. Each of the cultural group we serve has vast differences in education, incomes, faith practices, language, valued abilities, and lifestyles. The cultural groups in our school communities are as diverse as is the broader community. The differences *within* cultural groups often give rise to groups having more similar worldviews across cultural lines than they do within cultural groups.

5. To what extent do you know and respect the unique needs of cultural groups in the community you serve?

A one-size-fits-all approach to education fails to acknowledge students' different learning, cognitive, and information processing characteristics. A culturally proficient inclusive educator uses and supports colleagues to use differentiated instruction and universally accessible tiered supports to ensure every student access to the same educational benefits and privileges that previously had been afforded only to some.

6. To what extent do you know how cultural groups in your community define family and the manner in which family serves as the primary system of support for students?

A prevalent educational assumption has been that parents and other family caregivers who really care about the education of their children will avail themselves of opportunities to interact with the school. Increasingly, our schools have become adept at finding culturally inclusive ways of engaging parents and caregivers in support of student engagement and achievement. Culturally proficient educators look for community attributes and assets rather than community problems or issues.

We find, too often, educators and parents have different perceptions of what parent/community-school participation means. Effective and meaningful parent/community-school partnerships require sensitive, respectful, and caring educators who are willing to learn the positive nature and culture of the community and identify Barriers that have impeded progress in parent/community-school relations.

The traditional, often stereotypic, image of Euro-American homes of family identified as one mother, one father, and their children is now recognized as a limited view of "family." Today, culturally proficient educators acknowledge single parent families, multiple-generation extended families, same-gender parents, foster care families, and residential care homes as "family." Whatever the family configuration is for a student, that family is the family.

7. To what extent do you recognize and understand the bicultural reality for cultural groups historically not well served in our schools?

Parents and community members have to be fluent in the communication patterns of the school as well as the communication patterns that exist in their communities. They also have to know the cultural norms and expectations of schools, which may conflict or may be different from those in their communities, their countries of origin, or their cultural groups.

In ideal conditions, their children are developing bicultural skills to "code switch" to meet the cultural expectations of their environments. However, parents and guardians may not yet have these skills for adapting to new and different environments and are penalized if they fail to respond to norms set by educators because they do not navigate well the school system. Therefore, our responsibilities as educators are to adapt to our communities and their needs and help families and students successfully navigate their multiple worlds.

8. To what extent do you recognize your role in acknowledging, adjusting to, and accepting cross-cultural interactions as necessary social and communications dynamics?

We have encountered few educators who fail to recognize the historical and current impact of racism and other forms of oppression on current school environments. It is also our experience that our educator colleagues who do recognize and understand the huge toll that oppression takes also understand how people not affected by those same systems benefit in unwitting ways. This awareness and understanding of the dynamic nature of oppression versus entitlement enables such educators to be effective in responding to the educational needs of cultural groups within their schools and districts.

Unless one has experienced intentional or unintentional acts of discrimination or oppression, a person cannot fathom the everyday toll it takes on one's day-to-day life experiences. The over-representation of students of color in special education and other programs and their under-representation in advanced programs is not new information. Educators who are aware of such dynamics employ strategies and tactics that engage parents and community members as partners to ensure inclusive, equitable, and beneficial opportunities for their children.

9. To what extent do you incorporate cultural knowledge into educational practices and policymaking?

Experienced educators recognize the need to learn the culture of any new organization they join. Their very survival depends on appropriate responses to cultural norms of the school community. Effective educators are aware of their own cultures and the impact their culture has on their school or district.

Knowledge about school culture, our individual cultures, and the cultures of our community rarely arrives to our laptops as a PDF file. Cultural knowledge is possessed by those who are keenly aware of themselves, their community surroundings, and the legacies and challenges experienced by cultural groups in our country and local communities.

Educators who possess this self-awareness and are effective in cross-cultural settings avoid phrases such as, "Doesn't everyone know that?" "I would hope parents see that as their responsibility;" or "It's the way we do things around here. They'll just have to adjust." Phrases such as these marginalize and serve to perpetuate an "us against them" mentality.

Culturally proficient educators share their own cultural knowledge, engage with the community, and invite community experts, knowing that over time such actions will lead to appropriately institutionalizing cultural knowledge. Such educators recognize that re-culturing schools to be responsive to diverse constituencies is an internal, intentional, and ongoing process.

So, What's Your Response?

The Barriers presented in Chapter 3 are the typical narrative we face in schools. The Guiding Principles, as examined in these nine questions, can be the counternarrative to overcome these Barriers. Shifting the culture of a school or district from responding to Inclusive Education as a compliance issue to responding in ways that transform organizational culture relies on use of educators' internal assets of reflection and dialogue. This intentionality is a two-step process of personal reflection and purposeful dialogue with colleagues. Response to these nine questions provides the basis for developing core values intended to serve a diverse community.

BARRIER-BUSTING PARADIGMS PRIOR TO SPECIAL EDUCATION REFERRAL

What do general educators do when their instructional strategies seem not to work for some students? Often, they hear their colleagues say, "His behavior is so bad, refer him to special ed." Or another teacher might say, "I really can't understand what she is saying and she can't even read at grade level, so I'm referring her to special education." What if student learning differences were viewed and accepted as a natural part of human diversity rather than the majority of students being thought of a *normal*, a few celebrated as *gifted*, and others viewed as *disabled*? Are there structures, schooling practices, or student and family empowerment strategies that can turn dispositions, habits, traditions, and unexamined biases around to create truly inclusive learning environments where a culturally proficient view and treatment of student learning variability prevails? Fortunately, the answers to these questions are *yes*. And the remainder of this book describes and provides living examples, using the five Essential Elements of Cultural Proficiency, of what these inclusive dispositions, practices, and behaviors could look and sound like in your school.

To prepare for the notions that follow in subsequent chapters, the authors are compelled to introduce you to an essential disposition for creating inclusive learning communities—the *presumption of competence*. The authors also introduce you to a notion of comprehensive system of support and school organizational structure known as the Multi-Tiered System of Supports (MTSS) that acknowledges and plans for student diversity by marshaling and deploying human resources to maximize the likelihood that any student can progress and succeed in the curriculum.

Setting the Stage: Presuming Competence

Biklen and Burke (2006) confront a particular manifestation of ableism in U.S. education, namely, "to assume incompetence of students who have severe communication impairments [and other pervasive support needs] . . . through the process of classification" (p. 166). They point out that each of us has a choice to presume a person with extensive support needs (historically referred to as students with moderate and severe disabilities) to be incompetent or "admit that one cannot know another's thinking unless the other can reveal it. The latter . . . more conservative choice . . . refuses to limit opportunity by *presuming competence*" (p. 166). Presuming competence in the absence of evidence to the contrary is not a new notion. In the early 1980s, Donnellan and Leary (1984) described the notion of presumed competence, naming it the *criterion of least dangerous assumption*.

Summarizing the notion, Jorgensen (2005) writes, "the least-dangerous assumption when working with students with significant disabilities is to assume that they are competent and able to learn, because to do otherwise would result in harm such as fewer educational opportunities, inferior literacy instruction, a segregated education, and fewer choices as an adult"

(p. 5). The most dangerous assumption is to fail to presume competence, intelligence, and potential for growth. The criterion of least dangerous assumption is the *presumption of competence at all times for all persons.* For students with more extensive support needs, this presumption can be operationalized by creating *"personally meaningful curriculum"* (Bambara, Koger, Burns, & Singley, 2016, p. 475) that blends opportunities to acquire academic and functional knowledge and skills within the context of general education and natural routines "driven by family and individual preferences, values, and vision" (Bambara et al., 2016, p. 475). For all students, *Inclusive Education **is*** presuming competence and holding the highest of expectations (National Alternate Assessment Center, 2006).

Taking Action: A Multi-Tiered System of Supports for Inclusive Education for All

The Multi-Tiered System of Supports or MTSS language has emerged recently as an umbrella concept and label for a comprehensive system of support, which strives not only to prevent unnecessary referrals for special education but to provide a comprehensive, school-wide and district-wide system of "high-quality first instruction, supports, and interventions in academics and behavior for all students, regardless of whether they are struggling or have advanced learning needs" (California Services for Technical Assistance and Training, 2015, p. 2).

MTSS, originally termed Response to Intervention (RTI), was introduced in the 2004 reauthorization of IDEA in response to suspicions that the increasing number of students being made eligible for special education, particularly in the eligibility category of Specific Learning Disabilities, could be reduced if efforts were made to detect and intervene with students struggling early in their schooling. The system is conceptualized as a three-tiered "pyramid" approach, with Tier 1 being high quality, evidence-based core instruction in general education, with frequent student progress monitoring. Tier 2 represents the supplemental targeted and strategic interventions, generally delivered in small groups to students not making adequate progress on expected curriculum benchmarks. Tier 3 represents the intensive (more frequent and individualized) interventions for students whose response to intervention at Tiers 1 and 2 are deemed inadequate (Villa & Thousand, 2011).

MTSS is presented within this context as a "Barrier-buster" for general educators, administrators, counselors, and parents, as they collaboratively seek to meet the student's needs prior to a referral for assessment for special education eligibility. MTSS provides an overarching organizing structure that braids Response to Intervention (RTI) processes with Positive

Behavioral Intervention & Supports (PBIS) systems that support student social-emotional-behavioral health and growth (Higgins Averill, & Rinaldi, 2011). Figure 4.1 offers a visual representation of a system of support that includes the three tiers of RTI and PBIS. What are the components of an effective RTI system and a comprehensive PBIS system? How do they work together in a comprehensive MTSS? Let's explore the answers to these questions for RTI. Chapter 6 explores these same questions for PBIS.

RTI Components and Tiers Described. RTI represents the academic side of the MTSS pyramid shown in Figure 4.1. RTI integrates resources from general education, special education, and other programs, such as English language development support programs, into a comprehensive system of core academic instruction and interventions to prevent failure of and quickly responding to students having difficulty making progress in the general education curriculum. Table 4.1 identifies the key elements to a strong RTI process (Villa & Thousand, 2016) executed through the three tiers of support.

Tier 1. RTI Tier 1 represents (a) regular (e.g., three times per year), school-wide, general screening of all students' progress in the general education curriculum and (b) classroom-based instruction and individualized and group interventions that represent the core instructional program. Through the use of differentiated instruction and research-based methods that have been demonstrated to be effective with a wide range of diverse learners to

Figure 4.1 MTSS Pyramid

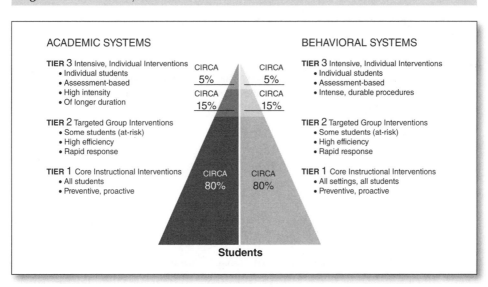

Table 4.1 Response to Intervention (RTI) Key Elements

1. Value and belief that every child can and does learn
2. Acknowledgement that a learning difficulty may lie in a "mismatch" between student characteristics and the teaching/learning environment rather than a deficit in the child
3. Regular, periodic (e.g., three times per year), "universal" screening of the entire school population
4. Early and swift intervention versus a "wait to fail" approach
5. Proactive, high-quality, evidenced-based instruction in general education classrooms
6. Regular team meetings to examine data and collaboratively problem solve (using established solution-finding and differentiation methods, such as those described in Chapters 6 and 7)
7. Data-based decision making by teams to determine appropriate interventions
8. Supplemental high-quality instruction by classroom teachers and specialists matched to student strength and needs
9. Research-based interventions provided at increasing levels of intensity
10. Continuous progress monitoring during interventions
11. Fluid and flexible grouping of students for instruction, remediation, and enrichment
12. Monitoring of instructional and intervention group composition to assure membership does not remain static and result in de facto tracking
13. Brings services to a student without having to label the student, make the student eligible for special education, or remove the student from the general education classroom or curriculum
14. Can replace the "IQ-achievement discrepancy model" to identify a Specific Learning Disability via documentation of a student having received research-based instruction and interventions and having failed to respond to increasingly intensified, specialized intervention
15. Active family involvement in decision making, with families being informed of student progress in their native language or preferred mode of communication

accommodate differences in students' natural learning differences, 80% to 90% of students should achieve predetermined benchmarks in expected time frames.

Hall, Strangman, and Meyer (2011), researchers at the National Center on Accessing the General Curriculum, describe differentiation of instruction as an instructional process that recognizes and *acknowledges the differences* among students' background knowledge, language, culture, and learning characteristics and then reacts *responsively and positively* to these natural differences. In differentiating instruction, general and special educators attend to the four *access design points* of Universal Design for Learning (UDL) to address the needs of diverse learners in the same classroom (Universal Design for Learning, 2013). Namely, teachers gather facts about the differences in students' background knowledge, readiness, language, culture, and learning preferences and interests (Design Point #1: Gathering facts about the learners). They provide students with multiple means of *representation* (Design Point #2: Content differentiation), multiple means of *expression* (Design Point #3: Product differentiation), and multiple means of *engagement* (Design Point #4: Process differentiation). Chapter 8 describes in great detail two proven processes for differentiating instruction—the reactive, *retrofit* process and the proactive, UDL process (Thousand, Villa, & Nevin, 2015).

If general educators co-teach with specialists (e.g., special educators, speech and language pathologists, English learner development specialists, literacy coaches), they can "double" their effectiveness in differentiating at Tier 1 by co-teachers meshing their diverse knowledge, expertise, and skills regarding content, instruction, management of materials and technology, human relations and motivation, and collaborative planning and problem solving.

Tier 2. Tier 2 is designed to address the approximately 15% of students who do not make adequate progress in Tier 1 instruction—failing to meet a predetermined expected benchmark performance level. Tier 2 intervention instruction is specially designed to accelerate learning in the area(s) of identified concern (e.g., decoding, reading fluency, reading comprehension). Tier 2 instruction typically is delivered to small groups of three to six students with similar learning needs during an *additional,* daily, thirty-minute instructional session. Progress monitoring occurs much more frequently (e.g., every two to four weeks) than Tier 1 assessment (e.g., three times annually). The duration of interventions may range from several weeks to an entire academic year.

At Tier 2, instructors use *parallel co-teaching* (described in detail in Chapter 6) to work with demographic groups of students in order to simultaneously deliver differentiated instruction to students homogeneously grouped for specific interventions. Tier 2 parallel co-teaching does not mean instruction is necessarily offered outside of the general education classroom. In fact, it should look like a classroom of three or four centers or stations with groups of students focusing on different learning. Placement in an instructional grouping is never based on students sharing a common label but rather it is based upon assessment data indicating that the students, at this particular moment, share a common instructional need and are likely to benefit from the same additional differentiated instruction.

Tier 3. Tier 3 intervention support addresses the fewer (approximately 5%) of students who do not make adequate progress with Tier 1 and 2 instructional supports services. More intensive (i.e., more frequent, for longer periods of time) interventions are crafted and provided. Tier 3 interventions often are administered individually or in groups smaller in size than at Tier 2 (i.e., groups of two or three). If, at Tier 2, the intervention time had been one 30-minute period, at Tier 3 that time might be increase to 2, 30-minute sessions. Tier 3 interventions are long term, enduring over weeks and months, so as to ensure there is adequate time for interventions to yield positive outcomes.

Tier 3 intervention is NOT special education or an automatic referral for assessment for special education. However, if Tier 3 interventions prove ineffective, assessment for special education eligibility may be considered as part of a deeper examination of the health, vision, hearing, social/emotional, language development, and information processing status of the student. As at Tier 2, Tier 3 intervention relies upon parallel co-teaching among the broad range of school personnel who share intervention responsibility.

MTSS is a systems approach to creating Inclusive Schools aimed at activating district-wide (rather than school-by-school) identification and alignment of internal and external agency (e.g., social services, continuing education, community college, university, juvenile justice) resources and partnerships to achieve high expectations for *every* student, from perceived high achievers to the 10% to 15% of students requiring intensive interventions. To achieve the highest performance of every student, an MTSS approach requires educators to learn and use *positive behavior support* approaches and *differentiated instruction (DI)* and *Universal Design for Learning (UDL)* principles and strategies to differentiate the content, product, and process of learning for all students examined in Chapters 6 through 8. MTSS also relies upon collaborative planning and decision making represented by the seven-stage *Decision-Making Cycle* shown in Figure 4.2. Through this cycle, team decision making is driven by ongoing student progress monitoring and data-based collaborative problem solving. The collaborative teaming and creative problem-solving processes introduced in Chapters 7 and 8 can be used at each stage of the cycle to increase team solution finding.

Progress in National Policy and Practice

Until 2014, the U.S. Department of Education was largely concerned with ensuring schools were in compliance with *procedures* for determining

Figure 4.2   MTSS Decision-Making Cycle

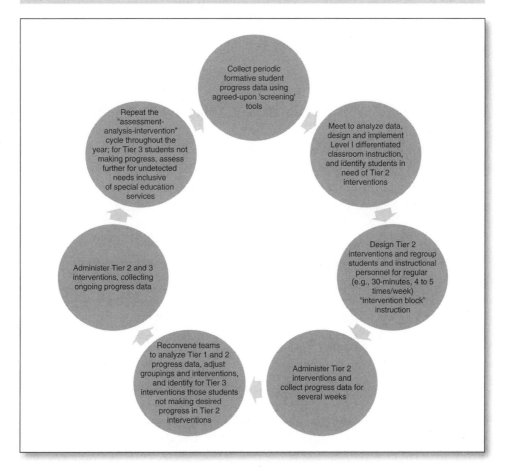

eligibility and delivering special educations services. However, today the key shift in oversight has been from checking for compliance to monitoring *student outcomes*. To quote former U.S. Secretary of Education Arne Duncan, "Every child, regardless of income, race, background, or disability can succeed if provided the opportunity to learn. . . . We know that when students with disabilities are held to high expectations and have access to the general curriculum in the regular classroom, they excel. We must be honest about student performance, so that we can give all students the supports and services they need to succeed" (U.S. Department of Education, 2014, para. 3). Secretary Duncan's statement acknowledges what over forty years of research have demonstrated: the power of providing students with disabilities access and support to succeed in the general curriculum (IDEIA, 2004). It takes (a) culturally proficient assumptions of competence for all learners, (b) structures such as MTSS for integrating resources, (c) instruction that genuinely differentiates, and (d) personalized adaptations and specialized academic instruction, when needed, for any learner.

DIALOGIC ACTIVITY

What are some Barrier-busting strategies that you and your colleagues might consider? Based on your reading in this section, what new ideas are surfacing for you? What surprised you about your own reactions? Of what do you want to be mindful in your own practice as a result of reading this chapter? What might be some collaborative actions that you and your colleagues can take at this point in your reading and thinking?

_____

_____

_____

_____

SUMMARY

The purpose of this chapter was to provide you with strategies for Overcoming Barriers to Inclusive Education through the use of the nine Guiding Principles of Cultural Proficiency and a Barrier-busting paradigm prior to special education service delivery. Part II of this book gives a description of Lakeside, the community where the people in our examples and case stories reside. Chapters 5 through 9 deeply examine how the five Essential Elements of Cultural Proficiency can be activated to promote Inclusive Education and guide you to develop an action plan for installing Inclusive Education.

Part II

How to Become Inclusive Using the Five Essential Elements of Cultural Proficiency

The five chapters that comprise this Part II section of the book examine ways to transform a school into a Culturally Proficient Inclusive School by using each of the five Essential Elements of Cultural Proficiency introduced in Chapter 2, outlined in Table 2.2, and identified here by the chapter in which each is featured. We present the Essential Elements in separate chapters to facilitate deep study and mastery of each element.

- Chapter 5: Assessing Culture
- Chapter 6: Valuing Diversity
- Chapter 7: Managing the Dynamics of Difference
- Chapter 8: Adapting to Diversity
- Chapter 9: Institutionalizing Cultural Knowledge

Together, the Essential Elements provide interdependent standards for being intentional about behaving, teaching, learning, and adjusting policies and practices so as to actualize genuinely inclusive learning communities where every student and adult is welcomed, valued, and supported to enjoy equitable access to success. As performance standards, the five Essential Elements can be used to plan for and evaluate change toward culturally proficient inclusive classrooms and schools.

Chapter 10 brings the Essential Elements together and provides guidance for educators to engage in an action planning process for installing Inclusive Schooling.

LAKESIDE AND LAKESIDE UNIFIED SCHOOL DISTRICT

Lakeside is the city where the people in our illustrative examples and case stories live and work. The stories we tell about Lakeside and the examples we use are a composite of the experiences of the authors and people we know as well as data we have collected through observations of and personal interviews with students, families, educators, and community members. Lakeside Unified School District (LUSD) represents a composite of actual individuals and groups from schools and districts across the United States and Canada who have actively engaged in developing culturally proficient inclusive learning communities. The composite characters and situations are presented to help you explore your own journey in becoming a culturally proficient community member and to provide practical applications of the two concepts of Cultural Proficiency and Inclusive Education.

The Lakeside Community

Lakeside is an urban/suburban community with a population of 125,000 residents. The population is comprised mostly of middle income and working-class folks who work in Lakeside or businesses in neighboring suburbs. About 15% of Lakeside families are considered working poor and rely on some sort of government assistance for child and health care. About 5% of Lakeside residents are in the upper tax bracket, commuting to top-paying management positions in the metropolitan center 20 miles away.

For the most part, families in Lakeside, regardless of income, send their children to the local public schools, shop in the area businesses, bank at the local banks and credit unions, obtain health care at the community hospital and neighborhood clinics, and worship in their respective local faith communities.

Lakeside's population has grown recently because of a community initiative begun six years before. Working with Welcoming America, a national organization that helps local communities work on immigrant-friendly initiatives, the mayor, city council, chamber of commerce, and local business owners launched the "Welcome Lakeside" campaign to make Lakeside an immigrant destination by developing and advertising (a) jobs that provided more than a living wage, along with high quality training and supportive working conditions and (b) family networking and other community resources (e.g., free adult English language instruction with free child care). City officials and leaders also partnered with the LUSD and public agencies to anticipate the need for English language development and other instructional and social support services (e.g., counseling and social work services) that students and families transitioning from countries in which they may have experienced trauma might need.

In the six years since the *Welcome Lakeside* initiative began, Lakeside's foreign-born population has jumped 65%, one of the largest gains in any locality of 100,000 or more residents. Much of this growth has been because of secondary migration, movement of immigrants who relocate after initially settling elsewhere. Lakeside's Pakistani, Somali, Indian, and Honduran populations have increased particularly rapidly.

"It's really great to see the change from 5 years ago to now," Lakeside mayor Bernie Sandoval says. "Changes are very visible in the vitality of the city, especially the downtown, where most people shop, eat, and enjoy our free community events." Not all residents have responded with such enthusiasm. A recent city-sponsored survey found that Lakeside neighborhoods with more immigrant families actually reported less welcoming attitudes than others. Lakeside responded by convening community dialogue events, block parties, and even an international soccer tournament.

Lakeside Unified School District

The increasing ethnic diversity of Lakeside's population is reflected in the student population of LUSD. Of the 15,000 public school students, 40% are European Americans; 22% are Latino from Central America, including Honduras, South America, Mexico, and the Caribbean; 18% are second- and third-generation Asian Americans from Vietnam, Cambodia, Korea, and the Philippines; 8% are African Americans; and 2% are Native Americans or Pacific Islanders. The remaining 10% of students represent the recent secondary migration of Pakistani, Somali, and Indian families. Of the school-aged population, 18% are eligible for special education services, a percentage that is 5% greater than the national average. Students learning English represent 20% of the student population.

LUSD serves its 15,000 students through two comprehensive high schools, East High and West High. Four Grade 6 through 8 middle schools—Central, Mission, Twin Oaks, and Lincoln—feed into the two high schools by geographic region. Eight elementary schools, each named after one of the first eight U.S. presidents, feed into the four middle schools, again by geographic region. Teachers and administrators in the elementary and middle schools are predominantly female and Caucasian. The staff and administration of the high schools are an even mix of males and females, again primarily Caucasian.

Given the steady growth of Lakeside's population, class sizes across all grades increased by 10% on average, a small percentage increase but an increase about which many veteran teachers complain and "blame" students with IEPs (Individual Education Programs) who are spending more and more time in general education—and the children of the new immigrant families. Funds are being raised to build additional classroom space, but the building program is not set to break ground for at least three to four more years, as the city and district are still coming out of the recession that hit Lakeside's small business community particularly hard.

As part of the *Welcome Lakeside* initiative, Trinity College, the local community college, and LUSD have taken advantage of state Early Start and Head Start funding to include a university-community childcare center for infants, toddlers, and preschoolers in the newly constructed School of Education complex on the university grounds. Program admission priority is given to children of university faculty, preschoolers eligible for early childhood services, children of families that rely upon federal assistance for childcare, and children of newly arrived immigrants. The program offers a clinical practice experience for the College of Education, Health and Human Services students studying to be elementary and early childhood general and special educators at no cost, other than supervision and couching, to the childcare program. The partnership is a win-win community effort that brings professionals, families, educators, and future educational professionals together to create an inclusive teaching and learning community.

Twin Goals: Inclusive Education and Culturally Proficient Community Learning and Action

The educational leaders of the LUSD have been deliberately engaged in the journey toward equity and Inclusive Schooling for students with and without disabilities for the past five years. Like many districts across the United States and Canada, administrators and teachers have been seeking ways to create a unified system of support for students that would break down the historical categorization of students as being either general education or special education students. To address the new support system, district administrators focused on two interrelated goals:

- Developing and implementing site-base Inclusive Education improvement plans that include (a) meaningful *incentives* (e.g., professional learning, opportunities to plan and reflect, sharing of

successes at school board meetings or national conferences) for personnel to take risks to try new inclusive practices and (b) adequate *resources* (e.g., human, technological, and organizational structures, such as MTSS) to expand and sustain inclusive educational learning communities
- Using Cultural Proficiency as an approach for teachers and administrators to examine how their *beliefs* about learning, including perceived disability, impact students and families and how district *policies* and *practices* facilitate or thwart student opportunities to access and success in the general curriculum

A LUSD central office and building leadership team, affectionately dubbed by teachers and school board members as *The Visionizers*, have been deliberate in defining and communicating the vision of welcoming, valuing, empowering, and supporting the diverse academic, social/emotional, language, and communication learning of all students regardless of perceived ability, ethnicity, race, gender, faith, sexual orientation, immigrant status, or socioeconomic level of students and their families. Although progress has been made toward achieving the district's dual goals, LUSD has a distance to go to accomplish its goals for *all* students. The question facing The Visionizers and district personnel is, "How do we use the Essential Elements and other Tools of Cultural Proficiency to continue and accelerate movement to create truly inclusive educational experiences for every student?"

How did LUSD get to the place in its journey toward equitable and Inclusive Education that you are learning about in this Part II Introduction? To answer this question, let us introduce you to two key *LUSD Visionizers*—Superintendent Dr. Patricia Alvarado and District Special Education and Pupil Personnel Services Director, Alyce LaPlant.

Dr. Patricia Alvarado, Superintendent. Dr. Patricia Alvarado came to Lakeside four years ago after completing a Juris Doctor (JD) PhD program at Northwestern University's Pritzker's School of Law with an emphasis in Human and Civil Rights and Mediation. She pursued her law degree after practicing as a special educator in a variety of positions in Chicago and neighboring public school district for twenty years. Prior to attending law school, she had risen through the ranks to become an special assistant to the superintendent charged with the responsibility of working with families and school staff to keep students with significant support needs in their local neighborhood schools rather than sending them to separate special classrooms in regional cluster classrooms, which had been the district's past practice. She had pursued the establishment of this position because of her own personal family experience. She is one of three children of an El Salvadoran father, who immigrated to the United States in the early 1960s, and a mother who has been a French and Spanish language high school educator in the Chicago public schools for her entire career. Because her parents strongly believed that all children should be fluent in more than one language, she was raised and became fluent in both of her parent's native tongues, English and Spanish, as well as French. The eldest child in the family, Michael, who had multiple disabilities, did not live at home. Shortly after he was born, Patricia's parents had been advised by the family physician to send Michael to be cared for in a well-known Chicago-land residential facility for children and adults with severe disabilities. Michael was born before the 1975 Public Law 94–142, the Education for All Handicapped Children Act (now called the Individuals with Disabilities Education Improvement Act), which opened schoolhouse doors for children with disabilities, including students like Michael. At the time of his birth, federal law did not require that a child with disabilities had the right to a free and appropriate education, and it was common practice for children with multiple disabilities to be place in a facility for care, with little educational dimensions to the care program.

Patricia visited Michael with her family on weekends and developed a deep love and respect for her older brother. She grew to hate the conditions under which he was living and, as a young teen, began a campaign to get Michael out of the facility and into a supported living arrangement near her family home. After more than five years of advocating for his independence, her family accomplished their goal. By the time Michael was 30, he was living in his own apartment with a roommate and a staff of supporting employees. As it turns out, in his many years of institutionalization, Michael had incidentally learned a great deal by observing and listening to others and watching TV shows, such as *Sesame Street*. With Patricia's advocacy, a variety of augmentative communication devices and procedures were introduced to Michael, and he began to learn to type entire words and then sentences using a keyboard. He enjoyed life in the community near his family for several years, until his early passing in his mid-30s because of undetected pneumonia, which took his life suddenly. Patricia's brother motivated her to become a teacher and to ultimately go to law school and get her doctorate, so that she had the knowledge and credentials to take on a leadership role in policymaking, school reform, and systems change. In her six years of doctoral studies, she immersed herself in studying the works of Paolo Freire, starting with *Pedagogy of the Oppressed* (1970), literature on systems change for Inclusive Education (e.g., Villa & Thousand, 2000, 2005), and the works of Delores and Randall Lindsey and colleagues on Cultural Proficiency (e.g., CampbellJones, CampbellJones, & Lindsey, 2010; Lindsey, Jungwirth, Pahl, & Lindsey,

2009; Lindsey, Nuri-Robins, & Terrell, 2009; Nuri-Robins, Lindsey, Lindsey, & Terrell, 2012). Her studies yielded a dissertation entitled "Uniting Critical Pedagogy, Cultural Proficiency, and Inclusive Education for Social Transformation," which mapped a process for transforming school districts and other institutions into inclusive communities.

In Patricia's last year of school, she came upon a *New York Times* article that described the Welcoming America national organization and featured Lakeside as one of the local communities that was working on immigrant-friendly initiatives. She had vacationed in the area as a child and had loved the lakes and the waterskiing and the camping she had done there. She decided to visit and see about opportunities to use her new degree and skills. Within three months, she interviewed for the superintendent position, secured it, moved, and was on her path to employ her passion and knowledge of social justice and organizational change to help move LUSD to becoming a culturally proficient inclusive schooling community of teachers and learners.

Alyce LaPlant, LUSD Special Education and Pupil Personnel Services Director. From as early as she can recall, Alyce, the elder of two siblings, loved playing school with her younger brother. She was very proud of her Abenaki Native American and First Nations lineage, both of her parents having a mix of French Canadian and Abenaki ancestry. As a special education teacher in a small northern Vermont town, she had joined her parents in campaigning for official State of Vermont recognition of several Abenaki bands, one being the Abenaki Nation at Missisquoi, from which Alyce's family descended in rural northern Vermont. The town in which she served as a special educator had been one of the original national federal homecoming model demonstration schools, which brought back students and teachers of segregated regional special education classrooms to the general education classrooms of their local schools back in the mid-1980s. She had been a primary student in her rural community school at the time that this project reunited siblings in their local school, and she remembered being a peer tutor and buddy to her new classmates. The experience and friendships she made through this systems change effort, which led to Vermont becoming the most inclusive state in the United States, reinforced her desire to teach and led her into a dual general and special education teacher credential program, after which she returned to her home town to continue the work collaboratively planning and teaching with general educators. Encouraged by her special education director, who was looking to groom a future replacement, she returned to school part time, while she was working as a teacher, to obtain her master's degree in educational administration.

Ten years into her career, she married and relocated to Lakeside community, because of a promotion that required her and her husband to transfer to her husband's corporate headquarters in the Midwest. The couple found a home in Lakeside, and Alyce easily secured a job as a special educator in the school district. When she arrived at her assigned elementary school to review her students' records and IEP plans, she was more than surprised to find that the majority of her students spent little to no time in general education academic classes. Some attended specials, such as music, physical education, and art. Others spent no time in general education environments at all, except for lunch and recess. Even more shocking to her was discovering that a special entrance for students with more significant disabilities existed at the school. When she inquired about this, she was told that it was too overwhelming for the students to transition in and out of school with all of those other students.

Alyce spent her first year developing relationships with colleagues, families, and administrators and working with her students' IEP teams to change IEPs to increase the hours students spent in general education. It was not an easy year, but she had her past experience and stories of her students' successes in general education to win over teachers and families, one by one. In her first year, Alyce also volunteered to be a member of the district Professional Learning Planning Committee. She eventually became chair. As member and chair, she advocated for and sought out well-known trainers to deliver district-wide professional learning in differentiated instruction, culturally responsive pedagogy, positive behavior supports, co-teaching, and the rationale for and practices of Inclusive Schooling. When Dr. Alvarado delivered her inaugural opening day speech, which outlined a vision for a model district that truly practiced equity and quality in education for every child, Alyce was relieved and inspired, as she saw in Patricia Alvarado an ally. Alyce quickly made an appointment with the new superintendent. In the meeting, Alyce told Patricia of her Vermont experiences, her multiple credentials, and her efforts to promote change and asked what more she could do. Patricia asked her if she would be willing to leave the classroom and activate her administrative credential in order to interview for the LUSD Special Education and Pupil Personnel Services director position, which was being vacated by the retiring director, who had been in the position for 30 years. Alyce jumped at the chance, interviewed, and was hired to start the first day after school closed in the spring!

The LUSD Visionizers. Patricia Alvarado and Alyce LaPlant began their work together through the establishment of *The Visionizers* team, already mentioned. Included on the team is Brian Wayne, district assistant superintendent for instruction, a twenty-two-year veteran of the district who holds knowledge of the institutional history of the district. Building representatives included administrators and representative of stakeholder groups—parents, teachers' union, paraeducators, and students. Among the representatives are a counselor from each high school. Janice Hightower, a fifteen-year district employee represents East High School. Diego Flores, who is bilingual in Spanish and English and a five-year district veteran, represents West High School. The two counselors have taken it upon themselves, as a joint professional learning endeavor, to read as much about Cultural Proficiency as they can, attend conferences on the topic in the region, and think about how to integrate these concepts into their counseling practices with students. They started their study by reading Nuri-Robins and Bundy's (2016) *Fish Out of Water: Mentoring, Managing, and Self-Monitoring People Who Don't Fit In,* which focuses upon strategies for working with youth who don't seem to fit in and who are targeted because they are different.

The group's members have been deliberate in spreading the vision of Inclusive Schooling and delving deeper into their understanding of Cultural Proficiency (CampbellJones et al., 2010; Lindsey et al., 2009; Lindsey, Kearney, Estrada, Terrell, & Lindsey, 2015; Nuri-Robins et al., 2012; Quezada, Lindsey, & Lindsey, 2012) by Assessing Cultural Knowledge as described in Chapter 5 and continually asking and answering the question, *How can we use the Tools of Cultural Proficiency to maintain and accelerate movement toward genuinely Inclusive Schooling for every student?*

Join us in following the various members of LUSD learn about and practice methods of culturally proficient community engagement, assessment, and instruction. In the chapters that follow, you are provided multiple opportunities to apply culturally proficient principles and practices in your own teaching and leadership. We invite you to immerse yourself in the getting centered, reflective, and other application exercises. We encourage you to try out the strategies and tools suggested in each of the chapters. Once you have tried the ideas or strategies for yourself, we further encourage to you reflect and assess how well they work to create more inclusive learning experiences for students, families, and members of your school. You may need to adapt some of the suggested approaches to fit your current situation, which is great. You may find your current school situation is not quite prepared to embrace some approaches, but you have them ready for their future use! So, take a "ready, *fire,* aim" rather than a "ready, aim, *fire*" approach, and engage with the chapters and offered activities. The more we try, the more we grow!

REFLECTION

What did you learn or what resonated with you from this Part II Introduction? What thoughts and feelings come to mind about your own school and community context as you read about Lakeside and LUSD? What questions do you have now?

_____

_____

_____

_____

5 Assessing Cultural Knowledge Through Authentic and Differentiated Strategies

The question that educators and psychologists often struggle with is: How smart is the student? Gardner suggested that this is the wrong question to ask. The question that needs to be addressed is: How is this student smart? This question presumes that all students are smart; they are just smart in different ways.

Mary Falvey, Mary Blair, Mary P. Dingle,
and Nancy Franklin (2000, p. 194)

GETTING CENTERED

What do you know about how you are smart? What do you know about how your students or your own children are smart? What do you know about how your personal cultural background and experiences affect your view of and how you assess what is smart? What do you know about how your students' cultural backgrounds and experiences influence their view of how they are or are not smart? What are ways to assess in order to get to know the "whole" of a child that goes beyond state and core standards?

_____

_____

_____

_____

The purpose of this chapter is to provide the reader with ways to assess the current dispositions and perceptions of members of a school community regarding culture and disability by taking actions identified in Table 5.1, which presents three columns of information. The first column displays a brief definition of the Essential Element of Cultural Proficiency: Assessing Cultural Knowledge. The second column offers five actions that culturally proficient members of an inclusive learning community may take to assess their cultural knowledge of themselves and others. The third column identifies, systems, practices, and strategies that are featured in this chapter to achieve each of the five actions.

REFLECTION

Take a moment and carefully read each of the five assessment actions of culturally proficient members of an inclusive learning community represented in column two of Table 5.1. What are actions you could take to become and be aware of the five dimensions of knowledge described? What are actions you have seen others take? How could expanding your knowledge of yourself, your school, your students, and your community benefit students with IEPs and students with other perceived differences or difficulties?

_____

_____

_____

_____

FIVE ACTIONS FOR ASSESSING AND DEVELOPING SPECIAL EDUCATION CULTURAL KNOWLEDGE

The following section offers descriptions of systems, practices, and strategies for engaging in the five assessment actions identified in column two

Table 5.1 Actions and Authentic and Differentiated Systems, Practices, Strategies for Assessing Cultural Knowledge

Cultural Proficiency Essential Element #1	Actions of a culturally proficient member of an inclusive learning community	Assessment systems, practices, strategies, and tools featured in this chapter
Assessing Cultural Knowledge Identifying the cultural groups present in the school and system	I/we . . . • Become and am/are self-aware of my/our own culture and the effect it may have on the students, families, and others in the school with whom I/we work • Become and am/are aware of what I/we know about others' cultures and about how I/we react to others' cultures and the diverse communities within my/our school • Become and am/are aware of how other educators in the school as a whole react to diversity • Extend my/our knowledge of what constitutes diversity • Become and am/are aware of what I need to learn, know, and do to be effective in a multicultural classroom and school that includes individuals with perceived disabilities and other learning, behavior, and communication differences	I/we . . . • Use mindfulness questions to prompt openness to new information about myself and others • Use *criterion of least dangerous assumption* and *presumption of competence* notions to assess my assumptions • Use the Cultural Proficiency Continuum and Van der Klift and Kunc's four views of and responses to diversity to assess my and colleagues' cultural knowledge • Use the Universal Design for Learning (UDL) "Gathering Facts About Learners" Design Point • Use data gathered at Tiers 1, 2, and 3 of the Multi-Tiered System of Supports (MTSS) • Use best practices and the spirit of IDEIA to implement the Individual Education Program (IEP) process with integrity • Use person-centered processes of intensive discovery • Learn and use Differentiated Instruction (DI) methods and strategies

of Table 5.1. The five actions could be thought of as steps of assessment. Therefore, each of the next five sections is identified as Assessment Steps 1 through 5. As you read each step and the examples provided, please remember that the examples are just that, examples. Many other ways are available to assess cultural knowledge and develop cultural proficiency. So, be mindful to avoid delimiting your own imagination by engaging in one or more barriers and blocks examined in Chapter 3, as you think of additional ways to assess cultural knowledge.

Step 1: Become Aware of My Own Culture and Its Effect on Students

Sounds easy, right? Not at all! As Lindsey, Nuri-Robins, and Terrell (2009) point out, developing Cultural Proficiency begins with oneself, as an *inside-out* process. Rather than thinking and speaking about "those students" or "those families," the culturally proficient member of an Inclusive School begins internally with herself and becomes aware and intentional of her own culture. She asks questions of herself such as the following:

- What do I bring to the school environment that might be a *Barrier* to healthy, supportive, and productive interactions with student and their families?
- What do I bring that manifests in my appearance, the language(s) I speak, and the cultures with which I identify that will *help* in creating a healthy, supportive, productive, and culturally proficient school environment and climate?

In their examination of culturally proficient practices for supporting educators of English learning students, Reyes Quezada, Delores Lindsey, and Randall Lindsey further offer a series of mindfulness questions for guiding inside-out thinking and prompting "openness to new information; and . . . awareness of more than one perspective" (2012, p. 58). The questions are modified here to reference and include students with disabilities and other perceived differences or difficulties.

My Inside-Out Learning Process

- Who am I in relation to the students I teach and serve?
- What am I learning about myself in relation to students with IEPs and other students with learning, behavior, and communication differences?

REFLECTION

Start your own inside-outside learning process! Reflect upon the observation: "This stuff is painful. . . . I never realized I had so much baggage and that it got in the way of my teaching. I learn so much from my students, and to think I used to be afraid" (Webb-Johnson, 2002, p. 67). Now answer the four Step 1 questions. What did you learn about yourself? Come back to these questions again in a few weeks and then, again, periodically. Do you notice any changes in your thinking? In what ways do the answers or indicators change or become refined or clearer over time?

_____

_____

_____

_____

Step 2: Be Aware of What I Know About and How I React to Others' Cultures

A next step for someone striving to assess her movement toward Cultural Proficiency regarding Inclusive Schooling is to ask herself questions that heighten her awareness of what she knows about and how she reacts to cultures other than her own, particularly the culture(s) of individuals with identified disabilities. One important question concerns two inclusive schooling notions introduced in Chapter 4; namely, the _criterion of least dangerous assumption_ and the _presumption of competence_. (See Chapter 4 for a review of these two notions.) The self-referencing question might be the following:

- To what extent do I genuinely embrace and apply the _criterion of least dangerous assumption_ and _presume competence_ for _every_ student, particularly the student who is considered to have significant disabilities?

Quezada, Lindsey, and Lindsey (2012) offer additional questions useful at this second step of becoming self-aware:

- How do I know (i.e., What are some indicators of success?) that I know about the cultures of my students and their families?
- How do I know (i.e., What are some indicators of success?) that I use the knowledge of my students' cultures, learning styles, behavior, communication preferences, and languages as _assets_ to support their academic, social/emotional, and interpersonal development?

REFLECTION

Consider the following scenario.

[A] pre-K teacher named Ms. Handley explained that because she does all of her assessments through observations, she was able to determine the interests and strengths of a student named Calvin, who is both an English language learner and a student with a disability. She revealed that by talking with Calvin's family and observing him in multiple natural contexts, her education team learned that he wanted to be a mechanic. They quickly realized that the only way they were able to engage Calvin in the curriculum was by "bringing in screws and hammers and discussing these as he played . . . "They learned "he had a lot of wonderful gifts, but we had to figure out how he was going to show his gifts." (Bacon, 2017, p. 43)

How is the notion of "presumed competence" introduced in Chapter 4 illustrated in this scenario? In what ways does Ms. Handley's approach to assessing Calvin and her other students reflect one or more of the five steps of culturally proficient assessment of cultural knowledge listed in Column 2 of Table 5.1 and described in this chapter? What are authentic ways you might use to get to know about your students' gifts, families, and cultures?

_____

_____

_____

_____

Step 3: Be Aware of How Other Educators in My School React to Diversity

The third step in Assessing Cultural Knowledge in Inclusive Schooling is to ask questions that reveal how other educators in the school community as a whole think about and react to diversity. At this step, Quezada and colleagues (2012) suggest posing open-ended questions about a school's culture such as the following:

- In what ways might we, all of the members of this school community, examine our current school culture, particularly regarding the inclusion of students with IEPs and other learning, behavior, and communication differences in all aspects of school life?
- Who do we say we are (e.g., deliverers of content, facilitators of access, advocates for social justice)?
- Are we who we say we are? How do we know? What are indicators?
- In what ways does our current school culture support or inhibit the inclusion and the academic, social/emotional, and interpersonal development of students with IEPs and other learning, behavior, and communication differences?

At this step, the six-phase Cultural Proficiency Continuum (introduced and described in Chapter 2 and illustrated in Table 2.1) becomes useful in assessing dispositions regarding diversity among the members of a school community. Table 5.2 combines the Continuum with observations of the respected Canadian human and disability rights advocates, Emma Van der Klift and Norman Kunc, to create an even more sensitive rubric for Assessing Cultural Knowledge through views of diversity and disability.[1]

Van der Klift and Kunc (2002) describe how, through their lifetimes, they have observed North American (Canadian and U.S.) societies and educators respond to diversity and disability differently based upon their view of diversity. At least four views and corresponding responses to human difference are noted in their work. The first view is that of *deviance*, which yields a response of *marginalization* expressed by avoiding, segregating, and in some cases, putting an end to the person who is different. This culturally destructive view and set of responses were prevalent in the pre-IDEA 1960s and early 1970s, when it was not unusual for a physician to advise the family of a children with extensive support needs to institutionalize their child. If the child remained home, absent IDEA protections to a free and appropriate public education (FAPE) in the least restricting environment (LRE), he will most likely have only a disability-only segregated school as a schooling option.

While U.S. society examined and changed such practices, the hurdle of the *ableist* perspective and *medical model* (described in Chapter 3) arose from the second view of diversity and disability as a *deficiency*. Remedial programs were developed expressly to minimize a child's disability and make her more like children without disabilities. The response to view disability as a deficiency is that of *reform*. Instead of thinking and saying "you can't be with us," educators now thought and said "you can be with us, but you must learn to be like us." A child with a disability was thought to need rehabilitation and assimilation in order to become a part of school and society. The reform response (the Cultural Continuum equivalent of *Cultural Incapacity*) remains today in many schools, although challenged by the mainstream schooling movement of the 1980s, and is still present today in some schools.

The third view of disability is that it is *unfortunate* and something *to be pitied*. This view yields a *tolerance* response. Tolerance may seem more appealing than the first two responses, as most view intolerance as morally unacceptable. However, although the intent of tolerance is to create greater acceptance, it fails to lead towards true social justice. Instead, it

---

[1] Meet Norman Kunc and Emma Van der Klift at http://www.broadreachtraining.com and http://conversationsthatmatter.org/. Learn more about what they do and offer to promote equity and inclusive community for persons with disabilities.

Table 5.2 Assessing Cultural Knowledge Through Views of Diversity and Disability

	Informed by Barriers to Cultural Proficiency Focus Is on *"Them"*			Informed by the Guiding Principles of Cultural Proficiency Focus Is on *"Our Practice"*		
Continuum Dimensions →	Cultural Destructiveness	Cultural Incapacity	Cultural Blindness	Cultural Precompetence	Cultural Competence	Cultural Proficiency
View of Diversity and Disability →	Deviant	Deficiency	Unfortunate To be pitied	Normal, natural, and typical		
Response →	Marginalization	Reform	Tolerance	Valuing (of diversity and disability as normal)		
Actions →	Segregation Avoidance Aggression	Rehabilitation Assimilation	Resignation Benevolence	Equal worth Mutual benefit Belonging		

leads to actions and words of resignation (e.g., "Sure, we'll include her, if we have to.") and benevolence ("I'll let her come into my class; I guess it's the right thing to do."). These statements represent tolerance and *Cultural Blindness* on the Cultural Proficiency Continuum, and simply being tolerated is hardly a life goal!

The fourth view of diversity and disability is that it is *normal, typical,* and part of the *natural* order of life. This view moves us beyond mere tolerance to the ultimate culturally competent response of genuine *valuing.* Educators who genuinely value diversity and others' cultures find it easy to envision and act to create Inclusive Schools and classrooms that welcome, value, and support any learner in ways described in the chapters that follow.

REFLECTION

Continue on your inside-out learning process by assessing the cultural knowledge of members of your school community through the lens of diversity and disability. With the Table 5.2 Continuum in front of you, think about how you and other educators in your school respond to students with disabilities, particularly students whose behavior are troubling or who have pervasive support needs (i.e., students with moderate and severe disabilities). Do you see actions or hear statements of marginalization, reform, tolerance, or valuing? What are they? Name them, claim them, and then commit to confront the underlying view of diversity and disability?

_____

_____

_____

_____

Step 4: Extend My Knowledge of Diversity—Use and Extend the UDL, MTSS, and IEP Processes

A fourth step in Assessing Cultural Knowledge is to extend our own knowledge of what constitutes diversity in our school and the community the school serves. At this step, Quezada and colleagues (2012) suggest exploring questions such as the following:

- Who and where are the cultural communities we serve inside and outside of the school (e.g., students with disabilities, students learning

English, students who identify as LGBTQ, students representing various ethnic and racial backgrounds, students who are athletes)?

- In what ways might we partner with the cultural communities inside and outside of the school to support the inclusion and success of students with IEPs and other learning, behavior, or communication difference?
- What are ways to get to know students in multiple ways that go beyond traditional academic performance assessments?

Extending knowledge about student diversity also means thinking about the assessment of student performance and success in multiple different ways. As the quote that opens this chapter suggests, it means shifting our thinking from simply asking "How smart are our students?" to asking "How are our students smart?" What are ways in which we can do this?

Extending Knowledge of Student Diversity Using the Universal Design for Learning (UDL) Design Point of "Gathering Facts About Learners"

Universal design refers to the creation and design of products and environments in such a way that they can be used without the need for modifications or specialized design. Universal Design for Learning (UDL) is the application of the universal design concept to education. With UDL, we take all of our students into consideration when designing curriculum, so that it may be accessed without the need for specialized adaptations for particular students, because the necessary adaptations in content (curriculum), product (assessments), and process (instruction) are built in. UDL is a way for educators to act on their perspective of diversity in students as natural and as an asset rather than a problem.

The first step or *Design Point* in the UDL process is to *gather facts* about learners in ways that let us know what they really know. Thousand, Villa, and Nevin (2015) describe and encourage teachers to use a broad variety of strategies and tools for gathering facts about students, ranging from home and community visits and student interest inventories to the use of technology or data-based observations of students engaged (or disengaged) in classroom and playground activities and other interactions (e.g., cooperative learning groups) to determine the communicative intent of behavior and interpersonal competence.

Accurate assessment of student learning requires students to have multiple means for expressing their understanding of the curriculum. Students who use assistive technology and augmentative communication systems to communicate and access learning also rely upon technological supports to show what they really know. Frameworks such as Multiple Intelligence theory (Gardner, 2011) and learning and thinking styles (Gregory & Chapman, 2013) assist educators to think about assessing students in various ways. For example, through his research, Gardner found a singular construct of intelligence to be too narrow. Instead he identified multiple (currently eight) dimensions of intelligence: visual-spatial, musical-rhythmic, bodily-kinesthetic, interpersonal, intrapersonal, naturalistic, verbal-linguistic, and logical-mathematical.

Particular Cautions Regarding Gathering Facts About Students With IEPs. In getting to know students with IEPs and identified disabilities, we caution educators to guard against focusing upon a student's disability label rather than learning about that particular individual. Culturally proficient educators ask for cultural knowledge as it relates to an individual learner (e.g., "Could you tell me about what really makes Amaya light up?") rather than about limitations (e.g., What is Amaya's IQ?). Educators striving to assess their and others' cultural knowledge must recognize and acknowledge that homogeneity within any category of disability is impossible and that specific information about a child from multiple perspectives (e.g., parent, siblings, friends, the student him- or herself) is the most beneficial to teaching and learning.

Disability-specific information can be gathered from any number of advocacy web sites that explain the educational implications for specific disabilities. However, the authors caution against overgeneralizing this information and losing sight of each student's strengths and uniqueness. We can get caught up in focusing on a medical condition, the challenging aspects of a disability, or the alphabet soup of eligibility categories (e.g., ED [emotional disorder], LD [learning disability], VI [visual impairment]).

Essential for the culturally proficient educator is to be aware that using a label to refer to a student objectifies and dehumanizes him. Norman Kunc, the recognized Canadian disability rights advocate—who also has cerebral palsy—refers to this dehumanizing phenomenon of seeing the person as the disability rather than the disability as a small part of a whole and complex person as "disability spread" (Kunc & Van der Klift, 1994). Figure 5.1 provides a visual representation of this phenomenon. The pejorative dehumanizing impact of labeling is so problematic that Individuals Disabilities Education Improvement Act (IDEIA) includes specific guidelines for using *person first language*—the practice (introduced in Chapter 4) of referring to an individual by name first and then adding a disability or other characteristic as a subsequent descriptor.

Figure 5.1 A Visual Representation of the Phenomenon of Disability Spread

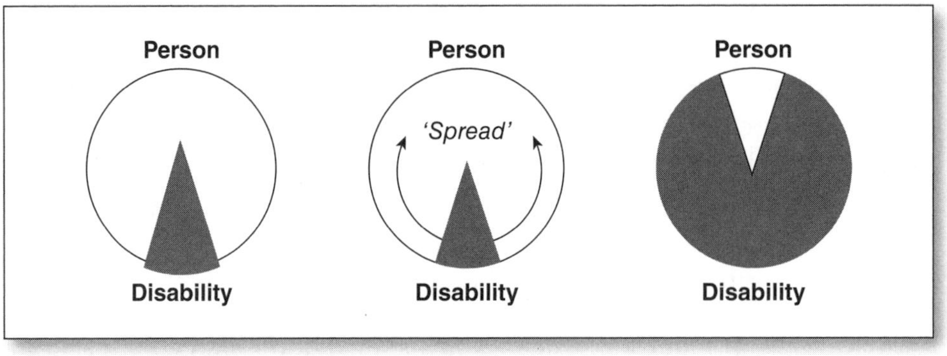

Source: Kunc, N., & Van der Klift, E. (1994). *Hell-bent on helping: Benevolence, friendship, and the politics of help.* Retrieved from //www.broadreachtraining.com/articles/arhellbe.htm. Used by permission.

Extending Knowledge of Diversity Through MTSS. As schools move to a culturally proficient Multi-Tiered System of Supports (MTSS) approach to anticipating and appreciating the learning community's natural student, we can extend our knowledge of our students' multiple dimensions if, in addition to the UDL Design Point #1 processes of getting to know our students, we also use Tier 1, 2, and 3 MTSS assessment structures as default ways for getting to know our students. What if we think about and ask ourselves questions such as the following:

- Within a Multi-Tiered System of Supports (MTSS) approach to academic and behavioral support and intervention for all students, how might we get to know our students in multiple ways by deliberately selecting diverse assessment measures that go beyond academic success (e.g., social skill competence, social/emotional well-being, creative thinking, and solution finding) and that are authentic, rich, and contextual in nature (e.g., curriculum-based assessment, artifact collections, portfolios, performance demonstrations, observations of student interpersonal interactions in cooperative groups)?
- Within a MTSS approach, how might we get to know our students in multiple ways by examining from multiple cultural perspectives the data generated from (a) periodic universal screenings, (b) observations of students engaged in high-quality evidenced-based instruction in general education classrooms, (c) continuous progress monitoring of interventions, and (d) conversations that occur in regular team meetings where student data are examined for the purposes of collaboratively problem solving? (Review the

data-based dimensions of MTTS in the Chapter 4 description of MTSS and the Table 4.1 list of key elements.)

Extending Knowledge of Student Diversity Through the IEP Process. Since first conceptualized in the 1975 Public Law 94-142 (now referred to as IDEIA), the assessment, eligibility determination, and progress monitoring dimensions of the IEP process have undergone several decades of refinement for the better. Any number of special education texts and websites can delineate the legal requirements of the IEP process from start to finish, the requisite components of an IEP plan, and the safeguards and steps designed to ensure due process and meaningful family and student input (e.g., Howard, Alber-Morgan, & Konrad, 2017). The results of any number of research studies can describe what can go wrong when the compliance *letter of the law* rather than the socially justice *spirit of the law* dominates the assessment and placement process. Things go wrong quickly when professional voices overshadow family and student voices and when professionals' behaviors disrespect and create confusion and intimidation among parents and students from culturally diverse backgrounds (Lo, 2012) or when the limited space on the computer-generated IEP plan form special educators are required to use literally "boxes out" what otherwise could be recorded as rich conversations and descriptions of a student strengths (Bacon, 2017).

In contrast, there are so many aspects of the IEP process that, when implemented in the socially just spirit of the law, highlight students' strengths and deepen trust, communication, and decision making among students, families, and professionals. For example, IDEIA requires that, on a student's IEP plan, the present level of performance (PLOP) statement be written in language that describes what the student *can do*—the student's current *strengths*, skills, preferences, talents—rather than what the student does not yet know or do. Another example is the requirement that every student supported with IEPs exiting high school develop a Summary of Student Academic Achievement and Functional Performance (SOP), which summarizes student strengths, interests, and learning preference as well as the adaptations, supports, and resources deemed necessary for the student to advocate for what is needed for success in post-school life. Carrying the SOP with them into their next schooling, work, and adult life experience, students can educate others and advocate for themselves the supports, accommodations, and differentiation that allows them success. Both are examples of the power of the IEP process. When implemented with integrity and heart, both requirements allow people to get to know the very best of a student's qualities and provide the appropriate and least restrictive supports.

Turnbull and colleagues (2015) provide several dozen tips and processes for engaging in the IEP process in ways that not only make it easy for students and families to exercise their rights under IDEIA but also make the IEP process one in which everyone—the student, family members, professionals, and invited others, such as friends and classmates—can easily discover and share a students' interests and gifts as well as their *great expectations* for a student's future. One of these processes is *person-centered planning*. Person-centered planning is a team approach for augmenting the IEP process to achieve what Beth Gallagher and Kirk Hinkleman (2012) refer to as *intensive discovery*. Person-centered planning gathers the diverse players in a person's life to engage in structured steps aimed at "finding new ways to listen and pay attention" (Gallagher & Hinkleman, 2012, p. 65). Person-centered planning helps everyone learn about a person's hopes and dreams, preferences, strengths and capabilities, goals, needed supports, and barriers to achieving a life worth living.

Available to educators are several well-established person-centered planning processes, such as lifestyle planning (O'Brien & Mount, 2005) and personal futures planning (Mount, 1995). The Planning Alternative Tomorrows with Hope (PATH) process is a unique process in that it works backward from a far-reaching dream—the North Star—to action steps in the present (Gallagher & Hinkleman, 2017, www.inclusion.com/path.html). The most widely used person-centered planning process is the **M**cGill **A**ction **P**lanning **S**ystem or **M**aking **A**ction **P**lans (MAPs) process (Falvey, Forest, Pearpoint, & Rosenberg, 2002; Villa, Thousand, & Nevin, 2010). The use of MAPs as a futures planning tool is illustrated at the end of this chapter with Evan's team, as his support circle plans for his transition from school to post-school life.

Common to all person-centered assessment and planning processes is the opportunity for the person who is the focus of the process to exercise self-advocacy. Having structured forums where self-advocacy can be nurtured and developed is important, particularly because research suggests a positive relationship between self-advocacy and the achievement of personal goals (Agran & Hughes, 2008; Arndt, Konrad, & Test, 2006).

Step 5: Be Aware of What I Need to Learn, Know, and Do to Be Effective in a Multicultural Diverse School and Classroom

The fifth step an educator can take to assess cultural knowledge is to take stock of what he, himself, needs to learn, know, and do to be effective in his multicultural school and classroom. At the very least, this self-assessment should lead an educator to learn about and try out methods for differentiating instruction, such as the Retrofit approach featured in

Chapter 6 and the Universal Design for Learning approach featured in Chapter 7. Why? Hall, Strangman, and Meyer (2011), researchers at the National Center on Accessing the General Curriculum, identify differentiated instruction (DI) as *the* instructional process that recognizes and acknowledges the differences among students' cultures, background knowledge, readiness, language, learning preferences, and interests and then responds *purposefully and positively* to these natural differences. The expressed goal of DI is to maximize each student's growth and individual success by meeting each student where he or she is in the curriculum and assisting each student to learn via his or her unique learning processes.

DI is not an easy strategy for all teachers to implement; teachers are required to adapt and modify materials, learning goals, instructional methods, and learning activities and identify what students are required to do and produce in a classroom (Universal Design for Learning, 2013). DI requires teachers and leaders to commit to changing and replacing familiar and comfortable teaching practices with new processes for shaking things up in the classroom so all students have access to powerful and effective learning. And DI most easily and naturally occurs when general educators and specialists (special educators) collaborate in planning and instruction to not only accommodate the learning differences of students with IEPs, English learners, students considered gifted and talented, and students otherwise considered at risk (e.g., impacted by homelessness), but to accommodate the learning differences experienced by all students through instructional delivery arrangements, such as *co-teaching* (examined in Chapter 6) rather than pull-out services.

What Exactly Is MAPs and How Does It Work?

Making Action Plans or MAPs (Falvey et al., 2002; Villa et al., 2010) is a person-centered, futures-planning process of intensive discovery that engages a group of people who have various relationships with a person (e.g., parents, siblings, neighbors, friends, teachers, classmates, administrators) to highlight what they know about that student's strengths, interests, and other learning, social, and emotional characteristics in order to creatively plan for the future. The MAPs process is a vehicle for empowering students to advocate for inclusion, respect, belonging, kindness, and friendship for themselves and their peers.

A MAPs gathering can be held anywhere—in a living room, backyard, classroom, office, restaurant—that is comfortable for the focus person (student) and those who are invited. The focus person determines the MAPs guest list. A neutral facilitator welcomes attendees, explains the process, and guides the group through the series of eight questions shown in Table 5.3.

Table 5.3 The Eight Key MAPs Questions

1. **What is a MAP?**

   A MAP is designed to assist people to get from where they are to where they want to be (goals). At a MAPs meeting, participants are asked what a MAP means to them.

2. **What is the person's history or story?**

   The person and the family are asked to describe their history or story.

3. **What is the dream?**

   This is in many ways the most important step of the process, because it identifies the goal(s) for which you will develop a plan of action. Again, the person and family members speak first and then others in attendance may add to the list of goals. The facilitator must be nonjudgmental in both words and body language.

4. **What is the nightmare?**

   This question helps those in attendance to understand the fears and concerns of the target student and family—the things they want to avoid. At times, this step elicits emotions and reactions that are strong and/or sad. The information is critical because the entire point of the process is to achieve the dream while avoiding the nightmare.

5. **Who is the person?**

   At this step, participants brainstorm and generate a list of words that describe the person for whom the MAPs is being held. The facilitator oftentimes groups descriptors into themes. The focus person is asked to describe him or herself and pick out three favorite words from the list.

6. **What are the person's gifts, strengths, and talents?**

   Here particular emphasis is placed upon the learner's "giftedness." The focus is not solely academic but designed to acknowledge the learner's strengths and interests.

7. **What does the person need?**

   Participants consider what resources and supports will be needed to assist the learner to reach the dream and avoid the nightmare. Those assembled may need to consider academic, communication, behavioral, biological, health, safety, and security needs of the person.

8. **What is the plan of action?**

   The final step is the development of a plan that includes the who, the what, and the when of actualizing the dreams and avoiding the nightmares.

The order of questions is flexible and can be altered to accommodate the dynamics of the group and the flow of contributions. A public record (e.g., on newsprint, projected from a computer connected to a projector) of contributions at each step is displayed for all to see. At each step, the focus person and those closest to that person—family members and friends—speak before any professionals attending the meeting.

MAPs is a forum that expressly solicits student voice and the voice of those who know best and care most about a student. For a student's teachers, the MAPs process offers valuable information about a student that could not be obtained by a standardized test or academic assessment. MAPs can be used with any student, and many teachers use a mini-version of a MAPs experience for every child in their classroom as part of student-parent-teacher conferences. Some states have incorporated components of MAPs as part of the IEP planning process for students eligible for special education. MAPs also can be used with organizations (e.g., schools, school districts) that are seeking new direction or focus (e.g., toward socially just Inclusive Schooling). MAPs, then, is an all-purpose self-determination vehicle for anyone, including students of all ages— kindergarten through college—for "giving direction, pointing out landmarks, showing routes and directions, and detours or things to 'get around'" (Villa et al., p. 142).

Evan's MAPs Meeting

Meet Evan! Evan is a seventeen-year old high school senior with autism who, in the upcoming year, is transitioning from high school to post-school life. Mr. Rosenberg, a teacher who has known Evan since he was a freshman, is facilitating Evan's MAPs meeting. Evan has strong convictions regarding environmental issues and what is "right and wrong." At times, these convictions put him in compromising positions. For example, when Evan notices schoolmates who litter, smoke, or otherwise disrupt the environment, he takes a strong stand and lets them know he is offended by these behaviors. For his MAPs meeting, Evan invited a wide circle of people, including current and past teachers, friends and classmates, his mother, and his long-time behavior support person.

So, how did the meeting go? What was discovered and planned as a consequence of Evan's giving focus to the MAPs meeting? See Figure 5.2 for a photograph of the summarized notes for each step of Evan's MAPs.

What Is Evan's History or Story? After three years of early childhood special education services, Evan started kindergarten in the LUSD at his local neighborhood school. To his family's disappointment, the special educators and school administrators argued that Evan was best served in a pull-out special education class for most or part of the day. Evan's family disagreed, and after two years of dissatisfaction with Evan's placement, the school district IEP team agreed that Evan would transfer to a Lakeside elementary site where the philosophy and practice was that special needs students would first be placed and supported in general education classes, with special education and related services (e.g., behavior support)

Figure 5.2 Evan's MAPs

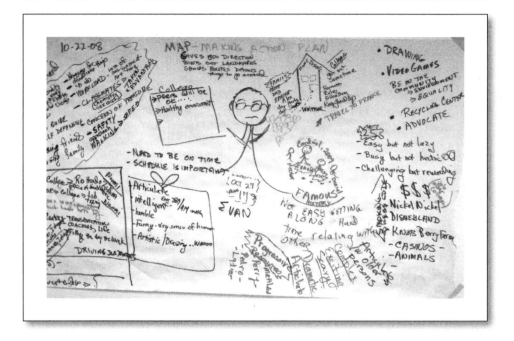

provided to the classroom teacher through consultation and co-teaching. With ongoing positive behavior support and counseling, Evan made it through and transitioned to one of the four middle schools, Lincoln Middle School (LMS), the district middle school with a visual and performing arts emphasis. At LMS, co-teaching among general educators and specialists (e.g., special educators; art, music, and theatre specialists) provides students access to the core curriculum, the arts, and for students with IEPs, specially designed instruction. At LMS, Evan was introduced to and discovered a passion for drawing and theatre staging.

Evan's transition to West High School was smooth. Because of the work of the district's Visionizer team and the professional learning the high school teachers had received regarding differentiated instruction, co-teaching, and the rationale for including high school students supported with IEPs in A to G content classes, West High School was transforming into an increasingly Inclusive School—with 78% of students with IEPs now attending co-taught core content classes, as compared to 10% three years before. Evan had attended general education classes throughout his high school years and had particular success in art. Evan has passed the requisite exit exams and will have earned enough credits to receive a diploma at the end of his senior year. Things are good at home with his mother, brother, and two dogs.

What Is the Dream? Evan, his family, friends, and teachers see Evan continuing his education. Evan wants to go to a campus where smoking is prohibited. Priority dreams are for Evan to continue to develop his drawing talent and be involved in community activities particularly focused upon social justice, such as organizations concerned with environmental issues, a recycling center, or an advocacy group. Other priorities are enjoying local entertainment venues (live theatrical productions; Disneyland; casinos, once he turns twenty-one), working around animals, and getting a job at age twenty-five or older that is "busy, but not hectic" and "challenging but rewarding."

What Is the Nightmare? Nightmares—frustrations, worries, and concerns that Evan anticipates—include time pressure and deadlines, workload in college and work, nagging from peers, classmates who do not really work, getting along with college peers and roommates, needing supported living services to live away from home, and relaxing with others (especially girls). In what ways might the team respond to these nightmares and anxieties?

Who Is Evan? What Are Evan's Gifts, Strengths, and Talents? Everyone in attendance agreed that Evan has a dry sense of humor, enjoys video games, and likes to draw and be around animals. He is articulate, intelligent, interested in going to community college, humble, funny, and an environmental advocate intolerant of smoking and littering.

What Does Evan Need? What Is the Plan of Action? With Evan's history, dreams, nightmares, and the gifts sections of the MAPs in mind as well as the question, *Who is Evan?* the team is able to identify Evan's needs and a plan of action so that Evan can reach his dreams and avoid the nightmares. Evan's team generates and prioritizes a long list of needs and actions. The list includes a range of activities: (a) agreeing to engage in senior activities and attend commencement in order to shake the principal's hand, (b) connecting with the Department of Vocational Rehabilitation for employment preparation and steps to reach employment goals, (c) visiting local community college campuses to explore enrollment as well as supports available from the Office of Disabled Students, (d) considering the pros and cons of conservatorship, and (e) revisiting progress on the plan of action developed at this MAPs meeting on a regular basis with Evan, his mother, and Mr. Rosenberg (see Figure 5.3 of Evan and Mr. Rosenberg).

For Evan, this MAP meeting is an important step in the development of his self-awareness about his strengths and post-high school dreams as well as his understanding of the complex maze of supports and services he might want or need to access to realize those dreams. MAPs provides a starting rather than an ending point, setting the stage for enlisting a network of

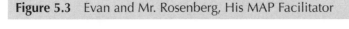

Figure 5.3 Evan and Mr. Rosenberg, His MAP Facilitator

people and community support services to help Evan execute a plan to address expected challenges and concerns (nightmares). The reality of the process is in the implementation and follow-up and the commitment of a team working together for the common goals and dreams of an individual.

REFLECTION

In what ways does Evan's story inform you about effective actions that can be taken or avoided in support of students? In what ways does Evan's story inform your work?

_____

_____

_____

_____

CASE STORY

We offer this case story as an example of how the Essential Element of Assessing Cultural Knowledge can be used to positively influence educators' actions.

Part 1: Pegah's Voice

John Adams is one of the eight elementary schools in LUSD. This school reflects the diversity of the district, although the teaching staff are primarily Caucasian and female. The principal of John Adams, Adam Watson, invites Pegah and her parents, Khan and Priya Patel, into his office for a brief welcome to the school. The school year is beginning, and Pegah's parents are among many immigrants who have just relocated to Lakeside as a result of the *Welcome Lakeside* relocation initiative. Pegah was born in the United States and attended kindergarten in the school district from which her family moved. She has just turned six years of age and comes to John Adams with an active IEP plan, which she has had since she turned three years of age. She and her family also received early intervention support services when she was a toddler. Pegah experiences significant expressive communication difficulty, and her previous special education support team worked with Pegah and her family to determine an augmentative electronic system that allows Pegah to communicate using an iPad. Since she was four, she has been using the device and apps loaded onto the device to communicate at home, in the community, and at school. Pegah's new first-grade teacher, Dora Johnson, and the primary grade special educator, Angela Teague, enter the principal's conference room and take seats around the table. Pegah gets up and joins another first grader, who is a new friend and neighbor, who invites her to try out the playground climbing structures.

Mr. Watson, the principal, suspects the iPad is the focus of the meeting and might be an issue with the teacher, Mrs. Johnson. Khan and Priya want Pegah to use the iPad for all communication, as this is her preferred mode of communication. Angela Teague supports the use of the iPad. Dora Johnson sees it as interfering with her using more normative ways to communicate. The parents are insisting that the school allow Pegah to use this method. The options presented to the parents are to send Pegah to a different school in which Pegah can use her iPad all the time or limit her communication modality in this school.

Adam Watson, Principal:	*Thank you, Mr. and Mrs. Patel, for coming in to meet with us. Welcome to Lakeside and to John Adams Elementary. We are excited to have Pegah join our school as a member of our first grade. We also are very proud of our special education support team, which will wrap support around Pegah from Day 1.*
Angela Teague, Special Educator:	*Thank you, Adam, for your kind words. Mr. and Mrs. Patel, I have reviewed Pegah's records and her IEP and know that she is using an iPad and the apps loaded onto it as a primary means of communication. And we see from her IEP quarterly progress reports that she has been very successful in using the iPad to communicate with peers and adults.*

Khan Patel, Pegah's Father:	*Thank you. We are happy to be here and find ways to help our daughter.*
	Actually, **all** *of her communication is through the iPad.*
Dora Johnson, First-Grade Teacher:	*All of it?*
Priya Patel, Pegah's Mother	*Yes. All of it.*
Dora Johnson, First-Grade Teacher:	*I know that I will be having Pegah in my class, so I need to tell you that in this school and most certainly in my classroom, we encourage children to use their voices to communicate. In our experience, it's the best way to develop language.*
Khan Patel, Pegah's Father:	*It's not that Pegah can't communicate, it's just that her "voice" is through the iPad. We have seen some great strides in her being able to express what she knows and what she wants and what she needs.*
Dora Johnson, First-Grade Teacher	*I am sure that there will be a place for the iPad, but I am wondering if we can encourage her to use her voice, at least with the other children? That way, she will be better able to keep up. She will have more opportunities to interact with the material and the other students.*
Priya Patel, Pegah's Mother:	*We prefer that the class become accustomed to Pegah and her communication modality.*
Adam Watson, Principal:	*I am not sure that an iPad or Chromebook has ever been used this way before in our school. I am concerned about a precedent that it might set.*
Angela Teague, Special Educator:	*Just as a reminder, Pegah has an IEP, and her IEP specifies as an expressive language accommodation her use of assistive technology—in her case the iPad and the apps loaded onto it. From what the IEP progress report and you, Pegah's parents, report, Pegah needs the iPad for communication at this point. At least for the first 30 days of her attendance here, our responsibility is to provide an interim placement that matches as closely as possible the supports, services, and placement Pegah had in her former district. Pegah attended kindergarten for at least 80% of her school day, so we are obliged to give her access to the use of her iPad when she is in general education and elsewhere, at least until we convene another IEP meeting in 30 days.*

REFLECTION

One of the actions of a culturally proficient member of an inclusive learning community identified in Table 5.1 is to become aware of how other educators in the school as a whole react to diversity. One way to do so is to assess community members' cultural views of diversity and disability using the Continuum presented in Table 5.2. From the conversation thus far, where on the Table 5.2 Continuum might the principal, the special educator, and classroom teacher fall. What evidence do you have for your conclusion? What might be questions you could pose or statements you could make as the special educator, parent, or principal to shift the first-grade teacher's view of and response to diversity toward culturally competent responses on the right side of the Continuum?

_____

_____

_____

_____

Another action of a culturally proficient member of an inclusive learning community identified in Table 5.2 is to become aware of how to be effective in a classroom that includes individuals with perceived disabilities and other differences, including communication differences. One way of doing this is learning and using Differentiated Instruction (DI) methods and strategies. Staff members of John Adams schools have received professional learning regarding DI. What might be questions that the principal or special educator could ask to remind themselves that DI requires teachers and leaders to commit to replacing familiar and comfortable practices with new processes for shaking things up in the classroom or the school with regard to use of technology in the classroom for Pegah and all students?

_____

_____

_____

_____

Part 2: Pegah's Voice for All

Adam Watson, Principal: *Thank you, Mrs. Teague, for reviewing our IEP responsibilities with us. Now that we have heard those responsibilities and the requests of Mrs. and Mrs, Patel, I am wondering if we could brainstorm some ways to work this out?*

Angela Teague, Special Educator:	*Yes, great idea, Mr. Watson. I am wondering if we could have Pegah start with using the iPad as she is accustomed to, and then we can meet again to discuss how it's working. Maybe we could come up with a specific list of observations that all of us are doing that gives us plenty of information to assess how Pegah is doing in the class and with her peers.*
Khan Patel, Pegah's Father:	*That would be acceptable. I want her to be successful.*
Dora Johnson, First-Grade Teacher:	*Well. It is a brand new technology for me, and I would be interested to see how successful it is.*
Priya Patel, Pegah's Mother:	*I could come in a talk with the other students to help with the introduction.*
Dora Johnson, First-Grade Teacher:	*Well, first, I'd like to see how Pegah uses it just with me. You know, maybe you and I and Pegah could meet and she could teach me, first. (nervous laughter). That would be helpful for me. I would be willing to give it a try.*
Khan Patel, Pegah's Father:	*I think this will be a good place to start. I think that you will see how well she does with the iPAD.*
Dora Johnson, First-Grade Teacher:	*So we can start this and then evaluated after 30 days?*
Priya Patel, Pegah's Mother:	*That would be acceptable.*
Adam Watson, Principal:	*Well, we do have the new Chromebook initiative that will fund every student having an iPad-like device. So, I believe that it might help us all think differently about what Pegah and other student need.*
Angela Teague, Special Educator:	*With all of us on board, we can be better advocates for Pegah.*

REFLECTION

Take a moment to reflect upon the proposed actions of the team. How do these actions reflect culturally proficient core values? How do the actions reflect an inclusive leaning community represented in column two of Table 5.1. To what extent do actions represent becoming aware of the five dimensions of knowledge described? What actions would you include? How could expanding your knowledge of yourself, your school, your students, and your community benefit students with IEPs and students with other perceived differences or difficulties?

_____

_____

_____

_____

DIALOGIC ACTIVITY

Consider the following observation of Paolo Freire, the author of *Pedagogy of the Oppressed*: "In the process of the ongoing education of teachers, the essential moment is that of critical reflection on one's practice" (as cited by Sennett, 2004, p. 107). With the Paolo Freire quote regarding critical reflection and the chapter content in mind, engage with your colleagues in a dialogue. Using the following prompt questions

- What have you learned about *Assessing Cultural Knowledge*?
- What have you learned about yourself?
- What have you learned about the students and the professional colleagues that populate your school?

Now that you know what you know and you have examined your assumptions, what are you willing to do? How does the information in this chapter inform and influence how you teach? What might it take to create an Inclusive School that embraces and supports all learners?

_____

_____

_____

_____

PREVIEW OF CHAPTER 6

In this chapter, we examined the Essential Element of Assessing Cultural Knowledge through authentic and differentiated strategies. In the next chapter, Chapter 6, we will examine the Essential Element of Valuing Diversity and learn about systems, practices, and strategies culturally proficient members of an Inclusive School can employ to develop appreciation for the differences among and within the groups at their school and within their community.

6 Valuing Diversity Through Inclusiveness

We will not successfully restructure schools to be effective until we stop seeing diversity in students as a problem. Our challenge is not one of getting "special" students to better adjust to the usual. . . . The challenge of schooling remains . . . ensuring that all students receive their entitlement. They have the right to thought-provoking and enabling schoolwork, so that they might use their minds well and discover the joy therein to willingly push themselves farther. They have the right to instruction that obligates the teacher, like the doctor, to change tactics when progress fails to occur. They have the right to assessment that provides students and teachers with insight into real-world standards, useable feedback, the opportunity to self-assess, and the chance to have dialogue with, or even to challenge, the assessor—also a right in a democratic culture. Until such a time, we will have no insight into human potential. Until the challenge is met, schools will continue to reward the lucky or the already-equipped and weed out the poor performers.

Grant Wiggins (1992, pp. xv–xvi)

GETTING CENTERED

In what ways might members of your school and community see diversity in students as a problem? To what extend do members of your school community take the approach of getting "special" students to better adjust to the usual? In contrast, to what extent do your members of your school community see the diversity among and within its students as natural and expected? To what extent do members of your school community see differentiated curriculum, instruction, and assessment as a right? To what extent do members view the opportunity for a student to dialogue with and even challenge her teacher's assessment as a right of democratic culture?

_____

_____

_____

_____

VALUING DIVERSITY: AN OVERVIEW

Diversity is ever present. Just look around! What do you see as age, language, ethnic, gender, sexual identity, sexual orientation, class, religion, geographic, and "exceptionality" cultural and microcultural identities and group identities within your community and school? In a Culturally Proficient Inclusive School, community members develop appreciation not only for the commonalities shared by it members (e.g., everyone, including teachers is a learner; everyone has a need for belonging and mastery) but also for the differences among and within the groups that comprise the community (Nuri-Robins, Lindsey, Lindsey, & Terrell, 2012). Members of an Inclusive School learn to listen to and value the perspectives of groups whose members may hold viewpoints and have experiences different from their own or the dominant culture. Member of an Inclusive School learn to appreciate the diversity of the students, staff, and faculty that comprise the community. They welcome all students into the classroom and value the opportunities and challenges student diversity brings.

The purpose of this chapter is to provide readers with ways to develop an ongoing value for the differences among and within groups at their school and larger community by taking actions identified in Table 6.1. As we presented in Table 5.1 in the previous chapter, Table 6.1 has three columns. The first column presents a brief definition of the second Essential Element of Cultural Proficiency, *Valuing Diversity*. The second column offers three actions for culturally proficient educators to take to show their valuing of diversity. Notice the first action involves acting to realize our definition of Inclusive Schooling offered in Chapter 2. The third column identifies systems, practices, strategies, and processes featured in this chapter that operationalizes this Essential Element.

Table 6.1 Systems, Practices, and Strategies That Facilitate the Actions of Valuing Diversity Through Inclusiveness

Cultural Proficiency Essential Element #2	Actions of a culturally proficient member of an inclusive learning community	Systems, practices, strategies, and tools featured in this chapter
Valuing Diversity Developing an appreciation for the differences among and within groups	I/we . . . • Welcome, value, empower, and support the diverse academic, social/emotional, language, and communication learning of all students in shared environments and experiences for the purpose of attaining the desired goals of education • Appreciate the challenges and gifts that diversity brings and share this appreciation with students in order to develop a collaborative and naturally supportive learning community • Initiate and support formal and informal decision-making groups inclusive of parents/guardians, community members, people whose viewpoints and experiences are different from mine/ours, and students themselves, in order to enrich conversations, decision making, and problem solving	I/we . . . • Develop and apply an MTSS tiered intervention approach to diversity rather than referring for assessment for specialized programs • Use a School-Wide Positive Behavior Support (SWPBS) approach to teaching self-discipline rather than reacting with "discipline-ary" responses • Structure opportunities to foster friendships and engage students as collaborative natural peer supports through cooperative learning, partner learning and peer tutoring, and student co-teaching arrangements • Use a Retrofit Differentiated Instruction (DI) approach to adjust mismatches between classroom demands and student characteristics • Take a funds of knowledge perspective to students and families as community assets • Actively engage and listen to students and families in IEP and other decision-making forums

REFLECTION

Take a moment and carefully read each of the three actions for culturally proficient educators to show their valuing of diversity represented in the second column of Table 6.1. What are systems, practices, strategies, or processes you have employed to develop and show your valuing of diversity?

What are systems and strategies you have seen others employ? How could expanding your appreciation of the differences between and among groups within your school and community benefit students with Individual Education Programs (IEPs) and students with other perceived differences or difficulties?

_____

_____

_____

_____

VALUING STUDENTS' ACADEMIC AND SOCIAL/ EMOTIONAL DIVERSITY THROUGH MTSS AND POSITIVE BEHAVIOR INTERVENTIONS AND SUPPORTS

In Chapter 4, the authors proposed a Multi-Tiered System of Supports (MTSS) approach to student support as a Barrier-busting paradigm of pre-referral to special education service delivery. As a reminder, MTSS is the concept and label for an approach to prevent unnecessary and disproportional numbers of special education referrals by providing a comprehensive, unified school-wide system of high-quality evidenced-based initial Tier 1 instruction in general education and Tier 2 and 3 academic and behavior interventions for any student, regardless of whether that student is eligible for special education services, is learning English as well as academics, is struggling for the moment academically or behaviorally, or has advanced learning needs. The MTSS structure has both an academic and behavior support side—the Response to Intervention (RTI) academic side and the School-Wide Positive Behavioral Support (SWPBS) side. We invite you to return to Chapter 4 to see Figure 4.1, the visual representation of MTSS, and an accompanying narrative regarding the overall MTSS structure and the components of an effective RTI academic support and intervention system.

In addition to offering an alternative to the historically separate system of special education, MTSS is a powerful structure for culturally proficient members of an inclusive learning community to welcome, value, empower, and support the diverse academic, social/emotional, language, and communication learning of all students in shared environments and experiences, which is the first diversity valuing action listed in Table 6.1 and the aim of Inclusive Schooling. When members of a school community agree to install a proactive MTSS approach to student diversity, they signal their deeply held belief that diversity in student academic and social-emotional learning is natural, expected, and worthy of extraordinary attention and instruction. Schools that structure MTSS as the way of operating provide a strong message that an overarching goal for every child is to avoid school failure and to receive services without having to be labeled or made eligible for special education.

School-Wide Positive Behavioral Support as Valuing Diversity

In America they . . . talk of troubled children as "throw-away" children.

Who can be less fortunate than those who are thrown away?

Thom Garfat,
Cited in Brendtro, Brokenleg, & Van Bockern (1990, p. 12)

We described the academic side of MTSS in Chapter 4. We describe the behavioral side, School-Wide Positive Behavior Support (SWPBS), here, because adopting and implementing a SWPBS system requires a shift to inclusive values and behaviors toward students perceived as troubled or troubling. Specifically, SWPBS requires educators to value and work with students rather than suspending, expelling, or otherwise sending away or *throwing away* a child whose behavior is unsettling.

A primary purpose of a SWPBS system is to minimize and prevent behaviors that interfere with learning and interaction with others in positive ways (O'Neill & Jameson, 2016). SWPBS starts with setting school-wide and individual student behavioral expectations, teaching expectations, recognizing and rewarding norm-following behaviors, responding to student behavior in ways that help students see the relationship between a behavior and its consequences, and nurturing social-emotional learning by teaching alternative norm-following ways of communicating distress and getting needs met by "[s]caffold skills in real time" (Jones, Bailey, Brion-Meisels, & Partee, 2016, p. 66) via adult modeling and coaching. Whether school-wide or not, Positive Behavior Support (PBS) requires the examination of why challenging behavior occurs, what the function of the behavior is for the student, and what need the behavior is meeting or not meeting. PBS requires data collection to determine the impact of not only academic responses but Tier 2 and 3 behavioral interventions. Further individualized responses for students with more frequent or intensive disruptive behaviors occurs through direct instruction of impulse control, problem solving, and social skills; contracts; daily check-in and check-out systems with daily progress reports; and frequent and salient praise and positive consequences for achieving goals.

Committing to a SWPBS approach is to shift from a culture of *compliance* to one of *cultural competence*, where social-emotional learning is outright valued as of equal importance to academic success. Committing to a SWPBS approach is to "value challenging behaviors not as a distraction from the work of learning . . . but as typical developmental occurrences that provide adults and children with real-world opportunities to practice new or emerging skills" (Jones et al., 2016, pp. 65–66). A second purpose, then, of SWPBS is to teach responsibility, which has two dimensions (Villa, Thousand, & Nevin, 2010). The first dimension is *flexibility*—the *ability* to respond in rule-following ways or to exhibit "response-ability." The second dimension of responsibility is *accountability*—a sense of personal ownership or internal self-discipline. Educators can teach responsibility by constructing experiences that "seek the child's inner control, a self-efficacy that allows the child to do the right thing when he or she is not under surveillance" (Van Bockern, Brokenleg, & Brendtro, 2000, p. 71). This inner control and self-efficacy is also known as self-discipline. This second purpose of a SWPBS system allows educators to help students whose behavior is considered challenging to pursue a lifestyle change by increasing their behavioral flexibility and accountability. Chapter 7 describes social skills and problem-solving and self-control scripts that culturally proficient educators can teach and support students to use to make this life change and become more flexible and accountable. See Orsati (2016) and Villa and colleagues (2010) for additional idea joggers for educators to collaborate with students to develop responsibility and self-discipline.

REFLECTION

Consider the following observation made by Fernanda Orsati "When adults 'work with' students and do not use techniques of 'doing to' students, the process of finding solutions to behavior issues is likely to work better" (2016, p. 141). What does this quote mean to you and your work with students? After reading this quote and the MTSS and SWPBS content above, what are your thoughts about actions you might take to promote social-emotional learning and positive behavior supports in your classroom and immediate sphere of influence (e.g., grade-level team, special education support team) and school-wide?

_____

_____

_____

_____

APPRECIATING THE CHALLENGES AND GIFTS DIVERSITY BRINGS: ENGAGING STUDENTS AS NATURAL PEER SUPPORTS

A powerful way to harness the gifts of a diverse study body is to collaborate with them in decision making and instruction. Collaborating with students means fostering self-discipline and student use of responsible behavior as described earlier in the section about PBS. Collaborating with students means involving students as decision makers and problems solvers and as mediators of conflict and controversy, as we describe in greater detail in Chapter 7. Collaborating with students means involving students as advocates for themselves and others and as designers of their own learning, as we describe in Chapter 8. Collaborating with students also means structuring opportunities for students to be natural peer supports in cooperative learning groups, partners in tutoring and partner learning arrangements, and as co-teachers with their teachers. Let's examine these three approaches to tapping into the instructional talent of students as well as natural ways for fostering friendships and relationships.

Students as Instructors in Cooperative Learning Groups

Cooperative learning is the umbrella term used to refer to a family of instructional methods in which the teacher instructs and guides groups of students to work together. This instructional practice can be challenging to master, yet the overwhelmingly positive international research results yielded over the past several decades clearly indicate that teachers can increase student academic performance and interpersonal and social-emotional learning when they have students work on the tasks in groups of two to six under guidelines by which the pupils teach each other, coach each other, and succeed as a group. These gains occur only when teachers show their pupils how to do and think about these things (Murray, 2002, p. 179).

Cooperative learning has been recognized as the sixth of nine most powerful instructional strategies found to increase student performance (Marzano, Pickering, & Pollack, 2001). In other words, it is more than worth a teacher's while to learn *how* to effectively engage students as teachers in cooperative learning groups.

Several major approaches to engaging students in cooperative group learning are recognized as effective. All share the common attributes of (a) students engaging in a shared learning activity in small groups and (b) students being interdependent and accountable for one another (Davidson, 2002). We value all of the cooperative learning approaches that have emerged over the past several decades, because they result in increased student engagement and learning. However, we are most attracted to David and Roger Johnson's Learning Together approach (Johnson & Johnson, 1999; 2009), because it is the one approach that focuses upon the direct teaching of interpersonal and small-group social skills, the civic behaviors needed for survival in school and the larger society (Johnson & Johnson, 2002). Thus, Learning Together is the approach we selected to share with you in this chapter. We encourage teachers to use the Learning Together cooperative learning approach, because the approach directly teaches and holds students accountable for the skills that promote belonging, mastery, independence, and generosity (Brendtro et al., 1990). We also encourage teachers to use this approach, because it has been recognized as one of the "great success stories based on theory, research, and practice over the past 11 decades" (Johnson & Johnson, 2009, p. 365). Teachers who use this approach empower their students to learn and use the democratic virtues and social competence required of well-rounded citizens (Johnson & Johnson, 1996b).

What Cooperative Learning Groups Are Not. A tremendous instructional difference exists between simply having students work in groups and structuring effective cooperative group learning among students. Four students sitting at the same table doing their own work and talking while they work is not cooperative learning; it is individualistic learning with sidebar conversations. When students work together with teacher instructions, such as "Help others if you finish first," this is not cooperative learning; it is individualistic learning with an expectation that some students will tutor others without any training or teacher direction. When students are assigned a project on which one student does all of the work while the others put their names on it to receive a group grade, this is not cooperative learning; it is one student working and others getting away with what is known as academic hitchhiking or what David and Roger Johnson called "free riding" and "social loafing" (Johnson & Johnson, 1999, p. 74).

Five Essential Ingredients of Cooperative Group Learning: PIGS Face. For students to be empowered to instruct one another in cooperative groups, the teacher must have a solid understanding of the critical ingredients for success. David and Roger Johnson have used an acronym, PIGS Face, as a mnemonic to help teachers and students remember the five essential ingredients of the Learning Together cooperative learning approach. *P* represents "positive inter-dependence"; *I*, "individual accountability"; the *G*, "group processing"; the *S*, "social skills"; and *Face* represents "face-to-face interaction." All five ingredients briefly defined here must be included in a lesson if students are to be more productive than if they were to work alone or in competition with one another.

1. *Positive interdependence* involves clearly structuring and communicating to students that they are linked with one another in ways so they cannot succeed unless all members succeed.

2. *Individual accountability* involves structuring ways to assure that each group member is taking personal responsibility for contributing to accomplish the group's goals and assisting other group members to do likewise.

3. *Group processing* involves guiding students to reflect (group process) on how well the group members (a) accomplish the tasks and (b) maintain and develop their interpersonal skills to work effectively and enjoyably in small groups.

4. *Social skills* involve providing instruction, guided practice, and expectations to use the interpersonal skills that are needed to make collaborative work effective and enjoyable.

5. *Face-to-face interaction* involves structuring the cooperative groupings (e.g., group size and membership) and the environment (e.g., the room arrangement) so students have frequent opportunities to engage in positive and promotive face-to-face interaction.

Refer to Villa and colleagues (2010) to learn more about these five ingredients and how to translate these ingredients into a viable, cohesive learning experience, with students serving as the mediators of instruction.

Student as Instructors in Peer Tutoring and Partner Learning Arrangements

Another way to tap into the instructional talent of students, especially when the students come from diverse backgrounds and skill levels, is to arrange for students to learn how to be effective peer tutors and partner learners. When students become peer tutors and partner learners, they unleash their potential to delve deeper, learn more, and retain better the content they are tutoring. Many ways exist to structure effective peer tutoring and partner learning arrangements. Partnerships can be individualized, class-wide, or school-wide. Let's meet an individualized partnership and look in on a class-wide tutoring program.

An Example of an Individualized Partner Learning Arrangement. Julietta and Michelle are fifth graders at Lincoln Elementary in the Lakeside School District. Julietta, a recent immigrant and English learner, is nervous about speaking in front of her teachers and classmates. Upon entering her language arts class, Julietta was seated next to Michelle, where there was an available desk. Julietta tripped and dropped her books as she neared her desk. She felt her face flush as she bent to pick up her books. Michelle quickly got out of her desk and assisted Julietta with picking up her belongings. Julietta was immediately comforted by the assistance and Michelle's reassuring smile.

Mrs. Robinson, the language arts teacher, soon realized that Julietta did not understand what she was saying. Mrs. Robinson also noticed how anxious Julietta appeared, except when she was working with Michelle. When the teacher asked Julietta if she liked receiving assistance from Michelle, Julietta beamed and vigorously nodded her head as she said, "*Si. Si.* She is my *maestra* [teacher] too." Mrs. Robinson arranged for Michelle to receive two 30-minute training sessions to learn how to peer tutor from Mr. La Due, the guidance counselor, who managed a peer-tutoring program. She knew an important part of peer tutoring was to be sure that Michelle knew how to support and empower Julietta and not simply do the work for her.

The two students really appreciated learning about *reciprocal teaching*. Reciprocal teaching is a well-researched method of teaching students to be active readers. Originally developed by Palincsar and Brown (1988) as an explicit metacognitive procedure to increase reading comprehension for students with learning disabilities, reciprocal teaching has been demonstrated to be effective with all students, including students learning English, as well as content material. Reciprocal teaching is useful for any task that requires reading comprehension (e.g., reading to solve math problems, reading to gain information from a science or social studies text). Each peer models each of four reciprocal teaching steps.

Step 1: Question—Ask a question about the main idea of a selected reading;

Step 2: Summarize—In a brief sentence or two, paraphrase the main idea and details;

Step 3: Clarify—Identify any words or concepts that need to be defined; and

Step 4: Predict—Anticipate what will happen next by using prior knowledge and making connections. (Lovitt, 1991)

Teachers often ask their students to generate and post on their desks a Reciprocal Teaching Guide with the following cues: question, summarize, clarify, and predict. These cues help students remember to pose the questions to themselves and their partners while they read to learn the content.

Michelle and Julietta also attended the same math class. One day over lunch, Mrs. Robinson was speaking with Ms. Hussein, the math teacher, about how well Julietta and Michelle worked together in her language arts class. Ms. Hussein noted that Julietta had no difficulty at all in math and as a matter of fact, Michelle was struggling in math. Ms. Hussein decided to speak with the two girls to see if they would like to sit near each other in math so Julietta could assist Michelle with grasping the math facts, principles, and concepts they were learning. They loved the idea! In fact, they decided to use the reciprocal teaching method to help each other solve the word problems that had always vexed them! Michelle's grades on quizzes and tests began to improve.

Michelle and Julietta developed a close friendship. They gained a new respect for each other when the roles of tutor and student were reversed and they realized that each had unique strengths. They were both moving to the middle school for sixth grade. Michelle was learning a little Spanish from Julietta. Spanish happened to be one of the electives available to middle school students in the arts rotation. Michelle was planning to take the Spanish class and knew that Julietta would be a great after-school tutor, if she needed support to learn, speak, and practice her Spanish language.

An Example of Class-Wide Peer Tutoring. In the same school, Ms. Planter, a special educator, and Ms. Zane, a general educator, collaborated to ensure that the third graders in Ms. Zane's inclusive classroom mastered their math facts. Ms. Planter first taught the steps of reciprocal teaching. Ms. Zane then scheduled at least one opportunity a day for reciprocal tutoring, which required about ten minutes to allow for each partner to play the role of tutor and tutee. The students focused on six math facts per session (four known and two unknown or unmastered) and practiced until they achieved mastery using auditory, visual, and kinesthetic activities.

The teachers became concerned about the way in which two students were treating each other while reciprocal tutoring. They noticed the students frequently used "put-down" statements and failed to use the reinforcement, feedback, and other social skills they had demonstrated during training. They fought over the materials as well. However, their progress in acquiring math facts as well as their written feedback indicated they perceived the sessions to be going well academically. When interviewed about their teachers' concerns, they each made accusations about the other.

With additional training, modeling, and supervision of the tutoring sessions, these two students developed their skills in making positive statements and sustaining positive interactions with one another. In addition to the math facts, they kept track of two items as part of their data collection procedures: "saying nice things" and "saying thank you." Both students kept a graphic representation of their performance and set up a contract with their teacher whereby they could collect jointly accrued points based on the number of times they both made positive statements.

The points could be traded later for activities they both enjoyed (e.g., learning games, lunch with a favorite teacher, etc.). With this slight adjustment to the class-wide peer tutoring program, the students improved their positive social interactions even as the supervision was gradually reduced. They consistently increased the number of math facts mastered, and they were able to sustain more positive interactions with each other.

Benefits of and Ways to Structure Peer Tutoring and Partner Learning Arrangements. What do these two examples have in common? Peers are teaching and learning from each other, guided by their teachers, and they are learning to be accountable for their own and their partner's achievements. Cross-age and same-age peer tutoring are methods of instruction in which learners help each other and in turn, learn by teaching. Peer tutoring is the process by which a student, with minimal training and with teacher guidance, instructs one or more students to learn or master a skill or concept. Webb (1989) identified six conditions that must be met to effectively transmitting knowledge through peer tutoring. The tutor must

(1) provide relevant help that is

(2) appropriately elaborated,

(3) timely,

(4) understandable to the tutee, and

(5) provide an opportunity for the student to use the new information.

The student must

(6) take advantage of that opportunity.

Peer tutoring and partner learning situations can be same-age or cross-age arrangements. They can be arranged as a whole-school activity in which all classes are involved during a specific time of day, a whole-class activity, or an activity that involves two specific students. The most effective peer tutoring and partner learning programs have a well-defined process for recruiting, training, monitoring, and evaluating instruction delivered by students.

Note that students with IEPs who may receive tutoring from a same-age or older tutor can and should be given the opportunity to tutor. Consider Chang, a fifth grader with an IEP who reads independently at a first-grade level. Chang tutors in the kindergarten and first grades, providing mentorship to younger students while working on his literacy skills.

His recall and comprehension of content is strengthened as he teaches the content to another person!

Why does peer tutoring and partner learning work? Tutors, tutees, and partners are contemporaries and speak "the same language." Peers in the instructional role are closer in time and experience to the learning than their adult teachers, so can recall their own struggles and teach their partners strategies they learned to overcome those struggles. Peers receiving instruction may feel freer to ask questions or express their opinions with a peer rather than a teacher. Further, partners have more opportunities to respond and practice content as compared to learning only through teacher-directed instruction.

Students as Co-Teachers With Their Teachers

As you will learn in Chapter 7, co-teaching is a way to restructure the traditional teacher role of stand-alone deliverers of instruction to joint endeavors, where the skills of two or more people are merged to share instructional responsibility for the students assigned to a classroom (Villa, Thousand, & Nevin, 2013). A common co-teaching arrangement is for a special educator or an English language development specialist to co-teach in order to provide students with IEPs and English learners access and support to succeed in the general education curriculum. An emerging practice is for students to serve as co-teachers with their own credentialed classroom teachers. Consider these following two examples from Lakeside High School:

Mr. Kyle, a drama teacher, co-teaches with Reanna and Ryan, two drama students who have previously taken the class in which they co-teach. The students and drama teacher have met and co-planned the lesson. During the lesson, all three co-teachers rotate, explaining and modeling drama exercises to the class of forty-five students. While the class members move around the room and engage in the exercises in pairs and triads, all three co-teachers walk among the groups to provide feedback and encouragement. Periodically, the three huddle together to adjust their lesson on the spot based upon what they are observing through their joint monitoring.

Jessica, a senior, co-teaches with Ms. Boykins, a math teacher. While Ms. Boykins provides an overview of what the students will do during the day's algebra lesson, Jessica passes out materials to students. When Ms. Boykins transitions into direct instruction of the content, Jessica walks among the students, checking for comprehension of the new concept and skills being taught. Next, students are given problems to solve. At this point, Jessica and Ms. Boykins co-teach; students hold up whiteboards showing their answers and receive a "yes" or "no" response from either co-teacher. To assist students in finding the correct answer, Jessica is masterful at providing prompts such as "Talk to your neighbor and see if you agree." Later in the lesson, Ms. Boykins and Jessica instruct the whole class together as they alternate roles of problem explainer and the person who creates a visual representation of the algebraic equations on the board.

A school interested in establishing a student co-teaching program must attend to the same dimensions as peer tutoring and partner learning programs; namely, recruitment, training, monitoring, and evaluation of student co-teachers. It should be noted that although students may function as co-teachers, they do so under the supervision of a credentialed teacher. Villa and colleagues (2010) provide additional examples of how two school districts, one on the East Coast and one on the West Coast, address the recruitment, training, monitoring, and evaluation dimensions of their student co-teaching programs.

Fostering Friends Through Natural Peer Interactions

To create friendship is tough. After all, friendship cannot be mandated. At best, it seems to be made up of 1/3 proximity and 2/3rds alchemy! No one has the power to conjure up friendship at will. Friendship is about choice and chemistry. This is precisely its magic. Realizing this, we can acknowledge without any sense of inadequacy that we are not friendship sorcerers. . . . Teachers and others, however, do have influence over the nature of proximity. . . . to create and foster an environment in which it is possible for friendship to emerge . . ."

Emma Van der Klift & Norman Kunc (2002, p. 23)

What might be some reasons the authors chose to introduce the fostering of friends with this quote? This quote comes from a chapter in which Van der Klift and Kunc (2002) assert that true inclusion depends on teachers fostering, as much as possible, meaningful *reciprocal* relationships between children. What they and we, the authors of this book, have noticed is that when a student with more intensive support needs transitions into an inclusive general education classroom from a segregated special program often structures such as a Circle of Friends (Falvey, Forest, Pearpoint, & Rosenberg, 2002) or peer buddy system are set up to promote interaction and inclusion. While increased interaction may result from such structures *during* school hours, friendship often remains elusive, and the student who was intended to benefit from the structures remain friendless when the bell rings at the end of the day.

When children without disabilities are placed in a *helping* role, reciprocity is *not* built into the interaction. Van der Klift and Kunc urge culturally proficient educators to acknowledge that help *without* reciprocity is *not* the basis for friendship and to guard against constructing one-way helping relationships or overemphasizing the helper-helpee aspect of any relationship. To foster relationships *without* reciprocity teaches students that disability is something to be pitied, tolerated, and worthy of little more than benevolent help. (Recall Table 5.2 and the discussion of responses to diversity described in Chapter 5.) We offer as alternatives collaborative learning structures, such as the cooperative group learning and reciprocal partner learning described in this section, in which reciprocity and natural peer support is or can be built in.

APPRECIATING THE CHALLENGES AND GIFTS DIVERSITY BRINGS: USING RETROFIT APPROACHES TO DIFFERENTIATION INSTRUCTION

Culturally proficient educators who are new to Inclusive Schooling but who appreciate the challenges and gifts their diverse student population brings with them often find themselves initially using a *retrofit* approach to correcting mismatches between the skills of particular students and the way they traditionally made content accessible. The word "retrofit" is derived from architecture and the practice of making a building accessible for everyone, by performing a retrofit: widening doorways, adding an elevator, reconfiguring rest rooms to be physically accessible. In education, retrofitting occurs when students join a classroom and encounter conditions preventing them from accessing the curriculum (e.g., when a sixth grader who reads independently at second-grade level encounters the class text written at a sixth-grade readability level).

To maximize the retrofit approach to correct mismatches between learner characteristics and classroom demands, educators must compare information about a particular students with the content, process, and product demands of the classroom. In gathering facts about a student, a teacher must get to know and consider that student's strengths as well as his or her challenges. The more challenging a student is perceived to be because of academic, social, language, or movement differences, the more important it is to identify and use that student's strengths.

To illustrate the power of a retrofit approach in addressing mismatches between the facts about learners and the classroom's demands, we introduce you to a middle-level team and Tina, a student who is struggling to learn. We describe how the team addressed mismatches by examining the facts about the learner and retrofitting changes in the content, process, or product demands of the classroom. This team recognized that they could not change the facts about their student overnight, but that they could adapt content, process, and product demands so Tina could successfully participate and learn in a general education classroom.

Addressing a Mismatch in Middle-Level Science

Ms. Swanson, a middle-level science teacher in her second year of teaching, has firm mastery of the curriculum content. She has, however, great difficulty establishing discipline and facilitating her students' learning of the content. She is concerned about poor test results, daily discipline referrals to the office, parental and administrative complaints about her classroom, and the sheer exhaustion she feels at the end of the day. Ms. Swanson had taught a different science course to most of the students in her class the previous year. She is upset to hear that this year she will not only be assigned a co-teacher to help her differentiate instruction, but she will also be assigned Tina, a student who has more significant disabilities than any student she has ever taught.

Ms. Tac is a speech-language specialist who has been assigned to co-teach with Ms. Swanson. She has previously co-taught with both math and science teachers at the middle level. She has experience teaching a wide range of students with communication, cognitive, academic, movement, and behavioral difficulties. She knows that Ms. Swanson is reticent about co-teaching with another professional.

At their first planning meeting, Ms. Swanson states that she does not believe a student like Tina should be in a general education classroom. Having taught most of the students the previous year, Ms. Swanson shares with Ms. Tac that these students are probably the "dumbest group of students" that Ms. Tac will likely encounter. Ms. Tac asks why Ms. Swanson feels that way. Ms. Swanson says that "they are just plain slow," and everything must be repeated over and over. The teachers decide to begin their co-teaching journey slowly by having Ms. Tac observe the class for a few days.

At their second planning meeting, Ms. Tac shares her observations as well as assessment data she has gathered. Together, they review the information in Table 6.2. Ms. Tac suggests that the two of them apply a retrofit approach to address the mismatch between the facts about Tina and the content, process, and product demands of the classroom.

REFLECTION

Use Table 6.2 Retrofit Planning Matrix With Student and Class Summary for Tina to support your reflections.

Table 6.2 Retrofit Planning Matrix With Student and Class Summary for Tina

Facts About the Student Name: <u>Tina</u>	Facts About the Class/ Lesson Class: <u>Science</u>	Mismatches Between Student Facts and Class/ Lesson Facts	Potential Solutions to Mismatches Between Facts
Strengths	**Content Demands**	1.	2.
Background Knowledge and Experiences:	Teacher lecture		
Previously assigned to self-contained classrooms with limited access to the general education curriculum	Reading from the textbook		
Prior attempts to develop a communication system (e.g., communication board, sign language) have not worked	**Process Demands**		
	Lecture		
	Student note taking of lecture		
Interests:	Extensive use of worksheets		
Enjoys Internet research	Students assigned seven- to ten-step tasks without written reminders or questioning for understanding		
Likes music and poetry			
Learning Style(s):			
Auditory and multisensory learner	No hands-on activities		
Uses facilitated communication	No projects		
Uses a computer with portable printer	No group work		
Slow response time	**Product Demands**		
Multiple Intelligences:	Rapid fire questions with no think time		
Verbal/linguistic	Frequent use of tests and quizzes		
Logical/mathematical	Competitive goal structure (i.e., grading on a curve)		
Musical/rhythmic			
Important Relationships:	**Other:**		
Father and two instructional assistants with whom she has long-term trusting relationships	Frequent behavioral disruptions in class		
Other:	Repeated explanation of content in response to students saying they don't understand the content or assigned tasks		
Grasps material quickly			
Nonverbal			
Tactilely defensive, does not like to be touched			
Engages in hand-wringing and body-rocking behavior	Teacher loses patience and blows up (i.e., yells) when students continue to ask for clarification		
Limited eye contact with others			

(Continued)

Table 6.2 (Continued)

Facts About the Student Name: <u>Tina</u>	Facts About the Class/Lesson Class: <u>Science</u>	Mismatches Between Student Facts and Class/Lesson Facts	Potential Solutions to Mismatches Between Facts
Frightened of tests Dislikes homework **Goals/Concerns** Provide increased opportunities to establish peer relationships Enhance communication via assistive technology (e.g., voice to speech) Tantrums when bored, frustrated, or stressed	Students seem to enjoy the teacher's losing patience; it is not clear if they do not understand the task or are purposefully frustrating the teacher		

What mismatches do you identify between Tina's characteristics and the class demands in science? Record your own observations of mismatches here or in the third column of Table 6.2.

In what ways might Ms. Swanson and Ms. Tac address each mismatch? Record your ideas for resolving each mismatch in the fourth column of Table 6.2.

_____

_____

_____

_____

Although skeptical, Ms. Swanson is so impressed with the accuracy and thoroughness of the data Ms. Tac has gathered about her class, her constructive comments, and enthusiasm for figuring out how to include Tina, that she is convinced to try the retrofit approach to differentiate instruction for Tina. They agree to meet with Tina, her father, and a paraeducator with whom Tina has had a long-term relationship. Tina's father explains and the instructional assistant verifies that Tina is a student who grasps information quickly. However, it can take her ten minutes or more to generate two to three sentences on her computer. She does not type unless her dad or an assistant with whom she is familiar and comfortable is seated next to her with a hand placed on her shoulder. Her father explains that, in the past, many educators made unwarranted assumptions about Tina's capabilities, because she does not make eye contact, wrings her hands, rocks her body, and does not communicate verbally but instead uses facilitated communication (http://disabilitystudies.syr.edu/what/fcinstituteresearch.aspx) to type her words.

After the meeting, Ms. Swanson acknowledges that perhaps Tina could successfully participate in her class. Ms. Swanson and Ms. Tac add a number of new ideas to their initial list for addressing the mismatches between Tina and the classroom demands, resulting in the list shown in Table 6.3. After examining these ideas, Ms. Swanson agrees to start with four changes from the list that she thinks would benefit and provide alternative access options to all students (e.g., requiring wait time after asking their students questions). She is so encouraged by the positive outcomes that, after three weeks, she agrees to work with Ms. Tac to figure out how to implement the remaining eight changes.

After six weeks of implementing all 12 strategies, Ms. Swanson has stopped referring to this class as "just plain slow." She even made a special trip to her principal's office to report, "Having Tina in my class has been the best thing that has ever happened to me for my own professional growth. It is so exciting to see how Tina's classmates know how to communicate with her. Now we all know how smart she really is. By becoming a better teacher for Tina, I am becoming a better teacher for all of my students."

REFLECTION

In what ways might you use the retrofit approach to differentiating instruction to resolve a mismatch between facts about a student and facts about the content, product, and process demands of a class or a disciplinary system?

How might you build the retrofit approach for solution finding for student-curricular/behavioral mismatches into gatherings and conversations at the grade level, discipline specific (e.g., special education, English learner), or school-wide (e.g., professional learning community, faculty) levels?

_____

_____

_____

_____

Table 6.3 Brainstormed Solutions to Address Mismatches Between Tina and Facts About Demands of the Middle-Level Science Classroom

1. Use the LCD projector for the classroom. Scan worksheets, quizzes, tests, and so forth into Tina's computer and "hook it up" to the projector.

2. For homework, provide Tina with a minimum of two questions that she will be asked during class the next day; have her type her responses so when she is asked the questions during class, she can project her typed answer on a screen for everyone to read.

3. Ask some questions that students, including Tina, can respond to quickly through a signal to indicate whether something is true or false.

4. Institute a 3- to 5-second wait/think period between the time when a question is asked and when students are called on to answer.

5. Reduce the amount of class work and homework that Tina is expected to complete but be sure to give her the more sophisticated questions to address.

6. If the volume of the class is too loud for Tina, allow her to move to an auditory learning station where she can listen to differentiated or enrichment activities on headphones.

7. Be mindful of traffic patterns, and be strategic about where Tina sits and which students are seated next to her.

8. Reduce the amount of worksheet activities.

9. Increase the frequency of hands-on activities and partner and group work.

10. Change from grading on a curve (a norm-referenced assessment) to grading for mastery of preset criteria (a criterion-referenced assessment). Create grading rubrics with the class. Determine at a later time if Tina will need a different rubric and, if so, include it within her IEP.

11. Develop classroom rules and set consequences for breaking the rules with the students. Assign Tina the role of monitoring students' adherence, including her own, to classroom rules.

12. Pursue or schedule an Assistive Technology Assessment to explore additional tools to enhance verbal communication.

VALUING DIVERSITY OF FAMILY AND COMMUNITY ASSETS THROUGH ENGAGEMENT IN DECISION MAKING AND PROBLEM SOLVING

One of the most powerful interventions for meeting the needs of any child is a strong home-school partnership characterized by equity and parity in decision making. The legal mandate driving Inclusive Education in the United States, which originated with the 1975 promulgation of Public Law (Pub. L.) 94-142, now reauthorized as the Individuals with Disabilities Education Improvement Act (IDEIA) not only required the design and delivery of a free and appropriate public education for every child with a disability, but it also provided for strong parent/guardian involvement and input. The architects of the original legislation were astute in their recognition of the critical role that families play in determining and evaluating the appropriateness of academic and behavioral/social-emotional supports and interventions for their children. The U.S. Congress recognized the power of family in the findings of the 2004 reauthorization of the IDEIA, noting that, "nearly 30 years of research and experience has demonstrated that the education of children with disabilities can be made more effective by strengthening the role of parents and ensuring that families of such children have meaningful opportunities to participate in the education of their children" (IDEIA, 2004).

Barriers to Family and Community Engagement

For a variety of reasons, the establishment of meaningful partnerships is not always easy. Some parents have had negative experiences themselves in school. Previous patterns of interaction with the school may have consisted primarily of meetings or calls home to report how poorly their child was doing, academically or behaviorally. School personnel have not made themselves available when family members are able to meet (e.g., in the evenings, on weekends). At times, parents/guardians may be overwhelmed with life circumstances and unable to participate more actively in their child's education. School personnel may have, intentionally or unintentionally, communicated that the family was failing at supporting their child or that their child did not belong in their school or the general education classroom.

Clearly, culturally proficient educators committed to Valuing Diversity and the education and inclusion of a diverse student population must confront and attempt to overcome these obstacles by asking and honestly answering questions such as these, which are most relevant to families of students with IEPs:

- ✓ Do we have established *structures and procedures* (e.g., holding meetings at times when family members can attend, home visits) to facilitate *communication* between families and teachers, not only at IEP meetings but on an *ongoing basis* throughout the year?
- ✓ Do educators solicit and genuinely *consider family* members' *perspectives* regarding their child's strengths, interests, and learning preferences when making IEP-related decisions?
- ✓ Do we solicit the voice of families in larger school considerations? For example, do our school-based parent-teacher associations, site improvement councils, and other similar *decision making and*

advisory groups have a *designated position* for a family member of a child with an IEP?

✓ Are families of children with IEPs routinely *included* in all invitations to *school-based functions* and volunteer/service opportunities?

Adopting and Applying a Knowledge Perspective

What else can educators do to tear down Barriers and overcome obstacles to genuine valuing and collaboration? One approach is to learn about and adopt an asset-based *funds of knowledge* perspective, a perspective that assumes and appreciates that families are educated by their life experiences and that students and their families bring a wealth of personal and culturally connected knowledge, resources, and assets to the decision-making and problem-solving table. Educators who focus upon student (and family) assets rather than deficits are more successful in facilitating student success (Rios-Aguilar, 2010).

Embracing a funds of knowledge perspective enables culturally proficient educators to not only appreciate but tap into families' accumulated and culturally developed skills that have allowed them, their households, and communities to function and thrive (Gonzalez, Moll, & Amanti, 2005). Actions educators can take to not only learn about but capitalize upon students' and families' funds of knowledge include (a) developing lessons using students' funds of knowledge, (b) inviting families and community members into the classrooms to co-teach and share their experiences, and (c) actively encouraging family members to seek out leadership roles, such as membership on various school advisory committees (e.g., the principal's advisory council, parent-teacher association, building committee for a new school facility, the school's wellness planning team) or serving as a student mentor or tutor.

Providing Desired or Needed Information to Families and the Community. Culturally proficient educators also ask families what they want to learn and know about their children's schooling. What are they confused or curious about with regard to the IEP process, the academic and behavioral supports and interventions their children can or are receiving, or any other topic of interest? When inquiring, remember that families may have very different views about their child's difficulties or gifts than professional educators. For example, in some cultures, families may believe that God or a past sin or acts of kindness brought their child to them as a punishment or a special gift. Knowing this, refrain from being taken aback by a parent's questions, curiosities, and beliefs or making assumptions that all members of a cultural or ethnic group share the same experiences or beliefs.

When providing families and community members with information, be sure to do it in ways that are safe and empowering, such as through an after-school informational spaghetti dinner, where childcare and games are provided for families' children, or a community science education night, where student-made experiments, games appropriate for all ages, and take-home science activities and materials are featured and provided. Also, it is highly recommended that information be delivered through a co-teaching arrangement of a parent/guardian and a professional, so parents see in the esteemed instructor role another parent/guardian with whom they can identify and who had credibility because of similar experiences. The parent-professional co-teaching arrangement models equity, parity, and an asset-based perspective.

Establishing Strong School-Community Collaborations. Schools, students, and families also benefit from educators valuing the funds of knowledge of the broader community and establishing diverse *school-community* collaborations. Schools that organize partnerships with local businesses, public service agencies, private foundations, volunteer organizations, YMCAs and other youth organizations, university teacher preparation programs, and other service-oriented organizations both expand the potential services available to their students and create opportunities for family members to become involved in school and community activities.

CASE STORY

Let's return to the Lakeside Union School District and one of the two high schools in the district, West High.

Part 1: A Dramatic Dilemma

Zen is a tenth-grade student at West High School. Staff and administration of the high school are an even mix of primarily Caucasian males and females. The school is well known for its performing arts programs and performances. One of the highlights of the school year is the annual spring play, which is performed under the leadership of the theater arts program. West High School also is known for its project-based approach to learning, which extends to this annual school drama production.

Rather than performing traditional published plays, students write and submit their own plays for consideration for performance. A committee of faculty and students involved in the theater arts program select one entry. Students take responsibility for managing all of the staging of the play—casting, costumes, stage props, and publicity. This year, the play is about an archaeologist searching for an ancient city. Along the way, the lead character, an archeologist, meets characters representing Greek gods and goddesses. Zen, a student with autism, specifically Asperger's Syndrome, has been cast as the lead character, the field archaeologist. Zen is known for his attention to detail and ability to focus, making him an ideal person to play the role. After the first week of rehearsals, a meeting was held that included Ms. Kipson, the drama coach; Mr. Larson, the special educator on the school's Student Support Team, who coordinates Zen's special education supports; and four members of the cast and crew—Rick, Maggie, Jay and Kayla.

Ms. Kipson, Drama Coach:	*So, we have a week of rehearsals under our belt. How are things going?*
Rick Student Director:	*We have read through the entire play a few times. We are fixing the script in places, and we have the cast learning their lines.*
Maggie, Character in the Play:	*We are blocking the first scene next week. Um . . . I'm sorry, but I'm a bit concerned about Zen.*
Mr. Larson, Zen's Student Support Team Teacher (SSTT):	*Why? I thought that casting Zen for the lead was brilliant. He does that role so well.*
Jay, Character in the Play:	*Yes, except that he has trouble when the part he is playing calls for him to change.*
Ms. Kipson, Zen's SSTT:	*What do you mean, Jay?*
Kayla, Character in the Play:	*Well, like when he meets the god, Aries, he is supposed to get very excited and he doesn't do that. He just reads the lines.*
Ms. Kipson, Drama Coach:	*I am sure that with time he will get it. We just need to be patient with him until he practices more.*
Rick, Student Director:	*I don't know. He doesn't seem to be able to do it even when I ask him to. We are really concerned. It's not just me. We don't want to be embarrassed.*
Ms. Kipson, Drama Coach:	*So, what are you thinking? This is really serious! Should we recast the part?*
Mr. Larson, Zen's SSTT:	*Wait, wait, I thought you said he was perfect for the part? Let's not move too quickly here.*

REFLECTION

One of the actions of a culturally proficient member of an inclusive learning community is to appreciate the challenges and gifts that diversity brings and share this appreciation with students in order to develop a collaborative and naturally supportive learning community. How might the cast and crew respond differently to Zen's way of being? How can the entire learning community encourage and support new ideas regarding leadership from diverse perspectives? In what ways might the team examine their behaviors and assumptions to better support Zen and present a stellar production?

_____

_____

_____

_____

Part 2: Zen's Unique Gifts

Let's continue listening in the conversation.

Ms. Kipson, Drama Coach:	*Ok. So the options are to recast the part or have Zen play it without emotion?*
Mr. Larson, SSTT:	*Well, I am sure that he is doing the best that he can. I know he was so proud to be cast in the lead, and he has memorized almost all of the play.*
Maggie, Character in the Play:	*Yes, that's true. He's such a great guy. But we really need him to play the part well. You know this character is over the top!*
Kayla, Character in the Play:	*Sometimes Zen is really funny. He can mimic anyone. Do you know he does great impressions?*
Jay, Character in the Play:	*Hey, what if we show Zen what someone who is very excited looks like. You know, his facial expressions would change? Like this is the face of someone who is very excited. (Makes a face.) That way he could do an impression of the character.*
Rick, Student Director:	*Jay, that's a great idea. That might work! I would be willing to give it a try.*
Ms. Kipson, Drama Coach:	*We could even write it in. Like stage blocking! He'd see it as part of the play itself. Everyone would.*

Mr. Larson, Zen's SSTT:	*Well, there you go. He would get that down better than most.*
Ms. Kipson, Drama Coach:	*That's exactly what we want. He has such great talent, which is why we cast him in the lead.*
Kayla, Character in the Play:	*All the kids really like Zen. I bet that they would be willing to help.*
Jay, Character in the Play:	*Wait! This sounds good to us. But, shouldn't someone ask Zen first?*
Mr. Larson, Zen's SSTT:	*Right, we should. It's ultimately his choice. But I think he will enjoy the support from all of you.*

REFLECTION

In this case story, guided by their drama coach and Zen's student support team teacher (SSTT), a group of students are learning how to problem solve. Reflect on Webb's (1989) six conditions of quality tutoring and support; namely, (1) relevant help that is (2) appropriately elaborated, (3) timely, (4) understandable to the student, (5) structured to provide opportunities for the learner to use the new information, with the learner (6) actually taking advantage of that opportunity. In what way does the support for Zen suggested by the end of this problem-solving meeting meet or not meet these conditions?

Some school sites use drama teams, peer counselors, peer buddy support teams, and/or school ambassadors as peer-to-peer support approaches. What might be other examples of natural and structured peer supports you have used or can envision using that meet the Webb support criteria and reflect true valuing of diversity and inclusiveness?

_____

_____

_____

_____

DIALOGIC ACTIVITY

Before moving on to Chapter 7, let's pause and reflect upon the dispositions, practices, questions, and stories provided in this chapter to assist us to assess and consider actions for demonstrating the valuing of diversity of our students, selves, and communities. With your grade-level team, your department group, and your faculty and paraprofessionals, engage in a dialogue using the following prompts:

- What is our shared understanding of demonstrating our value for diversity?
- What evidence do we have that Valuing Diversity is a shared priority for all educators within our school?
- In what ways do we demonstrate that we have an Inclusive School? In what ways has this chapter informed our work?

We further invite you to read the following six bulleted statements about student-family-school-community partnerships.

To what extent is each statement true for your school and school district?

- Families have frequent opportunities to *visit* their child's *classroom*.
- Teachers and administrators in our school *welcome* families *into decision-making processes* for student achievement and instruction.
- Families and students are provided *clear information* about whom to contact and what *steps to take* when they have an educational concern, and they are offered *ready access* to records they seek in a manner consistent with district policies and procedures.
- When school policies and procedures are updated, *input* is *solicited* from *family members*, *community partners*, and *students* as well as staff.
- The school collaborates with a variety of *community partners* (e.g., businesses, public service agencies, private foundations, volunteer organizations, youth organizations, universities, service-oriented organizations) *to expand* community *resources* and services to meet student and family needs.
- The school *connects families* of students with IEPs with *community resources* and partnerships relevant to family support interests and needs.

If your reaction to a statement is, "This is our routine practice," think about and discuss with others ways in which you could expand or share this practice with other schools and communities. If your reaction to a statement is, "I am not sure if we do this," or "We are doing some of this," think about and discuss with others ways to better listen to and collaborate with students, families, and community members to demonstrate valuing of their funds of knowledge.

_____

_____

_____

_____

PREVIEW OF CHAPTER 7

In this chapter, we examined the Essential Element of *Valuing Diversity* through inclusive dispositions and practices. In the next chapter, Chapter 7, we will examine the Essential Element of *Managing the Dynamics of Diversity* and learn how members of an Inclusive School can restructure their roles to better deal with differences and engage conflict management and problem-solving processes to manage the inevitable differences that accompany change.

7

Managing the Dynamics of Diversity Through Collaboration, Creative Problem Solving, and Conflict Management

The principle goal of education in the schools should be creating men and women who are capable of doing new things, not simply repeating what other generations have done; men and women who are creative, inventive, and discoverers, who can be critical and verify, and not accept, everything they are offered.

Jean Piaget (as cited by Sennett, 2004, p. 9)

GETTING CENTERED

What thoughts, feeling, or emotions do you experience as you read this Jean Piaget quote? What's your hunch about why we might begin this chapter on managing the dynamics of diversity through collaboration, role redefinition, creative problem solving, and conflict management with this quote? What personal and collective reflections need to happen before problem solving begins?

_____

_____

_____

_____

MANAGING THE DYNAMICS OF DIVERSITY: AN OVERVIEW

The purpose of this chapter is to provide readers with ways to understand and manage the changes and conflicts that inevitably occur within a school community committed to becoming more culturally competent. We offer actions identified in Table 7.1. Similar to Table 5.1 and 6.1 in the previous two chapters, Table 7.1 has three columns. The first column presents a brief definition of the third Essential Element of Cultural Proficiency of Managing the Dynamics of Diversity. The second column offers actions for helping culturally proficient educators with ways of responding effectively to the issues that arise in a diverse environment that is transforming to be a genuinely Inclusive School. The third column identifies systems, practices, strategies, and tools featured in this chapter for accomplishing these four actions.

REFLECTION

Take a moment and carefully read each of the four actions for culturally proficient educators to understand and manage change and conflict presented in Table 7.1. What are systems, practices, and strategies or processes you have employed to understand and manage conflict and controversy and creatively problem solve issues that have arisen in your school and community? What are the strategies and processes you have seen others employ? In what ways might expanding your skills in managing change and conflict between and among groups within your school and community benefit

Table 7.1 Systems, Practices, Strategies, and Tools That Facilitate the Actions of Managing the Dynamics of Change Through Collaboration, Creative Problem Solving, and Conflict Management

Cultural Proficiency Essential Element #3	Actions of a culturally proficient member of an inclusive learning community	Systems, practices, strategies, and tools featured in this chapter
Managing the Dynamics of Change Learning to respond appropriately and effectively to the issues that arise in a diverse environment	I/we . . . • Appreciate conflict as a natural and normal process, with cultural contexts that need to and can be understood and that contribute to creative problem solving • Help students understand that what appear to be conflicts may be cultural clashes • Teach students to detect and manage the feelings associated with conflict and develop self-management and conflict resolution strategies to manage their own unresolved conflicts • Learn and use creative problem solving, conflict resolution, and instructional differentiation approaches as natural and routine processes to manage conflict; accommodate differences in student learning, behavior, and interpersonal relations	I/we . . . • Restructure traditional roles, rules, and relationship for collaboration • Use co-teaching arrangements • Teach students and adults the natural sources of conflict and controversy • Teach anger management and impulse control strategies and scripts (e.g., identifying triggers, engaging in calming strategies) • Teach and support students' social skill and social-emotional learning and development for conflict management • Teach students and adults variations of the Creative Problem Solving (CPS) process to resolve conflicts, mediate peers' conflicts, and differentiate instruction

students with Individual Education Programs (IEPs) and students with other perceived differences or difficulties?

_____

_____

_____

_____

APPRECIATING CONFLICT AND CONTROVERSY AS NATURAL, NORMAL, AND DEMANDING OF NEW COLLABORATIVE ROLES

Given the cultural proficiency lens offered in the previous chapters, the authors hope that educators now can picture the transformative actions needed to shift from an exclusion culture to an inclusion schooling experience as doable. We already know a lot about change. For example, we know that schools are cultures comprised of diverse microcultures and that to actualize a new vision of schooling, a new culture must replace the existing culture. We know that change inevitably creates cognitive and interpersonal conflict and that conflict can be managed. Chapter 5 prepares us for managing the dynamics of change toward Inclusive Schooling by having us assess our own and others' beliefs, experiences, assumptions, and cultural experiences. Chapter 6 further prepares us by offering ways to show our valuing of the perspectives, attributes, challenges and gifts of others through Inclusive Education. This first section of Chapter 7 presents the dynamics of change by alerting us to what David and Roger Johnson, cooperative group experts from the University of Minnesota, have for years researched and taught; namely, that "conflict occurs all the time They are a natural, inevitable, potentially constructive and normal part of school life" (Johnson & Johnson, 1991, p. 58). Our job, as culturally proficient educators, is to acknowledge that conflict is a natural and normal process that occurs within the context of a school culture. We also are conscious that, among the microcultures of a school, conflict can be understood and managed. Additionally, culturally proficient processes can be used to value and manage our natural differences in opinions, perspectives, and experiences and use them as assets and as catalysts for creative problem solving.

One source of conflict among some adults within a school is a perception that educators lack the time and human resources to support the diversity of the students within the classroom. We might hear a general education teacher say, "I already have so many students in my class that I'm not sure how to reach all students. How can I possibly do my job by adding students with IEPs to the mix?" This teacher likely has been and expects to continue to work alone, without the support of another professional or paraprofessional. Many educators are well versed in the *lone ranger* way of operating—one teacher teaching thirty-five students without communication or support from others. The notion that the so-called self-contained classroom and the lone teacher can somehow meet the needs of an increasingly diverse student body is a myth. Despite the obvious absurdity of teaching in isolation, traditions and organizational structures of many schools perpetuate segregation of staff and students with somewhat standard and inflexible expectations of the roles of people with different labels—administrators, teachers, and specialists of all sorts, including paraeducators, and parents.

Role Redefinition for Everyone to Eliminate Conflicting Responsibilities

Even in the late 1990s, teaching was characterized as the "lonely profession," which needed to be viewed differently (Sarason, Levine, Godenberg, Cherlin, & Bennet, 1996, p. 74). We now know that fundamental change in schooling requires a redefinition of the roles, rules, relationships, and responsibilities of everyone, students included, so that everyone collaborates to share their ideas, materials, resources, professional expertise, problem-solving abilities, and responsibility for the instruction of all students. Through such collaboration, educators not only can survive but thrive and transform general educators' thoughts and comments to "Wow, the integrated and collaborative support from my English learner, special education, and related services team not only helps me with these three students, but all of my other students, as well!"

For educators to most readily access the resources of other educational personnel, everyone in the school system must relinquish traditional roles, drop distinct professional labels, and redistribute their job functions across any number of people. Table 7.2 illustrates how job functions change in Inclusive Schools that meld human resources through dynamic, system-wide role redefinition. Flexibility and fluidity are the keys to role redefinition. Exactly who does what from one year to the next should always be subject to change and determined by students needs and the complementary expertise (and needs) of the educators distributing job functions among themselves. People behave in ways that reflect their job titles and formal descriptions. When people think they have conflicting job roles, conflict in perceived responsibilities are likely to occur. For example, we might hear a professional say, "I'm only assigned to work with students eligible for speech and language services. It is not my responsibility to teach students who cannot read the grade-level science text used in our district." This conflict does not need to occur if culturally proficient educators further signal a change in culture by formulating new job descriptions that expect, inspect, and respect an ethic of collaboration and shared responsibilities as well as co-learning and co-teaching.

Co-Teaching to Eliminate Conflicting Responsibilities and Increase Effectiveness

What Is Co-Teaching? In Chapter 6, you met Ms. Swanson, a middle-level science teacher, and her co-teacher, Ms. Tac, a speech-language specialist

Table 7.2 Job Responsibilities of School Personnel Before and After Role Redefinition

Role	Traditional Responsibilities	Redefined Responsibilities
General Education Administrator	Responsible for the management of the general education program Special programs are "housed" within general education facilities, but program responsibility is that of special education rather than general education administrators	Responsible for management of educational programs for *all* students Articulates the vision and provides emotional support to staff as they experience the change process Participates as a member of collaborative problem-solving teams inventing solutions to Barriers inhibiting the successful inclusion and education of any child Secures supports and resources to enable staff to meet the needs of all children
General Educator	Refers students who do not "fit" into the traditional program for assessment for diagnosis, remediation, and possible removal Teaches children who "fit" within the standard curriculum	Shares responsibility with special educators and other support personnel for teaching all assigned children and problem-solving solutions when students struggle to learn Collaboratively plans and co-teaches with other members of the staff and community to meet the needs of all students Recruits and trains students to be peer tutors for one another
Special Educator	Provides instruction to students eligible for services in resource rooms, special classes, or special schools	Collaborates with general educators and other support personnel to meet the needs of all students Co-teaches with general educators in general education classes Recruits and trains students to be peer tutors for one another
Psychologist	Tests, diagnoses, assigns labels, and determines eligibility for students' admission to special programs	Collaborates with teachers to define problems, creatively design interventions, co-teach, teach social skills, conduct authentic assessments, train students to be conflict mediators; provides counseling

Role	Traditional Responsibilities	Redefined Responsibilities
Related Service and Other Support Personnel (e.g., speech and language therapist, physical therapist, social worker)	Diagnoses, labels, and provides direct service to students in settings other than the classroom Provides support only to students eligible for a particular special program	Assesses and provides direct services to students within general education classrooms and community settings Collaboratively plans and co-teaches with classroom teacher Supports students not eligible for special education Trains classroom teachers, instructional assistants, volunteers, and students to deliver support services Shares responsibility to meet the needs of all students
Paraeducator/ Paraprofessional (instructional assistant)	Works in separate programs If working in general education classrooms, stays in close proximity of and works only with student(s) eligible for special services	Provides services to a variety of students in general education settings Facilitates natural peer supports within general education settings
Student	Primarily works independently and competes with other students for "best" performance A passive recipient of learning	Often works with other students in cooperative learning arrangements Actively engages in instruction, advocacy, and decision making for themselves and one another

who has been assigned to co-teach with Ms. Swanson. These co-teachers experienced how their collaborative use of the retrofit approach to differentiating instruction yielded positive outcomes, not only for Tina but the entire class. Co-teaching is defined as two or more people sharing responsibility for teaching all of the students assigned to a classroom. This instructional approach involves distributing responsibility among people for planning, instruction, and evaluation for a classroom of students and is an engaging approach for students to learn from two or more people with different backgrounds and experiences as well as ways of thinking and teaching.

Co-teaching has many faces. In a national survey, teachers experienced in teaching in diverse classrooms reported that they used four approaches to co-teaching—supportive, parallel, complementary, and team co-teaching (National Center for Educational Restructuring and Inclusion, 1995), briefly defined in Table 7.3. The success of a premier co-teaching team is measured by the students' view of each teacher as equally knowledgeable and credible.

Table 7.3 What Do the Four Approaches to Co-Teaching Look Like?

SUPPORTIVE
Supportive co-teaching is when one teacher takes the lead instructional role and the other(s) rotates among the students providing support. The co-teacher(s) taking the supportive role watches or listens as students work together, stepping in to provide one-to-one tutorial assistance when necessary, while the other co-teacher continues to direct the lesson. Teachers new to co-teaching or who are short of planning time often begin with this approach.
PARALLEL
Parallel co-teaching is when two or more people work with different groups of students in different sections of the classroom. Co-teachers may rotate among the groups, and sometimes, there may be one group of students that works without a co-teacher for at least part of the time. Teachers new to co-teaching often begin with this approach. Key to parallel co-teaching is that each co-teacher eventually works with every student in the class.
COMPLEMENTARY
Complementary co-teaching is when co-teachers do something to enhance the instruction provided by the other co-teacher(s). For example, one co-teacher might paraphrase the other co-teacher's statements or model note-taking skills on a whiteboard. Sometimes, one of the complementary co-teaching partners pre-teaches the small group social skill roles required for successful cooperative group learning and then monitors as students practice the roles during the lesson taught by the other co-teacher. As co-teachers gain in their confidence and acquire knowledge and skills from one another, complementary co-teaching becomes a preferred approach.
TEAM CO-TEACHING
Team co-teaching is when two or more people do what the traditional teacher has always done—plan, teach, assess, and assume responsibility for all of the students in the classroom. Team co-teachers share leadership and responsibility and are comfortable alternately taking the lead. Team co-teachers simultaneously deliver lessons in ways that allow students to experience each teacher's expertise. For example, for a lesson on inventions in science, one co-teacher with interests in history explains the impact on society. The other, whose strengths are with the mechanisms involved, explains how inventions work.

Co-teaching has a rapidly expanding research-base demonstrating academic language and social-emotional benefits to all students in heterogeneous inclusive classrooms (Villa, Thousand, & Nevin, 2013). So, co-teaching is *the* organizational arrangement of human resources to make schools and classrooms both inclusive and more effective.

Who Are Co-Teaching Partners and How Can They Manage Conflict?
As we learned in Chapter 5, credentialed professionals are not the only school personnel who can co-teach; students can be trained and coached to be terrific co-teachers. And as Table 7.2 highlights, practically anyone with an instructional role in a school can co-teach—general and special education; specialists, such as reading or English language development specialists or interventionists; related service personnel, such as speech and language, occupational, and physical therapists; counselors and school psychologists; and volunteers.

Co-teachers are often partnered precisely because of their differences, at least their differences in professional preparation. For example, special educators and teachers of English learners often are partnered with general educators in order to better include and provide meaningful instruction to students who are perceived as having learning, language, and other differences. Because co-teachers often come from different disciplines or instructional cultures, they may have conflicts because of differences in their professional training and unconscious biases, deeply held assumptions, beliefs, subjectivities, and positions associated with their training backgrounds (e.g., "I am a general educator; I'm not trained as a special educator," or "I am a special educator, not a bilingual educator."). Conflicts can also occur out of feelings of personal vulnerability. The feelings of not being an expert about everything needs to shift to the mindset where teachers have an opportunity to learn from and co-teach with others, where individual teachers can blend and complement each others' instructional strengths.

Co-teaching can actually serve as a vehicle for co-teaching partners to become more culturally proficient as they dialogue and question, surface, and identify their own unconscious biases and assumptions. Co-teachers can also manage the dynamics of differences by recognizing sources of conflict that stem from differing values. For example, beliefs about and orientation toward time are culturally embedded. When beliefs are clarified, co-teachers develop understanding and appreciation for culturally based differences and focus upon conflict resolution to eliminate obstacles to the learning of the students they share and serve. Although a research base exists for collaboration between general and special educators in multicultural classrooms (e.g., Nevin, Harris, & Correa, 2001), limited studies have been conducted on the dynamics between and among the cultural diversities of co-teachers. In other words, co-teachers who come from differing cultural and linguistic heritages need to invent ways of working together that emphasize the strengths they bring from their unique heritages, languages, and knowledge bases. Becoming culturally competent means becoming intentional about gaining a deeper understanding of how one's own culture might influence differences that arise as the co-teachers go through developmental stages of relationship development. Villa, Thousand, and Nevin (2013) offer additional strategies for managing the dynamics of relationship development and employing co-teaching strategies to facilitate student learning and organizational change toward Inclusive Education.

REFLECTION

Review the changes in roles, rules, and responsibilities presented in Table 7.2.

In what ways might you and your colleagues facilitate transformation of one or more of these or other roles in your school? Now review the four approaches to co-teaching presented in Table 7.3. With whom can you envision co-teaching? Under what circumstances can you envision using each of the four co-teaching approaches?

_____

_____

_____

_____

HELPING ADULTS AND STUDENTS UNDERSTAND AND APPRECIATE SOURCES OF CONFLICT AND CULTURAL CLASHES

Students, no matter how young or how old, are involved in conflicts every day. The question is not "Will I have a conflict today?" but "How do I handle conflict?" Students can be bullied, "dissed," harassed, or treated as outcasts. Boys and girls alike are exposed to name-calling (e.g., "Re-tard." "D-uh!" "You tramp!" "Stupid!") or threats (e.g., "I'll get you after school, just wait."). When students bring these conflicts to their teachers or parents, they are often told, "Just ignore it," or "Walk away." When students ask their friends, they are often told, "Get 'em back!" And when the students' conflicts reach the principal's desk, the consequences often are detention or suspension for all involved. None of these responses help students get the conflicts resolved, nor do these responses help students develop conflict resolution skills. Thus, conflicts continue and often escalate.

A *conflict* is a disagreement between people. A *controversy* is a disagreement of opinion or ideas. Everyone can name examples of student conflicts (e.g., teasing, put-downs, bullying, being excluded, rumormongering, stolen or damaged property, threats) and controversies (e.g., fighting over who is the best sports star or pop singer, arguing over which game to play during recess). Some schools have more conflicts and controversies than others, often due to how the faculty and administration handle them.

An important first step in helping students and adults alike to view and appreciate conflict as normal and natural is to make them aware of the natural sources of conflict. What are sources of conflict? William Glasser (1986, 1990) suggests that conflict arises when students (and adults) cannot satisfy their *basic internal psychological needs*: (a) the need to belong (loving, sharing, and cooperating), (b) the need for power and authority (being recognized and respected, achieving), (c) the need for freedom (making choices in their school activities), and (d) the need for fun (laughing and playing). When students (or adults) feel excluded or discriminated against, are unrecognized, have no freedom to make classroom decisions, or stop having fun, there will be more conflicts in the classroom. *Limited resources*, such as sharing scarce materials or equipment or getting the teacher's attention for help, can also be a source of school conflict.

Differences in values can give rise to conflict and cultural clashes. People and cultural groups within a school and community can have different convictions, and when they interact, their values are represented in their words and actions. When a student proclaims "It's not fair!" or "I'm right and you're wrong!" or "He's not telling the truth," often, she may be responding to cultural differences within the concepts of honesty, equality, and fairness. Clashes because of different values may be bias based and expressed as ableism (described in Chapter 3), racism, classism, sexism, and homophobia. Because adults and children bring learned biases and ethnocentric views to the negotiating table, the processes for developing Cultural Proficiency offered in this book must be a part of the context for safe and productive conversation and dialogue rather than destructive argument and conflict.

Generally speaking, people do not change their beliefs and values easily. We strongly recommend against trying to "change" another person's value set, and it's impossible and undesirable to attempt to change anyone's culture. To manage conflicts arising from these differences, first notice that differences *do* make a difference. Then, seek to understand the differences causing the conflict. Effective communication skills and a desire to discover differing values help create shared sets of values. The next two sections of this chapter examine skills and processes for communicating, negotiating, problem solving, and mediating conflict.

REFLECTION

To what extent do you agree with William Glasser's (1986, 1990) supposition that conflict arises when people cannot satisfy their *basic internal psychological needs* of belonging, power and authority, freedom and choice, and fun? In what ways might you teach students about and construct experiences inside and outside of the classroom to help students meet their psychological needs of belonging, power, freedom and choice, and fun? In what ways might you teach colleagues and families about how to get their psychological needs met? What are actions you can take to ensure that your interactions with colleagues and family members help to get their psychological needs?

To what extent have you experienced differences in values giving rise to conflict and cultural clashes? What so far in this chapter and book helps you to understand and better manage conflicts and cultural clashes arising from differences in values?

_____

_____

_____

_____

TEACHING AND SUPPORTING STUDENTS TO DETECT AND CONSTRUCTIVELY MANAGE FEELINGS AND IMPULSES

At times, everyone has experienced difficulty managing feelings, impulses, and anger. Clearly, it is not adequate to simply remind someone in distress to "stop and think" prior to acting. Instead, culturally competent educators offer direct, quality instruction in impulse control and strategies for managing feelings and anger, such as the following:

1. Teach students to recognize and monitor the dimensions and cycle of anger and conflict—the external triggers (e.g., someone saying or doing something you do not like) and internal triggers (e.g., internal dialogue about the external trigger, such as "That's not fair, I'll get her!") and the physiological signals of fear, anger, and anxiety (e.g., sweaty palms, increased heartbeats). This instruction includes teaching students the sources of conflict and controversy already described in the previous section of this chapter.

2. Teach students a series of stress and anger reducing techniques, such as conjuring up pleasant images, deep breathing, counting backwards from ten, relaxation and mindfulness strategies, and new internal dialogue scripts and self-control scripts, such as the ones we will highlight in the next section.

3. Teach students to use tools such as "hassle logs or journals" for self-assessment, self-monitoring, and self-reinforcement.

Toomey (1990) offers an explanation for students having difficulty with impulse control. She describes a student's inability to "stop and think" prior to an interaction as a lack of *tentativeness*. Tentativeness is "the disposition or ability to identify all of the relevant information in order to make the best possible response" (pp. 15–16). To be tentative, a person needs to know how to do five things:

1. Differentiate between tasks that provide all of the necessary information in an explicit way and tasks that require searching for information

2. Differentiate between closed (one right answer) and open (many possible answers) tasks

3. Differentiate between relevant and irrelevant information

4. Discriminate what constitutes the best response

5. Decide at what point a search must stop and a commitment should be made to some response

Students demonstrating poor impulse control experience difficulty in one or more of these five areas. Culturally proficient teachers may promote tentativeness and impulse control by offering choices on how to approach tasks, teaching and encouraging self-correcting procedures, teaching the difference between open- and close-ended tasks and offering opportunities to do both, teaching students how to task analyze long-term projects, differentiating expectations and acknowledging differing levels of students performance, and asking students to think and teach out loud.

Of course, critical to any of these instructional elements is deliberate structuring of opportunities for newly learned skills and strategies to be practiced and generalized through role-playing, coaching, and ongoing practice and reinforcement in a broad range of contexts. Specific instructional strategies include script writing and rehearsals to prepare student and adult learners to manage the dynamics of differences.

Self-Control Scripts

A *self-control* script is a problem-solving script in which a student engages in self-talk to exert self-control. Scripts can use acronyms to assist recall of the steps. Two scripts, STOMA and WIN, are described by Curwin, Mendler, and Mendler (2008, p. 151). The third script, POP, is used by preschool and primary school teachers in Nebraska (Personal communication, Richard Villa, April 17, 2009).

STOMA

Stop before you do anything.

Take a breath; think about what happened and what you want to do.

Options: What are the consequences of each choice?

Move on it (make a choice).

Appreciate yourself (for not losing control and doing your best).

WIN

What is the problem?

Identify possible solutions.

Narrow it down to the best choice.

POP

Problem?

Options?

Plan?

The "What Are You Doing?" Script. The *What are you doing?* script is specifically designed for adults to collaborate with students to help them take ownership of their behavior when it does not conform to the classroom or school social contract and expectations. Ideally, all students and adults in a school learn, rehearse, and systematically use the script to interrupt behaviors outside of the norms. This script leads to a plan and a commitment for engaging in alternative behaviors in the future that are within the boundaries of the agreed-upon expectations. Systematic use of this script turns violations of norms into learning opportunities for students as well as opportunities to get back into alignment with social contract expectations. The ultimate goal of learning and using a self-control script systematically is for students to stop and think before acting and realize that it is easier to make a good behavioral choice rather than having to go through the script with an adult if they make a bad behavioral choice. The script goes as follows:

1. What are you doing?

2. Is it helping? Or, Does it comply with expectations? If not, Which expectation does this behavior violate?

3. How will you solve the problem? Or,

   What could you do instead that falls within our expectations?

4. Is this something you can really do?

   (Optional: Do you need help or a reminder to do this? What would help?)

5. When will you start? For how long can you do this?

6. What will you get out of following this plan?

7. Congratulations, you made a good plan/choice/decision!

If you reword the "What are you doing?" script above so that *you* is changed to *I*, the script now is a "What am I doing?" self-control script, which a student can memorize, internalize, think through alone, and even memorialize as a written commitment to action.

The STAR Script. We particularly like a variation of the "What are you doing?" script known as STAR—**S**top, **T**hink, **A**ct, **R**eview. The STAR script is easy for students to first complete on their own at their desks or in a *cool down* spot. As you examine the script presented in Table 7.4, notice the addition of the affective questions at the beginning and end of the script (i.e., "Right now I am feeling . . . ," "Now I am feeling . . . .") that acknowledge and honor the emotions students experience when they are in distress and make poor choices. The addition of these affective questions helps students to recognize that making a better choice can lead to feeling happier and less frustrated, angry, worried, sad, or bored. Students also can feel more deeply respected when teachers ask, "Is there anything else you would like to say?"

REFLECTION

To what degree do you agree with the supposition that impulse control can be taught and nurtured? In what ways might you incorporate the self-control strategies and scripts, such as described in this section, in your

Table 7.4 STAR Review Plan

Student _____

Teacher _____

Date _____

Right now I am feeling: (circle one)

happy	OK	frustrated	angry	worried	sad	bored

Stop	What did I do? What happened because of what I did? What expectations (rule[s]) did I forget?
Think	What else could I have done? 1. 2. 3. What might have happened if I acted differently? 1. 2. 3.
Act	What do you plan to do the next time?
Review	Is there anything else you would like to say?

Now I am feeling: (circle one)

happy	OK	frustrated	angry	worried	sad	bored

teaching? In what ways might you teach and use the strategies and scripts to manage your own feelings and impulses in difficult conversations and interactions with colleagues or family members of students with and without IEPs or other designated support needs?

_____

_____

_____

_____

SOCIAL SKILLS AND CREATIVE PROCESSES FOR SOLVING PROBLEMS, MANAGING CONFLICT, AND ACCOMMODATING STUDENT DIFFERENCES

When students bring conflicts to their teachers or parents, they are often told, "Just ignore it," or "Walk away." When students ask their friends, they are often told, "Get 'em back!" And when the students' conflicts reach the principal's desk, the consequences often are detention or suspension for all involved. None of these responses help students get the conflicts resolved, nor do these responses help students develop conflict resolution skills.

Culturally proficient educators acknowledge that conflict is a natural and ongoing part of human existence, offer alternate responses, and promote student responsibility by

a. directly teaching young people social skills and safe and healthy ways to get their needs met;

b. making the development of social skills, social-emotional learning, creative problem solving, and conflict management a part of the school's curriculum, and

c. learning, modeling, and coaching ongoing thought, reflection, on the part of school staff.

Teaching and Expecting the Use of Social Skills

None of us are born with social skills; instead, social skills, including conflict management skills, are learned. Most of the approaches described in this book work only if students and adults have and use a repertoire of self-directed, self-assessment, self-management, self-monitoring, interpersonal, and small-group social skills. We often hear teachers, pressured to cover the requisite academic standards, holding students accountable for using social skills, claiming that it takes too much time away from the real curriculum to actually teach them appropriate social skills. We would argue that teachers cannot afford *not* to teach social skills. These skills enable students to not only abide by the social norms of the classroom and school but also contribute to their current and future quality of life. The goal of social skill development is to teach children and youth how to communicate their thoughts, feelings, and needs in ways that allow adults and peers to hear and respond to them.

The culturally proficient educator is knowledgeable that prosocial skills encompasse a wide range of instructional strategies that include behavior, cognitive, and affective approaches. Curwin, Mendler, and Mendler (2008) and Hazel, Schumaker, Sherman, and Sheldon (1995) suggest several basic but essential social skills. For example, the co-authors emphasize greeting others and initiating a conversation, making eye contact, making a request, getting someone's attention, actively listening, accepting and giving positive feedback (praise), accepting and giving constructive feedback (criticism), and resisting peer pressure. Kagan, Kyle, and Scott (2004) identify nearly two hundred resources for developing not only social skills but also other skills in personal (self-knowledge, goal setting, organization), affective (expressing feelings, relaxation), motivational (learned optimism, self-talk), cognitive (memory, moral reasoning), and physical (nutrition, play) domains important to self-knowledge, self-management, and interpersonal competence and social-emotional development. As reiterated throughout this book, these strategies and approaches must be culturally appropriate, responsible,and inclusive.

To effectively teach social skills, teachers collaborate with students so that they (a) learn, (b) see a model, (c) practice what the social skill looks like and sounds like, (d) understand why a particular social skill is important to learn and use now and in the future, and (e) practice using it in multiple school and community contexts. Posters/anchor charts explaining the steps involved in using the learned skills can serve as reminders to students of what they know and can prompt self-correction when a social skill is lacking. Paul Tough, reporting on the work of innovative educators and psychological researchers, describes seven additional strengths "likely to predict life satisfaction and high achievement" (2013, p. 76). The strengths, listed in alphabetical order, are the following: curiosity, gratitude, grit, optimism, self-control, social intelligence, and zest. These strengths have been operationalized and can be identified, nurtured, and taught like any other social skill.

Educators often hear this claim: "we remember and understand 20% of what we hear; 50% of what we hear and see; 70% of what we hear, see, and do; and 90% of what we hear, see, do, and teach to another person." Given this general knowledge, culturally proficient teachers who collaborate with students to help them learn and use self-directedness and conflict resolution skills also are likely to become skilled in working with colleagues to manage the issues that arise as the school moves to become more inclusive of everyone. What a *win-win* outcome for including social skills and a solution-finding orientation within the curriculum!

Teaching and Using Creative Problem-Solving and Conflict-Resolution Processes

For students to have flexibility and accountability in problem solving at any level of the self-discipline pyramid, they must have familiar tried-and-true processes that they can activate for themselves or others to overcome the many potential Barriers to creative thinking, problem solving, controversy, and conflict management (Adams, 2001; de Bono, 1985, 1992; Leff, 1984; Osborn, 1993; Parnes, 1992a, 1992b; Thorpe, 2000; Treffinger, 2000; von Oech, 1986, 1998). We believe that we have an obligation as teachers to model how to use these processes and to guide students to apply them, because they are necessary for negotiating life's challenges during and after their school years.

One very powerful and flexible generic process that has had extensive application in education and business over the past several decades is known as the Osborn-Parnes Creative Problem-Solving Process or simply CPS. The six stages of the CPS process outlined in Table 7.5 are based on the process described by Alex Osborn (1993/1953) and his protégé, Sid Parnes (1992a, 1992b), as well as applications employed by Giangreco, Cloninger, Dennis, and Edelman (2002) and one of our co-authors (Villa, Thousand, & Nevin, 2010). CPS can be easily customized for multiple purposes. A key feature of the *Osborn-Parnes* CPS is that at each stage, problem solvers alternate between divergent and convergent thinking. Each stage begins with divergent thinking activities, like the broad exploration of possible issues, problems, options, criteria, and actions. Each stage closes with convergent thinking activities, such as, a narrowing of focus through the sorting, organizing, evaluation, and selecting of preferred ideas or actions. The ability to easily move back and forth between divergent and convergent thinking is an identified attribute of highly creative people (Parnes, 1992a, 1992b).

Four CPS variations that help adults and students to problem solve and resolve conflicts are (1) the SODAS IF problem-solving process and tool, (2) a more complex CPS variation for guiding conflict resolution, (3) a variation for peer mediation, where a student rather than adult guides peers to resolution of their own conflicts, and (4) the use of the "idea-finding" stage of CPS, with students to guide them to solve curriculum and instructional mismatches for themselves and peers.

The SODAS IF Application of CPS to Problem Solve. SODAS IF (Hazel et al., 1995) is a simplified variation of the CPS process that has been successful in helping adults and students as young as preschool identify and solve their own problems and disputes. SODAS is an acronym for Situation-Options-Disadvantages-Advantages-Solution. A template for

Table 7.5   Stages of the Osborne-Parnes Creative Problem Solving (CPS) Process

Stage 1: Challenge finding. Look around and become alert to situations in need of improvement. Realize something should be done and make a decision to work for improvement. First, be divergent and consider a variety of possible challenges. Then be convergent, selecting one challenge upon which to focus that is small enough to be solved in the time allowed.
Stage 2: Fact finding. Start divergently, asking questions to collect data on what is and is not happening with regard to the situation in order to improve understanding of the challenge. Be sure to record and save all facts. It is important to acknowledge that two people may have contradictory perceptions about the exact same event. If so, accept both as facts, as they are the personally true facts for each individual involved. End convergently by sorting, organizing, and reviewing of facts most relevant to the selected challenge.
Stage 3: Problem finding. Consider different ways of viewing the problem. When rephrasing the problem statement, restate the challenge in *positive* words, by using the starter phrase "In what ways might we …? Continue this until a bite-sized problem is teased out that everyone is comfortable tackling. This is the convergent close to this stage.
Stage 4: Idea finding. Engage the rules of brainstorming to generate many possible solutions to the problem. Brainstorming is a divergent idea-generating process in which judgment (even praise) is deferred to stretch thinking beyond the obvious. Here, facts revealed at Stage 2 can be used to jog ideas by asking questions such as "How might this fact be reversed, made smaller or larger, eliminated, or altered to improve the situation? Note that some ideas won't be usable. This is OK, as the process of brainstorming to loosen up thinking is the point of Stage 4.
Stage 5: Solution finding. Now it is time to judge ideas. First, engage in *criteria finding* and identify, refine, and finally select criteria for judging and electing the most promising Stage 4 ideas. In a school situation, criteria, stated in question form, might include the following: (1) Is this proposed solution feasible? (2) Is it time efficient and cost effective? (3) Do the users (e.g., student, teacher, parties in a conflict) like the idea? (4) Is the idea consistent with the school's values and values of the teachers and students who will implement it? Next, be convergent when applying the selection criteria.
Stage 6: Acceptance finding. Make promising solutions ready for use and determine what needs to be done, in order for the solutions to actually work and be accepted by those who are involved. Craft the needed steps to achieve the agreed-upon solutions by taking the facts (i.e., the perceptions of those involved) into consideration. Stage 6 begins divergently, asking and answering "who," "what," "where," "when," "why," and "how" questions. End convergently by preparing a step-by-step plan to turn the plan into action.

the SODAS IF, shown in Table 7.6, identifies the stages of CPS (i.e., Stages 3–6) that parallel the SODAS IF steps.

To illustrate the use of SODAS IF in the classroom, imagine Ms. Cordova, a third-grade classroom teacher randomly drawing from the

Table 7.6 SODAS IF Problem-Solving Template With Corresponding CPS Stages

---

SITUATION (CPS Stage 3: Problem Finding):

_____

_____

_____

_____

OPTIONS (CPS Stage 4: Idea Finding):

1. _____ 2. _____ 3. _____

DISADVANTAGES (Stage 5: Solution Finding)

a. _____ a. _____ a. _____

b. _____ b. _____ b. _____

c. _____ c. _____ c. _____

d. _____ d. _____ d. _____

ADVANTAGES (CPS Stage 5: Solution Finding)

a. _____ a. _____ a. _____

b. _____ b. _____ b. _____

c. _____ c. _____ c. _____

d. _____ d. _____ d. _____

SOLUTION:

IF you agree to a solution, MAKE A PLAN (CPS Stage 6: Acceptance Finding)
(Who will do what, when? How you know if the plan is working?)

---

class meeting suggestion box the problem, "A student calls another student's sister a name, and the students get into a shouting match in the hallway." Ms. Cordova projects the SODAS problem-solving template from the document projector, as she asks the students to identify the problem situation. Ms. Cordova calls on a student who correctly identifies the problem situation and writes the identified situation on the template form. She then asks students to identify some options for solving this problem and calls upon students to share their ideas. Five different options are generated, and the teacher adds a sixth, all of which are recorded on the template.

The next step involves identifying disadvantages for each of the options. Ms. Cordova models an example of a disadvantage of the first option and records the disadvantages on the template. Then, she asks the students to turn to a neighbor and discuss possible disadvantages of the second option. After a minute, she calls on various learners and records the disadvantages shared by the students. She repeats this process for the remaining options, calling on students and recording.

Ms. Cordova repeats the process for the advantages. This time she tallies responses and puts a circle around the advantages with the most votes. She directs the students to turn to a different partner to identify the possible solution(s) that would achieve the best advantages and avoid the worst disadvantages. After a couple of minutes, she asks the students to report out and tallies the results. She explains that if the scenario were real, the two students who had fought would be expected to use SODAS to come up with an alternate response to fighting if a problem like this were to occur again.

Ms. Cordova asks students how the SODAS IF problem-solving process might help them solve problems on the playground, in class, and at home. She closes the lesson by each sharing an example of how they could use SODAS IF in their personal lives and telling the students that they will use SODAS IF to solve problems throughout the year.

The Conflict Resolution Application of CPS. As already noted, conflict is a natural part of the human experience. It is how we perceive conflict and how we act during conflict that brings either distress and frustration or satisfaction and growth in our work worlds and lives. Although none of us has absolute control over the behavior, thoughts, or feelings of others, we do have great influence, particularly if we engage in the actions and steps of constructive conflict resolution.

To manage a successful conflict resolution encounter is complex and sophisticated in terms of the several social skills and steps participants must employ and the alternative perspectives they must take on. Ensuring that a conflict is constructive requires practicing the skills and steps of

Table 7.7 A Comparison of the Stages of CPS and the Steps of Conflict Resolution

Creative Problem Solving	Conflict Resolution
Stage 3: Challenge Finding	Step 1: Decide to Confront
Stage 3: Problem Finding	Step 2: Jointly Define the Conflict
Stage 2: Fact Finding	Step 3: Communicating Positions and Feeling
Stage 4: Idea Finding and Criteria Finding	Step 4: Negotiation
	4a Communicate *Cooperative Intent*
	4b Take Other's *Perspective*
	4c Coordinate *Motivation* to Negotiate in Good Faith
Stage 5: Solution Finding	Step 5: Agree
Stage 6: Acceptance Finding	Step 6: Make a Plan With Back-Up and Follow-Up

conflict resolution. Table 7.7 compares the stages of CPS with the steps of conflict resolution. Table 7.8 details the actual steps, actions, and dispositions for constructively resolving a conflict or controversy. Conflict resolution is an area of human relations that affords us the opportunity to test our individual and collective capacity to facilitate something of which the world is in desperate need, peace. Conflict resolution is a basic life skill. Learn it (i.e., study the steps outlined in Table 7.8), practice it, model it, and pass it on.

An abundance of research is available to support the notion that conflicts have value. For example, achievement, problem solving, positive social development, flexibility in the face of change, and the experience of fun all can be improved when a conflict is constructive (Johnson & Johnson, 1989). A good example of constructive conflict is illustrated in Chapter 6, when Ms. Swanson (the middle-level science teacher) and Ms. Tac (the speech-language specialist) negotiated and tried out the retrofit differentiation approach to generate and implement ideas for including Tina in science. How do you know that a conflict is constructive and has value? You will know when a problem is solved, the relationship among those involved is strengthened, and when the people involved increase their ability to resolve conflicts in the future.

Table 7.8 Elaboration of the Steps of Conflict Resolution and Corresponding CPS Stages

---

Step 1: Confrontation (Challenge Finding)

The very first step in seeking a constructive resolution to a conflict is to make the *decision* to confront the other person or persons involved. In this context, confronting is a positive term meaning "the expression of my perceptions and feelings about a conflict and inviting the other person(s) to do the same."

In terms of the CPS model, confronting requires first recognizing that a conflict of interest exists (i.e., challenge finding) and then acting (confronting) to set the occasion for discovering and airing differences (i.e., setting the CPS process into motion). A certain set of assumptions and ground rules operate in all successful conflict resolution negotiations.

Assumptions

1. Confrontation is a way to express concern for another person and to maintain or increase future involvement with that person.
2. I am willing to involve myself more deeply with the person(s) I am confronting.
3. The other person(s) has the ability and authority to change the situation of concern.
4. I think I can motivate the person to self-examine and consider change.

If, in a conflict situation, you can say "yes" to these four assumptions, then abiding by the following four ground rules helps increase the likelihood that solution finding and resolution will follow.

Ground Rules

1. **Do not "hit and run."** Confront only when there is time to define the conflict jointly and "schedule" a negotiation session.
2. **Honestly communicate** perceptions of and feelings about the issue. Do not threaten but do express anger, resentment, or any other feelings. The rule is to focus anger on the issue (or the other's behavior) not on the person's character or being. Essential is to express regard and concern for the other person as well as your commitment to the relationship.
3. **Comprehend fully the other person's view and feelings** about the conflict. Use those good social skills of actively listening and paraphrasing. Ask questions to negotiate a clear understanding of the person's *position* and *underlying interests* (e.g., fears, needs, desires, concerns). Although each party may come to a conflict with a particular position or stance, there likely are several alternative positions that can be negotiated that can satisfy both persons' interests.
4. **Unless you are God, do not demand** the other person(s) to change his or her behavior. You will request and negotiate changes but not demand them. The goal is to avoid "shark" behavior and minimize defensiveness.

Step 2: Jointly Define the Conflict (Problem Finding)

Once confrontation has been initiated, the next step is to arrive at a mutually agreed-upon definition of the conflict. In CPS language, this is the "problem finding" phase. The conflict must be defined in ways that do not make either party defensive by following the following five steps. A constructive definition makes any conflict easier to resolve.

1. Describe each other's ACTIONS without labeling or blaming each other.
2. Define the conflict as a MUTUAL problem you expect to resolve not as a win-lose struggle.
3. Define the conflict in the most SPECIFIC way you can.
4. Describe your FEELINGS and the effects on you and others using "I" statements.
5. Describe actions of both yourself and the other person that CONTINUE the conflict.

Step 3: Communicate Positions and Feelings (Fact Finding)

During any negotiation, stated positions may change. To come to agreement, you must know what you are disagreeing about. To come to a satisfactory solution depends on you BOTH understanding how the other person's feelings, thoughts, and needs are different from yours. Therefore, be sure both parties fact find by asking and answering questions like these:

1. What are the differences between us?
2. On what do we agree?
3. What actions of the other person do I find unacceptable?
4. What actions of mine does the other person find unacceptable?
5. What are possible solutions satisfactory to both of us?
6. What are things I need to do or change to resolve the conflict?
7. What are things the other person needs to do or change to resolve the conflict?

It is critical at this juncture to understand that there is a huge difference between a person's *interests* and current stated *position*! Interests or concerns are what fundamentally *motivate* a person. A *position* is something that for the moment seems to satisfy and express those interests and concerns.

Recognize that for every interest, there usually are several potential positions that could satisfy it. Further, just because the other person has an opposing position, realize that his or her underlying interests are not necessarily opposed. In fact, in most negotiations, there are more shared and compatible interests than there are conflicting ones.

Ways to discover common interests and modify positions are to

1. Acknowledge that each party may have multiple interests/concerns
2. Make a list of the other party's interest/concerns in order of importance
3. Remember that the same basic human needs (e.g., belonging, mastery, independence, fun, choice, safety, security, generosity) motivate each side's concerns

Step 4: Negotiate (Idea Finding and Criteria Finding)

Step 4a: Communicate Cooperative Intent

In what ways can you communicate that you genuinely intend to work toward a common solution? How can you communicate your trustworthiness and your trust in the other person?

Some ways to communicate what you want and why include the following:

1. Make your interests/concerns come alive; that is, be specific.
2. Demonstrate that you understand the other person's interests/concerns.
3. Describe the problem as you see it before you propose solutions.

(Continued)

Table 7.8 (Continued)

4. Look forward and focus upon the future by talking about goals rather than arguing about past failures.

5. Be concrete yet flexible.

6. Avoid blaming the other side; that is, be "hard" on the problem but "soft" on the person.

Step 4b: Take the Other's Perspective

Resolving conflicts constructively requires using active listening skills. Stop and view the conflict from the other person's shoes. To fully understand the other person's position and feelings, you MUST view the conflict from the other's perspective. No two people see a conflict in exactly the same way; each person interprets every event in life differently. Thus, to resolve a conflict you must keep in mind BOTH your own and the other person's perspective.

Role-playing is an excellent way to increase understanding of another person's perspective. Presenting, out loud, the other person's position and feelings as if you were the other person allows you insight into the other person's viewpoint. It also communicates to the other person that you really do understand his or her position and feelings. The more involved you get in "arguing" one another's positions, the more you understand how the conflict appears to the other person. This further enhances credibility of your intent to cooperate and come to a mutually agreeable solution. Research findings on perspective taking are clear; the more you understand, the more you are able to generate and settle upon solutions that are mutually acceptable.

Step 4c: Coordinate Motivation to Negotiate in Good Faith

Each party's motivation to resolve a conflict *can* be changed by highlighting and even increasing the gains of resolving the conflict and the costs of maintaining the conflict. Engage in answering the following series of questions. Equally important, engage the other person in doing the same.

Question 1:   What do I/you/we *gain* from resolving this conflict?
How might I *increase* these gains?

Gains from conflict resolution included such things as continued friendship, more effective outcomes for students through collaborative interaction, and a united front against outside enemy forces.

Question 2:   What do I/you/we *lose* if this conflict is *not resolved*?
How might I *increase* the costs of these losses?

Potential losses again may be friendship and effectiveness in work or teaching as well as respect from colleagues or students.

Question 3:   What do I/you/we *gain* from *maintaining* this conflict?
How might I *reduce* these gains?

In many situations there are some gains to maintaining a conflict. A classroom teacher in conflict with a special education co-teacher might gain from the conflict by increasing control and power over classroom activities and curriculum. If conflict is resolved, this support person might expect to be in the classroom, need the teacher's time to meet, and otherwise modify the classroom teacher's previous autonomous way of operating in the classroom. The trick here is to help that classroom teacher *see* autonomy and control as less desirable. This might take some outside influence from the co-teacher, colleagues, or a supervisor (school administrator).

Question 4: What do I/you/we *lose* if this conflict is resolved?
How might I *reduce* the costs?

The losses of conflict resolution are often the same as or similar to the gains from maintaining conflict. The classroom teacher in the previous example may lose autonomy and total control over students and classroom operation if a conflict is resolved. Again, the key is to help change the teacher's perception of the importance or benefits of the perceived loss of such things as autonomy, individualism, and isolated decision making. Answering the above four questions bring to a conscious level the motivational factors represented in each of the four cells of the following matrix.

Questioning What Is Gained and Lost if a Conflict Is Resolved or Maintained

	If We Resolve the Conflict	If We Maintain the Conflict
What do I gain? **What do you gain?**	How might I *increase* the *gains* of *resolving* the conflict?	How might I *minimize* the *gains* of *maintaining* the conflict?
What do I lose? **What do you lose?**	How might I *minimize* the *losses* of *resolving* the conflict?	How might I *increase* the *cost* of *maintaining* the conflict?

Step 5: Reach an Agreement (Solution Finding)

A conflict ends when you and the other person reach an agreement or in the language of CPS, you jointly solution find! All parties must be genuinely satisfied with the agreement and commit to abiding by the agreement. Any agreement should be put into writing and specify the details of each person's future actions and what needs to happen if the agreement "slips up." This formal commitment is the Acceptance-Finding and final step (i.e., Step 6) of CPS for conflict resolution.

Step 6: Make a Plan With a Back-Up and Follow-Up Plan (Acceptance-Finding)

Any agreement should be clearly articulated in writing and specify at least the following:

1. The joint position being adopted
2. Ways you will act differently in the future
3. Ways the other person will act differently in the future
4. Ways to restored the plan if one person slips up and acts *out of agreement*
5. Future meetings to monitor the plan, celebrate successes, and fine-tune pieces that are not working well or could be improved to enhance cooperation

It is essential that you both understand what triggered the distress, anger, or resentment in the other person. Criticism, put-downs, sarcasm, and other "belittling" behaviors trigger conflict. If the two of you understand and commit to what NOT to do as well as what TO DO, it is possible to permanently resolve the conflict.

In summary, you can judge if a conflict has been resolved successfully if both parties can answer "yes" to the following six questions:

1. Was a solution generated?
2. Do parties perceive that the conflict was resolved *con*structively versus *de*structively?
3. Do the involved parties consider the solution satisfactory?
4. Is there liking or respect among involved parties?
5. Is the ability to work together restored or increased?
6. Is the possibility of future conflicts reduced?

The Peer Mediation Application of CPS. Fred Schrumpf, a national leader in peer mediation, made the following observation about conflict in schools:

> Conflicts are part of everyday life for most children in school. Unresolved conflicts, however, can hurt a school climate and can result in violence, absenteeism, and vandalism. Knowledge of how to handle a conflict in an appropriate way is a life skill that can be learned cooperatively with peers; its application will benefit students beyond the school environment and school years. (Schrumpf, 1994, p. 275)

What can schools attempting to be culturally proficient do to handle student conflicts in a proactive, positive, and productive way? They can follow the lead of the many North American schools that have turned to teaching and employing students to be the mediators of their own conflicts. What does the research say about the value of conflict resolution and peer mediation training programs? David and Roger Johnson's comprehensive review of the literature on conflict resolution and peer mediation yielded five important findings:

1. Conflicts among students occur frequently but rarely result in injury.

2. Untrained students use strategies that create destructive outcomes that ignore ongoing relationships.

3. Conflict resolution and peer mediation programs can be effective ways to teach students to negotiate and mediate conflicts.

4. After training, students tend to use these conflict strategies, which generally lead to constructive outcomes.

5. Students' success in resolving their conflicts constructively tends to result in reducing the numbers of student-student conflicts referred to teachers and administrators, which, in turn, tends to reduce suspensions. (Johnson & Johnson, 1996a, p. 506)

Students who are trained to serve as mediators sometimes are called *peacemakers* or *conflict managers*. Peer mediation assumes that (a) conflict can be treated as learning opportunities and (b) conflict resolution skills are forces for positive personal growth and social change.

Peer mediation can be initiated within an elementary or secondary classroom or throughout a school. Common to all peer mediation programs are student mediators who are trained to apply with student disputants a mediation process, such as the CPS variation outlined in

Table 7.9, as a Peer Mediation Session Agenda. Notice that each step of the agenda indicates the CPS stage the student is applying. Notice also that the steps are a simplified version of the detailed conflict resolution process described in Table 7.8.

We advocate that all students be trained in the negotiation and mediation social skills students learn when they are trained to serve as peacemakers. For more information on how to build consensus for, initiate, provide students training, monitor, and evaluate a peer mediation program, see Chapter 8 of Villa, Thousand, and Nevin's (2010) text on collaborating with students in instruction and decision making.

Using the "Quick Brainstorm With Kids" CPS Variation to Harness Student Creativity and Solution Finding. Students who know how to use these tools are empowered to collaborate with their teachers to develop accommodations and modifications in curriculum, instruction, and assessment for themselves and their classmates, when what we as teachers have typically structured is not working. To illustrate, Michael Giangreco et al., (2002) described what happened when first graders, working in groups, were provided an overview of how their teacher typically taught an upcoming literacy lesson. The first graders were asked to use the creative solution-generating technique of *brainstorming*—that is, the Stage 4, Idea Finding dimension of CPS to generate as many ways in which the lesson could be changed so that all learners in the class, including Molly, a new student to the class who was deaf and blind, could meaningfully participate. As a reminder, the roles of brainstorming are as follows:

- Defer judgment; do not make evaluative comments until all ideas are generated.
- Be wild with ideas. Freewheeling is encouraged.
- Go for quantity; generate ideas with number versus quality as the goal.
- Set a short time limit.
- Assign a recorder or two to record key words and phrases.
- Do not admire problems or ideas; keep moving.
- Remember to follow the rules of brainstorming!

Students were clustered in groups of three and four. At the end of ten minutes, the six-year-olds had generated nearly seventy possible options! Subsequently evaluating the ideas, the teacher noted that at least sixty ideas could work to include Molly in this lesson and future lessons and activities. She recognized that many of the students' ideas not only allowed Molly's active engagement but also worked to help other students access the curriculum.

Table 7.9 Peer Mediation Session Agenda With Each Step's Corresponding CPS Stage

---

**Step 1. Open and Gain Commitment to Ground Rules
(Stage 1: Challenge Finding—Agreeing to Confront)**

*Make introductions.
*State the ground rules:

1. Mediators are neutral (they do not take sides).
2. Everything said is confidential (stays in this room).
3. No interruptions.
4. Agree to solve the conflict.

*Get commitment to the ground rules.

Step 2. Jointly Define the Conflict (Stage 3: Problem Finding)

*Ask each person, "Please tell me what happened."
(Listen and then summarize.)
*Ask each person, "Do you want to add anything?"
(Listen, summarize, and clarify with questions.)
*Repeat until the problem is understood.
(Summarize the problem.)

Step 3. Interest Finding (Stage 2: Fact Finding)

*Determine interests; ask each person,
"What do you really want?" "Why?"
"What might happen if you do not reach an agreement?"
"What do you have in common?"
(Listen, summarize, and question.)
*Summarize shared interests.
*State what disputants have in common.

Step 4. Generate Options (Stage 4: Idea Finding)

*Brainstorm solutions; ask disputants,
"What could be done to resolve the problem?"

Step 5. Evaluate Options and Agree on a Solution (Stage 5: Solution Finding)

*Evaluate options and decide on a solution.
*Ask each person,
"Which of these options are you willing to do?"
*Restate: "You both agree to...." (List all they agree to do.)

Step 6. Write an Agreement and Close the Session (Stage 6: Acceptance Finding)

*Write an agreement and sign it.
*Shake hands.

Source: Adapted from *Collaborating with students in instruction and decision making: The untapped resource* (p. 161) by R.A. Villa, J.S. Thousand, & A.I. Nevin, 2010. Thousand Oaks, CA: Corwin Press. Copyright 2010. By Villa, R.A, Thousand, J.S., and Nevin, A.I. Adapted with permission.

In a more recent experience, Richard Villa (personal communication, September 13, 2016) facilitated a student assembly in which 650 middle–level students were introduced to facts about various learners and classroom demands. They were asked to use the retrofit approach to differentiating instruction described in Chapter 5 to first identify mismatches between learner characteristics and classroom demands and then generate a minimum of three possible solutions for each mismatch. For each scenario, Richard stopped students after five minutes of brainstorming and sampled their ideas. His favorite part of the assembly was watching the expressions of surprise and pleasure on the faces in the adult audience members as the students shared their ideas. Following the assembly, several teachers who had been in the audience revealed that some of the students who had shared the best ideas were considered to be struggling learners in their classes. The teachers smartly concluded that they needed to collaborate with these students to identify potential solutions to the mismatches that exist between them and the demands of their classrooms.

REFLECTION

To what degree do you agree with the supposition that conflict has value and can strengthen relations of disputants? In what ways might you incorporate social skills and the problem solving, conflict resolution, and peer mediation approaches, such as those describe above, in your curriculum and instruction? In what ways might you teach and use the social skills and creative problem-solving approach in your interactions with students in distress, other educators in your school with whom you may have a difficult conversation, or family members of students with and without IEPs or other designated support needs?

_____

_____

_____

_____

CASE STORY

Let's return to the Lakeside Union School District and one of the elementary schools in the district, James Madison Elementary.

Part 1: Too Close for Comfort

James Madison Elementary School is located on the east side of Lakeside near the local community college, Trinity College. James Madison has always had an active parent teacher organization (PTO). The principal, Clarita Garcia, encourages parents and teachers to work collaboratively, especially as the district launches the Multi-Tiered System of Supports (MTSS) approach for "catching students before they fall" through swift and targeting interventions in general education. She has offered several professional learning sessions about MTSS and its relationship to special education services in the evening hours, so that parents as well as teachers and paraeducators can learn about the process at a time of day that does not conflict with most parents' work schedules.

One of the school's most active parents, Dr. Karen Tyler, a lecturer at Trinity College, has a fifth grader, Katlyn, who is both academically gifted and eligible for special education services because of significant physical limitations resulting from cerebral palsy, which adversely impact her access to the curriculum. Dr. Tyler contacted Ms. Garcia and requested a meeting with members of Katlyn's IEP team because she was concerned about comments she had heard from Katlyn's fifth-grade teachers regarding Mrs. Carter, a paraeducator who has supported Katlyn since kindergarten. The meeting begins with Mrs. Garcia welcoming everyone and giving an opening statement.

Mrs. Clarita Garcia, Principal:	*Thanks everyone for coming today. Dr. Tyler has asked us to meet with her today because of concerns she has about how we would like to address Katlyn's needs. We all know we want to do our best when it comes to supporting Katlyn.*
Dr. Karen Tyler, Katlyn's Mother:	*Thank you, Mrs. Garcia, for gathering this group together. Katlyn has done so remarkably well recently; my family is very proud of her and appreciates how everyone works to help her. As a matter of fact, that's why I'm here. I have concerns about what I've heard some of you say about how Mrs. Carter supports Katlyn. I hope you are all clear as to how much Katlyn needs Mrs. Carter's help. As a child with cerebral palsy, Katlyn does well physically, but has grown to depend on Mrs. Carter.*
Evelyn Williams, Fifth-Grade Team Leader:	*Dr. Tyler, I'd like to speak first about this issue. As you know, we all agreed last year to advance Katlyn forward a grade, because she is so academically advanced. This has been a good thing. And it has meant that Katlyn has lost her peer group from the past four years She has this entirely new group of classmates with whom to make real connections and potential friendships. Dr. Tyler, from my several observations of Mrs. Carter's interactions with Katlyn in the classroom, hallways, playground, and cafeteria, it appears as though she believes her job is to be Katlyn's "right hand assistant." Katlyn may have needed more direct adult support when she was very young but not any more. Bryan, you know Katlyn and coordinate her special education services this year. What have you observed?*

Bryan Thompson, Special Educator:	*Yes, Evelyn. What you have described is my experience as well. Dr. Tyler, I know Mrs. Carter cares very much for Katlyn; after all, she has supported her since kindergarten. Since we planned her transition to fifth grade at the end of last year, I have come to know Katlyn as a physically, socially, and academically determined girl who has figured out how to ask for and get what she wants and needs. At this point in Katlyn's development, a paraeducator's role is to be in the background, ready to facilitate natural peer collaboration and supports. This is a big shift for Mrs. Carter, we know. It is like watching your kids grow up and realizing you just have to let go and let them fly, even though it is scary and you are not sure what will happen. But you have to let go, nevertheless. I have been talking with her about what we have in mind for Katlyn, but she is stuck and resists letting Katlyn go anywhere or do anything without her nearby.*
Tonya Sommers, Fifth-Grade Language Arts teacher:	*Yes, I agree. As you know, Bryan and I are co-teaching this year during the period that Katlyn is in our language arts class. We have created lots of opportunities for our students to work together on projects and assignments. We have to intervene to let Mrs. Carter know that she is not to take Katlyn over to her desk and work with her alone. Mrs. Carter does not seem to know what to do with herself. To work with Katlyn alone defeats our purpose of making Katlyn a genuine member of this class. She is so social and is missing out on the great collaborative learning experiences her classmates enjoy when Mrs. Carter spirits her away. Her classmates are confused, too. Several have questioned if Katlyn really is a member of the class. Because she skipped a grade, they don't really know her yet and don't understand why she has an adult who keeps being by her side.*
Karen Tyler, Katlyn's Mother:	*I don't think you are trying to understand Katlyn's relationship with Mrs. Carter. They are close and Katlyn depends on her. I can tell we are getting nowhere. Mrs. Garcia, what are you going to do about this situation?*

REFLECTION

What are some Barriers that are getting in the way of a productive meeting? In what ways might the principal manage this conversation? What are some of the key issues of this story? In what ways might the Essential Element of *Managing the Dynamics of Differences* help resolve these issues? Knowing what you know about culturally proficient inclusive classrooms, what might you do if you were Mrs. Garcia?

Part 2: Managing Our Differences

For the resolution to this conflict, let us reflect on the actions of a culturally proficient member of an inclusive learning community. Let's join the conversation now, as Mrs. Garcia and the co-teachers use the systems, practices, strategies, and tools featured in this chapter.

Mrs. Clarita Garcia, Principal:	*So, I understand that Katlyn gets a lot of support from Mrs. Carter. Our differences seem to be about how Mrs. Carter provides support and how much support Katlyn needs from an adult.*
Dr. Karen Tyler, Katlyn's Mother:	*Like I said, I hope you are all clear as to how much Katlyn needs Mrs. Carter. It is because of Mrs. Carter, that Katlyn has had so much success in the past. I don't want her to be without Mrs. Carter.*
Evelyn Williams, Fifth-Grade Team Leader:	*We all know that Katlyn is a very bright, curious, and determined girl, who has a whole new group of peers to get to know, so she can benefit from their collaborative work. We are anxious for her classmates, Ms. Sommers, Mr. Thompson, and all of her other teachers to have the opportunity to get to know and work with Katlyn.*
Bryan Thompson, Special Educator:	*How about we see how Katlyn does in a leadership role in our next project group effort, which starts on Monday. We are trying to be deliberate about using cooperative group structures and roles and distributing roles among students based upon their observed strengths. And we could spend a little time with Mrs. Carter to explain about co-teaching and how she could join Tonya and me collecting engagement data while students are working and joining us as a team, providing every group support rather than hovering over Katlyn and her groups. My take is that we should assume that Mrs. Carter just doesn't yet know what to do if not by Katlyn's side. It is our job to model and guide her to be part of the team supporting all students.*
	Clearly, Katlyn has great social skills and would be a natural at the encourager and equalizer roles, where she would encourage team members to contribute and make sure everyone has had an equal opportunity to make contributions. It would really allow her to use her social strengths and contribute as a team leader. Wada say, Tonya, Dr. Tyler?

Tonya Sommers, Fifth-Grade Language Arts Teacher:	*Yes, how about we use the next group project to do just what you have suggested, Bryan. We can ask Mrs. Carter to observe and monitor what she sees, just like we do. We certainly can use another set of eyes and ears. I believe she can really reinforce Katlyn to be a team player, and she can give us insight into how to adapt our materials and instruction so Katlyn can best participate. She has a wealth of experience with this.*
Dr. Tyler, Katlyn's Mother:	*Well, as long as Mrs. Carter is still involved. She knows Katlyn so well. Thanks for acknowledging that. I'd be willing to give it a try, as long as we meet again soon and if you can give me regular reports, like a short note home on how the day has gone. Mr. Thompson, you offered that at the beginning of the year, but I did not see the need. What I am hearing is that you recognize Katlyn's strengths and want to focus upon building her independence and autonomy. However, I don't want this to happen too quickly. How will Mrs. Carter know how to manage her support for Katlyn?*
Bryan Thompson, Special Educator:	*Well, part of my job is to provide training, direction, and supervision to all of the paraeducators who work to support students in our classrooms. That includes Mrs. Carter. Tonya and I will sit down with Mrs. Carter and lay out a clear job description with regard to her role with Katlyn as well as all of the students in this and other classrooms where she provides support. I believe Mrs. Carter is just not clear as to how all of our roles have changed, with our emphasis on co-teaching and having students take the lead in cooperative learning arrangements that rely less upon adult direct instruction and more upon collaborative problem solving in alignment with the Career and College Readiness Standards we are implementing now.* *Tonya, are we are on the same page?*
Tonya Sommers, Fifth-Grade Language Arts Teacher:	*Absolutely, our fifth graders will soon be transitioning to the middle school where they are expected to be both independent decision makers and team players. Katlyn and all of her classmates have this year to develop these complementary skills through a focus on project-based and cooperative group learning experiences.*
Mrs. Clarita Garcia, Principal:	*Bryan and Tonya, thank you for thinking through and explaining how Mrs. Carter can continue to be involved in supporting Katlyn in a different way. Dr. Tyler, your bringing us together today signals to me that you haven't lost faith is us as a team. We appreciate that you will continue to help evolve Katlyn's schooling and work with other parents in our school community through our strong PTO.* *Thanks to everyone for staying open to airing and managing our differences in ways to best serve Katlyn.*

REFLECTION

Using Table 7.1 as a frame for action, what do you notice about the team members' actions in this part of the case story? What might have been some key actions in the story and why? What might have been other pathways team members could have taken to resolve this issue in a culturally proficient manner? What additional steps need to be taken following the meeting?

_____

_____

_____

_____

DIALOGIC ACTIVITY

A fair idea put to use is better than a good idea kept on the polishing wheel.

Alex Osborn (as cited in Parnes, 1992, p. 38)

As the Alex Osborn quote suggests, an important disposition shared by creative problem solvers is that they take action on what can be attempted. In other words, rather than taking a "ready, *aim*, fire" stance, where everything has to be perfectly organized and ordered in order to step out and attempt something, effective problem solvers take a "ready, *fire*, aim" stance and give ideas a try.

Now that you have read this chapter, take a moment and think about ways in which you, your colleagues, and students might adopt a "ready, fire, aim" disposition and try out co-teaching, self-management, conflict resolution, mediation, and other strategies described in this chapter. With your grade-level team, your department group, your faculty and paraprofessionals, engage in a dialogue using the following prompts:

- What is our shared understanding of Managing the Dynamics of Difference?
- What evidence do we have that Managing the Dynamics of Difference is a shared priority for all educators within our school?
- In what ways do we demonstrate that we have an Inclusive School? In what ways has this chapter informed our work?

- In what ways might we engage your colleagues, students, and families in talking about and planning for creative thinking and problem solving becoming default dispositions and processes to effectively address issues as they arise as your school transformations to a more Inclusive School?
- The key is to act and engage others in action as well. What might our collective next steps be?

PREVIEW OF CHAPTER 8

In this chapter, we examined the Essential Element of *Managing the Dynamics of Diversity* and learned how members of an Inclusive School more collaboratively manage differences by restructuring their traditional roles and by learning and using creative problem solving, self-management, and conflict resolution processes. In Chapter 8, we examine the Essential Element of Adapting to Diversity through advocacy for and adoption of practices and policies to eliminate inequities and facilitate Inclusive Schooling. We introduce frameworks for understanding students, enhancing the relevance of instruction through the use of Universal Design for Learning principles, and activating student self-determination.

8 Adapting to Diversity Through Advocacy and Universal Design for Learning

Cowardice asks the question, "Is it safe?"
Expedience asks the question, "Is it political?"
Vanity asks the question, "Is it popular?"
But conscience asks the question, "Is it right?"
And there comes a time when one must take a position
that is neither safe, nor politic, nor popular,
but it must be made because conscience says that it is right!

Martin Luther King Jr. (n.d.)

GETTING CENTERED

What thoughts, feeling, or emotions do you experience as you read this Martin Luther King Jr. quote? What might be some reasons to begin this chapter on adapting to diversity through advocacy and universal design with this quote? What is the right work for you?

_____

_____

_____

_____

ADAPTING TO DIVERSITY: AN OVERVIEW

The purpose of this chapter is to provide readers with ways to proactively plan instruction with student diversity in mind, tap student leadership and advocacy, and advocate for changes in policies and practices that support diversity and inclusion by taking actions identified in Table 8.1. Similar to the first table in each of the previous three chapters, Table 8.1 has three columns. The first column presents a brief definition of the fourth Essential Element of Cultural Proficiency, Adapting to Diversity. The second column offers four actions for helping culturally proficient educators to adopt practices and policies to eliminate inequalities and transform a school to a genuinely inclusive community. The third column identifies systems, practices, strategies, and tools featured in this chapter for accomplishing these four actions.

REFLECTION

Take a moment and carefully read each of the four actions for culturally proficient educators to understand and adapt to differences and diversity presented in Table 8.1. What actions, practices, and strategies are you curious about or want to learn more about? What are systems, practices, strategies, or tools you have employed to proactively plan instruction with student diversity in mind, tap student leadership and advocacy, and advocate for changes in policies and practices that support diversity and inclusion? What are systems and strategies you have seen others employ?

_____

_____

_____

_____

Table 8.1 Systems, Practices, Strategies, and Tools That Facilitate the Actions of Adapting to Diversity Through Universal Design and Advocacy

Cultural Proficiency Essential Element #4	Actions of a culturally proficient member of an inclusive learning community	Systems, practices, strategies, and tools featured in this chapter
Adapting to Diversity Changing and adopting new policies and practices that support diversity and inclusion	I/we . . . • Actively and continuously learn about marginalized and/or underserved cultural groups different from my/our own and use their experiences and backgrounds to enhance teaching and learning, student empowerment and self-advocacy, and home-school-community relations • Actively and continuously learn about and implement what is necessary to (a) enhance the relevance of my/our instruction, (b) differentiate instruction for any student, and (c) deal with issues caused by differences • Actively tap the leadership potential of members of cultural groups (i.e., students with disabilities) • Advocate for changes in school and district policies and practices so they reflect the Guiding Principles of Cultural Proficiency and challenge negative assumptions and stereotypes regarding disability	I/we . . . • Practice cultural reciprocity • Learn and use Multiple Intelligences theory and other frameworks for understanding students • Learn about and use Universal Design for Learning as the default approach to proactively differentiating instruction for all students • Structure opportunities for students to advocate for themselves and others and share leadership authority with adults in decision making regarding school issues • Have students with IEPs exercise self-determination by teaching and supporting them to lead their own IEPs • Advocate for personal learning plans for every student to counter the stereotype that only some people need or benefit from personalized learning plans • Learn how to facilitate organizational change

ACTIVELY LEARNING ABOUT CULTURAL GROUPS BY USING DIVERSE FRAMEWORKS FOR UNDERSTANDING STUDENTS AND FAMILIES

In Chapter 6, we examined some of the Barriers and facilitators to truly getting to know and valuing cultural groups different from our own (e.g., students and families with IEPs, students and families from marginalized and underserved cultural groups). We highlighted the importance of activating an asset-based *funds of knowledge* perspective of students and their families, appreciating that the wealth of personal and culturally connected knowledge and resources enhance the quality of schooling and enhance home-school-community relations. In addition to taking a *funds of knowledge* perspective, culturally proficient educators, in adapting to diversity, also must further demonstrate appreciating how values and belief systems differ from one cultural group to another and engage in what is known as *cultural reciprocity*.

Using the Adaptive Posture of Cultural Reciprocity

Within the context of schools and special education service delivery, *cultural reciprocity* is defined as a two-way recursive process for sharing information between families and school personnel. As was emphasized in Chapter 5, assessing culture begins with recognizing differences between our own perspective and those of members of other cultural backgrounds. For educators, particularly educational specialists, such as special educators and therapists (e.g., occupation, physical, speech and language), this requires first understanding the discipline's cultural underpinning and identifying "the cultural values that are embedded in the interpretation of the student's difficulties or in the recommendations for service" (Wang, McCart, & Turnbull, 2007, p. 28). Kalyanpur and Harry (2012) note how easy it is for European American educators to fail to realize to what extent many educational principles and practices have their origins in European American values and assumptions, particularly about disability being a condition that must be treated and remediated.

Wang and colleagues (2007) provide a case study of a Chinese American family. The study illustrates a culture clash and is an application of cultural reciprocity. In this case study, educators wanted to offer *positive* behavior supports, a best practice in the current "culture" of behavioral interventions, for a teenage girl with ADHA experiencing problem behaviors. The family preferred using a *punishment* response at home when she failed to complete homework. The school team proceeded to ask the "right questions" (Santa, Rothstein, & Bain, 2016) and learned about the family's (i.e., grandmother's) perception that the teenager's behavior problems were influenced by bad spirits because of something the grandmother had done in her previous life. With this knowledge and continued dialogue, the team honored the family's perspective and adapted their professional interpretations and recommendations to develop a culturally responsive intervention aligned with the beliefs and values of the family.

Beth Harry notes the critical value of using the adaptive posture of cultural reciprocity in learning about and using the experiences of families, particularly in special education, when she observes that "[u]nderstanding that our own beliefs and practices are but one cultural variation should make it easier to respect and, therefore, to serve the wide diversity of families whose children are served by special education programs" (2003, p. 138.) This cultural understanding clearly should do the same for any educator to respect, adapt, and serve the wide diversity of students who enter our classrooms and schools.

Getting to Know Students Through Learning Preference Frameworks

For every educator, the process of differentiating curriculum and instruction begins by getting to know the students. Learning preferences provide helpful frameworks for understanding and finding strengths in all students. One popular learning preference framework recommended by Dunn and Dunn (1987) suggests that teachers think about students in terms of auditory, visual, tactile, and kinesthetic modalities as well as other factors that affect learning, such as noise and light, motivation, and task structure (e.g., independent, self-directed, or cooperative). These factors provide educators opportunities to connect with students through a frame of culture and curriculum.

Multiple Intelligences Theory. Since the early 1980s a widely used framework for understanding, motivating, and finding strengths in all students has been derived form Howard Gardner's Multiple Intelligences (MI) theory (Armstrong, 1987, 2009; Gardner, 1983, 2011). MI theory assumes that all students possess an array of at least eight intelligences or orientations to experiences described in Table 8.2. In contrast to a modality learning style theory (Dunn & Dunn, 1987), which classifies students into separate categories (i.e., auditory, visual, tactile, kinesthetic), MI theory suggests that each person has all eight intelligences in different strengths or proportions that function in unique ways for each person. MI theory in the field of education has reminded educators that intelligence is neither fixed nor static. Any one of a person's "weaker" intelligence areas can become strengths when exercised and given an opportunity to develop. Identifying a student's strength intelligences allows educators to use those strengths to capture a student's attention and assist the student in learning new information. Examine Table 8.2 for details discussed in this section.

Numerous MI surveys have been constructed. A Google Internet search by the authors yielded hundreds of pages of results for the key words, *multiple*

Table 8.2 Definition of the Eight Multiple Intelligences

1. **Verbal/linguistic**—is word oriented; is sensitive to the sounds, structures, meanings, and functions of words; may show an affinity to storytelling, writing, reading, and verbal play (e.g., jokes, puns, riddles)

2. **Logical/mathematical**—is concept oriented; has capacity to perceive logical or numerical patterns; has a scientific or numerical nature to discover or test hypotheses

3. **Visual/spatial**—is image and picture oriented; is able to perceive the world visually and to perform transformations on those perceptions; may daydream and demonstrate artistic, designer, or inventive qualities

4. **Musical/rhythmic**—is rhythm and melody oriented; can produce and appreciate rhythm, pitch, timbre, and multiple forms of musical expression; may be animated or calmed by music

5. **Bodily/kinesthetic**—is physically oriented; uses one's body movements for self-expression (e.g., acting, dancing, mime); excels in athletics; uses touch to interpret the environment; can skillfully handle or produce objects requiring fine motor abilities

6. **Interpersonal**—is socially oriented; has strong mediation and leadership skills; can teach others and discern moods, temperaments, and motivations of other people

7. **Intrapersonal**—is intuitively oriented; can access and interpret one's own feelings; may be strong willed or self-motivated; may prefer solitary activities

8. **Naturalist**—has capacity to classify nature; has outstanding knowledge of or sensitivity to things that exist in the natural world; has ability to discern patterns in nature

intelligence surveys. Among the surveys, the Multiple Intelligences Developmental Assessment Scales (MIDAS) are endorsed by the MI theory originator, Howard Gardner, because of their development in accordance with valid research procedures and their track record of producing a valid and reliable profile (www.miresearch.org/). MIDAS has both teen and adult versions. Armstrong (2009) provides MI inventories and assessment checklists for adults and students. However, other less formal ways of gathering MI assessment information about students also exist. These methods include observations; record review; talking with students, parents, and other teachers; anecdotal records; and setting up special activities and centers for observing how students express their multiple intelligences. Thousand, Villa, and Nevin (2015) offer more about how to use MI theory to differentiate the content (materials, objectives), processes (way students engage with content and one another), and products (ways students show what they know) of a lesson.

REFLECTION

In *The Tao of Teaching*, Greta Nagel offers the following advice: "Do not hesitate to express your interest in getting to know others or to admit that you have much to learn from them" (1994, p. 179). Now that you have read about using the adaptive posture of cultural reciprocity and the Multiple Intelligences approach to learning about student and adult learning preferences, in what ways might you engage these processes to do as Greta Nagel suggests, get to know others (i.e., your students and their families) and show that you have much to learn from them? How might you use *cultural reciprocity* to discover how to be responsive to the cultural challenges your students might experience?

_____

_____

_____

_____

How might you assess your students to discover their multiple intelligences? Better yet, how might you structure experiences where students discover their own multiple intelligences and become aware of their greatness(es)? How might you use knowledge of your students' unique combinations of multiple intelligences to differentiate the content (materials, objectives), processes (way students engage with content and one another), and products (ways students show what they know) of your lessons? How might you research more about cultural reciprocity and MI theory? In what ways might you engage your colleagues about cultural reciprocity and MI theory to increase your school's flexibility in developing interventions and designing lessons?

_____

_____

_____

_____

USING UNIVERSAL DESIGN FOR LEARNING (UDL) AS THE DEFAULT APPROACH FOR DIFFERENTIATING INSTRUCTION FOR ALL STUDENTS

Differentiated Instruction (DI), though not a new approach for today's educators, is not often understood nor put into daily practice in all classrooms. DI is a process for providing students curriculum access whereby "educators *vary* the learning activities, content demands, modes of assessment and the classroom environment to meet the needs and support the growth of each child" (Thousand, Villa, & Nevin, 2015, p. 11). DI also is a frame of mind or philosophy that educators are responsible for adapting instruction to student differences, because one size does not fit all. DI is not individualized instruction, nor is it ability grouping of students. Further description is often needed for educators to fully understand the benefit of the instructional approach of DI for all students as first introduced by Carol Ann Tomlinson (1999).

Two Approaches to Differentiation

Retrofit. Two approaches to differentiating instruction exist for classroom instruction (Thousand et al., 2015). The first approach is the *retrofit* approach, where teachers alter preexisting curriculum and instructional methods to help students access the curriculum. The retrofit process was described and illustrated in Chapter 6 through the example of Ms. Tac, the speech and language specialist, and Ms. Swanson, the science teacher, collaborating to "after the fact" generate adaptations for Tina to succeed in science class. Retrofitting is a *reactive* process for remodeling instruction when teachers realize that what was planned or what they usually do is just not going to work for one or more students whose learning characteristics they had not considered when first designing the lesson.

The term *retrofit* is derived from architecture. Think of a multi-storied school building built in the 1950s. Was it built to allow access for all students? No! The building can be made accessible by retrofitting: adding elevators and ramps, widening doorways, and so on. A retrofit approach works but is expensive in terms of the valuable time and creative energy spent developing individualized adaptations, after the fact, for any number of students.

Universal Design. An alternative to retrofitting is an approach known as *universal design*. As a concept borrowed from architecture, universal design involves designing products and environments in ways that they can be used without need for modifications or special designs for particular circumstances. Curb cuts, which allow wheelchair access to sidewalks, are examples of universal design. They are expensive to add after the fact, but cost virtually nothing if designed from the start. Curb cuts also ease stroller access and reduce joint stress for joggers and faulty footing for all sidewalk users. Universal design requires preplanning and intention toward purpose and clear outcomes.

Universal Design for Learning (UDL): Planning and Implementation

Universal design applied in education is known as *Universal Design for Learning* (UDL). UDL is a *proactive* approach to differentiating instructional content (curriculum and goals), products (assessments), and processes (instructional methods) based upon "up front" assumptions of student diversity in multiple dimensions and investigation of students' varying characteristics. Differentiated materials, methods, and assessment alternatives are considered and created *in advance*, with the full range of students' differences in mind.

Planning for Four Access Design Points. UDL requires culturally proficient educators to attend to four *access design points* described in Table 8.3. These four design points are translated into an easy-to-use UDL Lesson Plan Template in Table 8.4, which guides educators through the planning, implementation, and evaluation phases of developing and executing effective UDL lessons and units. In the lesson template, gathering facts about students is shown as the first planning step, acknowledging that the process of UDL differentiating always begins with getting to know students in multiple ways. Equipped with this rich set of student data, educators then can consider differentiation options for the three remaining instructional design points of content product, and process, by asking the following questions at Steps 2, 3, and 4 of the planning phase:

- Step 2: Content—In what ways might we provide multiple options for students to take in information (content and materials differentiation)?
- Step 3: Product—In what ways might we provide multiple options for students to express what they know and be assessed on what they have learned (product differentiation)?
- Step 4: Process—In what ways might we engage multiple learning processes to help students make sense of the ideas, concepts, procedures, and principles being taught (process differentiation)?

Pausing to Reflect. Importantly, at each of the four design points, teachers—especially teachers new to using the UDL process—*pause and reflect* about all of the students in order to consider whether a specific student need or all students could benefit from additional individualization, the use of technology, or meaningful ways to connect content to students' culture, home, and community life. Notice that the pause and reflect aspect of considering student diversity is included at each step of the lesson planning phase. Fortunately, educational technology and web-based resources now are readily and easily available at little or no cost to assist teachers to differentiate instruction. For example, the Kansas State Department of Education (KSDE) in collaboration with the Kansas Technical Assistance Support Network (TASN) has created Co-teaching Differentiated Instruction Resource pages (found at https:// sites.google.com/site/ksdetasndi2/home), which offer links to a host of web-based apps and resources for getting to know student learners and

Table 8.3 The Four UDL Access Design Points

Access Design Point 1: Facts About the Students
Always begin by first *gathering facts* about the differences in and among students—their background knowledge, readiness, life circumstances, language proficiency, culture, learning preferences, strength, and interests.
Access Design Point 2: Content Demands
Given this information about students, differentiate content. Content is multidimensional, because it involves not only what is to be taught and differentiated for students but variations in learning objectives and levels of knowledge and proficiency different students are expected to demonstrate as well as variations in the materials to be used and how the materials are accessed (e.g., online, in print, accessed through the use of technology, such as "text to speech" software).
Access Design Point 3: Product Demands
The product access design point concerns how students show what they know and have learned and how their products are evaluated. A backward design approach is used to consider what students need to show about their learning before designing the processes by which they will access this learning. Information gathered about student learning preference (e.g., multiple intelligences) can be used to enable students to best show what they have learned. Standardized assessments are augmented with authentic assessment processes (e.g., portfolios, curriculum-based assessment, direct observation of performance).
Access Design Point 4: Process Demands
The process design point requires considering how best to help students make sense of what they are to learn. Various lesson formats and arrangements (e.g., discovery learning, cooperative group learning, direct instruction), technology, evidence-based instructional practices and scaffolds, and collaborative teaching arrangements provide access to learning.

assisting in differentiating at content, product, and process design points.

Inviting Collaboration. As you study the UDL Lesson Planning Template, in what ways do you detect differentiation considerations and practices identified in previous chapters? In what ways do the implementation and evaluation/reflection phases of the template invite teachers to tap the resources of their professional colleagues and students through co-teaching to enhance the application of universal design principles? Differentiation can be made easier and more effective when more than one person plans and delivers instruction. The literature on collaborative teaching and learning clearly suggests that two heads (and bodies) really can be better than one (Thousand, Villa, & Nevin, 2015; Villa, Thousand, & Nevin, 2010, 2013).

Table 8.4 UDL Lesson Plan Template

PLANNING PHASE

Lesson Topic and Name:

Content Area(s):

Standards and Goals Addressed:

Step 1: Discover Facts About the Student Learners Who are our students and how do they learn? What are our students' various strengths, languages, cultural backgrounds, learning styles, and interests? What are our students' various multiple intelligences (i.e., verbal/linguistic, logical/mathematical, visual/spatial, musical/rhythmic, bodily/kinesthetic, interpersonal, intrapersonal, naturalist)? What forms of communication (e.g., assistive technology) do our students use? ***Pause and Reflect About Specific Students*** Are there any students with characteristics that might require differentiation in the content, product, or process of learning?	**Step 3: Products Showing Student Success** How will students convey their learning? In what ways will the learning outcomes be demonstrated? ***Differentiation Considerations*** What are multiple ways students can demonstrate their understandings (e.g., multiple intelligences, multilevel, and/or multisensory performances)? What authentic products do students create? What are the criteria teachers use to evaluate the products? ***Pause and Reflect About Specific Students*** Are there any students who require unique ways of showing what they know?
Step 2: Content—What Students Learn What College and Career Readiness and English Language Development standards are addressed? What are the academic, language, and socioemotional learning goals? ***Differentiation Considerations*** In what order will concepts and content be taught? What multilevel and/or multisensory materials do teachers need to facilitate access to the content? What multilevel goals are needed for all students to meaningfully access the content? ***Pause and Reflect About Specific Students*** Are there any students who require unique or multilevel objectives or materials?	

(Continued)

Table 8.4 (Continued)

Step 4: Process of Instruction (how students engage in learning)

Instructional Formats (how students take part in learning)	Instructional Arrangements (methods for grouping students)	Instructional Strategies	Social and Physical Environment	Co-teaching Approach(es)
Differentiation Considerations	*Differentiation Considerations*	*Differentiation Considerations*	*Differentiation Considerations*	*Differentiation Considerations*
Adapted lectures?	Cooperative group learning?	Use research-based strategies?	Room arrangement?	Teaching with another professional or paraprofessional?
Experiential?	Same or cross-age peer tutors?	Apply MI theory?	Social norms?	Students as co-teachers? (e.g., cooperative learning peer tutors, arrangements)
Simulations?	Independent?	Integrate the arts?	Teach responsibility?	
Role-play?	Whole group?		Positive behavior supports?	
Group investigation?	Other? (tutorial, teacher directed small group)		Environmental (light, sound) alterations?	
Discovery learning?			Use of space outside of class?	
Online learning?				
Self-directed?				
Stations?				
Integrated cross-curricular thematic?				
Service learning?				

Pause and Reflect About Specific Students

What student-specific teaching strategies do selected students need? What specific systems of supports (e.g., assistive technology), aids (e.g., personal assistance, cues, contracts), or services (e.g., counseling) do selected students need?

IMPLEMENTATION PHASE

Date(s) of lesson?

Who are the co-teachers?

What Does Each Co-Teacher Do Before, During, and After Implementing the Lesson?

Co-Teacher Name:		
What are the specific tasks I do BEFORE the lesson?		
What are the specific tasks I do DURING the lesson?		
What are the specific tasks I do AFTER the lesson?		

REFLECTION/EVALUATION PHASE

To what extent were student needs met through planned (or incidental) differentiation?

How does this lesson inform the design of subsequent lessons?

If co-teaching, how effective was co-teaching in engaging and differentiating instruction for students?

Evaluating Adaptation Toward UDL. Finally, Table 8.5 offers schools striving to become Culturally Proficient Inclusive Schools a series of questions for assessing the extent to which educators' current dispositions and practices support the installation of UDL as a default adaptive response to student diversity. As with the five Essential Elements of Cultural Proficiency, these questions are intended to provide standards of practice, in this case for making UDL the instruction process, for eliminating inequalities and promoting success for all students. For sample lesson and unit plans and to learn more about how to use the UDL approach to Differentiated Instruction, we refer you to Thousand, Villa, and Nevin's 2015 text, *Differentiated Instruction: Planning for Universal Design and Teaching for College and Career Readiness.*

REFLECTION

Review the content of the UDL Lesson Plan Template in Table 8.4. Are you wondering if UDL is a complex, though powerful, process? Well, yes, it is! So, let's start somewhere. Where might you begin? What processes (MI, MAPs) might you use to more deeply get to know all or selected students? At which design point, content, product, or process might you try one or more of the differentiation considerations suggested in the lesson template? In what ways might you partner with a colleague to experiment with the UDL lesson plan template for a lesson and possibly co-teach that lesson? Which design point interests you most? In what ways might you advocate for professional learning to learn more about UDL and how to use it in your instructional practice?

Review the questions in Table 8.5 regarding current dispositions and practices for installation of UDL as a default adaptive response to student diversity. On a scale where zero represents an answer of "not at all" and five represents "absolutely yes," what would be your rating to each of the questions for your school community? How would teachers, administrators, students, and parents respond to these questions? Would they be in agreement or differ in their responses? What are actions you could take to promote an adaptive and collaborative response?

_____

_____

_____

_____

Table 8.5   Questions for Assessing Dispositions and Practices for Installing

UDL as the Default Proactive Responses to Student Diversity

Dispositions: Do instructional personnel understand that they have a *responsibility* to *proactively* adapt instruction to accommodate student differences?

Professional learning: Are instructional personnel provided explicit and extensive *training* to understand and apply what constitutes UDL?

Collaboration: Do instructional personnel collaborate to *develop* and *share* differentiated *lessons and unit plans*?

Getting to know learners: When planning for lessons and units of study, do instructional personnel *first* gather data (facts) about students from varying multiple sources (e.g., record review, interview, survey, interest inventories, observation, learning styles inventory, formative and summative assessment) in order to differentiate instruction *using* their students' varying background knowledge, interests, strengths, culture, language, learning preferences, and means of communication (e.g., alternative and augmentative communication)?

Content differentiation: In lessons and units of study, does *content and material* differentiation routinely occur, with students being offered *multiple options for taking in information* (e.g., texts with varying readability levels, text-to-speech/text reader software and apps, auditory and visual input, word walls, graphic organizers, layered curricula, curriculum compacting)?

Product differentiation: In lessons and units of study, does *product and assessment differentiation* routinely occur, with students being offered *multiple ways to express what they have learned* (e.g., written products, PowerPoint or Prezi products, podcasts, summary of interviews, oral presentation) and being graded in a variety of ways (e.g., benchmark assessments, contracts, IEP goal attainment, portfolios)?

Instructional differentiation: In lessons and units of study, does *process differentiation* routinely occur to help students make sense of the ideas, concepts, procedures, and principles being taught through

a. The use of *multiple instructional formats* (e.g., adapted lectures, hands-on, computer, and web-based; stations and centers; simulation; role play; thematic unit or lesson; community referenced; service learning; self-directed, culturally responsive techniques)

b. The use of *multiple instructional arrangements* (e.g., cooperative learning structures, same or cross-age peer tutors, teacher-directed small groups, independent study, large group instruction)

c. The use of *multiple instructional strategies* (e.g., Multiple Intelligence theory, integration of the arts, use of taxonomies, research-based strategies)

d. *Alterations of the physical environment* (e.g., room arrangement, accessibility of materials, preferential seating) *and/or social environment* (e.g., providing positive behavior supports and using problem solving, self-control, or behavior contracts, as needed)

e. Collaborative teaching among adults (co-teaching) and students (cooperative learning, partner learning, students co-teaching with their credentialed teachers)

TAPPING LEADERSHIP POTENTIAL: COLLABORATIVE ROLES FOR STUDENTS AS DECISION MAKERS AND ADVOCATES

In one of the authors' writing retreats, Cynthia Jew mused, "You know it seems that at my daughters' school, students with disabilities don't seem to be given the same opportunity to take on leadership roles as other students. As a matter of fact, it seems all but a few who get recognized for their academic, artistic, or athletic prowess seem to be visible or invited." Cindy's observation prompted us to make sure that in this chapter we examined ways in which schools have or could actively tap the leadership potential of all students by inviting them in as collaborators in changing the practices and policies of the school to be more inclusive.

Rationales for Empowering Students

Multiple rationales exist for enfranchising and empowering students as leaders in collaborative roles as (a) instructors—for example, members of cooperative groups and partner learners, described in Chapter 6; (b) inventors of adaptations for selves and classmates, as illustrated by the *quick brainstorm with kids* creative problem solving examples in Chapter 7; (c) decision makers—for example, problem solvers using any of the self-control, problem-solving, and conflict management tools and processes described in Chapter 7; and (d) advocates for themselves and others—the focus of this section of the chapter. First, given the diverse needs of a heterogeneous, culturally diverse student populations, schools need to take advantage of any and all available human resources; students offer a rich source of expertise, enthusiasm, and refreshing creativity at no extra cost for the school district. Second, for several decades, educational reform leaders have advocated for more opportunities for students to take the lead and use higher level reasoning skills through "a new collaborative role . . . in which students accept an active senior partnership role in the learning enterprise" (Benjamin, 1989, p. 9). Having students plan, problem solve, and evaluate educationally related activities responds to calls for student empowerment. Third, when students are empowered to advocate for their own and fellow classmates' education interests (e.g., through the MAPs person-centered planning process described in Chapter 5), they develop appreciation and empathy for others, while being contributing and caring members of society (Benjamin, 1989; Noddings, 1992).

Strategies for Enfranchising Students as Leaders

Culturally proficient educators can enfranchise students as responsible citizens and collaborative leaders in a school by inviting them to engage in roles such as those listed in Table 8.6. These are roles that traditionally have been performed only by adults. Roles included in this table are ones not yet described in previous chapters.

REFLECTION

The U.S. champion of democratic schooling, Maxine Green, is noted for reminding us that "It is an obligation in a democracy to empower the young to become members of the public, to participate and play articulate roles in the public place" (1985, p. 4). Review the student leadership roles suggested in Table 8.6. In what ways might you encourage, invite, and

Table 8.6 Collaborative Roles for Students to Take the Senior Partnership Role as Decision Makers and Advocates for Themselves and Others

- Friends and classmates serving as *members of a peer's IEP team*, suggesting age-appropriate and culturally meaningful goals, accommodations, and modifications; natural peer supports; and advocating for their peer's preferences, choices, and priorities
- Students invited to *coach teachers* and offer feedback on teachers' progress toward professional growth goals or offer feedback regarding the effectiveness, cultural-relevance, and flexibility (i.e., use of differentiation procedures) of teachers' instruction and discipline procedures
- Students serving as members of school *governance committees,* such as the school board, the inclusive education strategic planning committee, a student-operated "jury of peers" where students rather than adults address student behavior infractions
- Students serving as members of school *decision-making committees,* such as the School-Wide Positive Behavior Support and Multi-Tiered System of Supports development and leadership committees, the curriculum development committee, and the professional development planning committee
- Students serving as advising members of a *facilities committee* charged with inviting community participation to help design a new school building with shared spaces for classrooms, recreation areas, and cafeteria configuration as cross-aged and shared family space.
- Students serving in an advisory capacity on the *hiring committees* for new administrators, teachers, paraprofessionals, office, and outdoor supervisory staff
- Students from different cultural groups within the school (e.g., students with IEPs, students who frequently received behavior interventions and supports or are at risk for being recruited as a gang member, students who self-identify as LBGTQ) serving on the *principal advisory group* advising administrators and teachers on how to make the school more welcoming and inclusive
- Students establishing *peacemaking*, peer mediation, anti-bullying, and violence prevention organizations or clubs
- Older students *teaching peacemaking*, peer mediation, anti-bullying, and violence prevention information to younger students
- Students serving as rotating members (so each child serves) on their teacher's regularly-convened, classroom-based *caring classroom committee* to develop ways to make the classroom more emotionally safe, supportive, caring, and communal

engage students to become members in the public place as leaders suggested in Table 8.6? What additional empowering collaborative leadership roles can you imagine? What are other ways to teach and support students to better advocate for themselves and one another?

_____

_____

_____

_____

TAPPING LEADERSHIP POTENTIAL AND EXERCISING SELF-DETERMINATION THOUGH STUDENT-LED IEPS

Although some students become self-determined seemingly on their own, most need or at least benefit from careful guidance and coaching from adults and peers. What is self-determination? Self-determination can be described as a basic understanding of one's strengths and limitations together with a belief in oneself as capable and effective (Field, Martin, Miller, Ward, & Wehmeyer, 1998). The promise is that students who are self-determined become adults who can enjoy an enhanced quality of life, because they have an increased likelihood of being able to manage, advocate for, and receive needed services as an adult. What this means for educators is that students, particularly those with identified disabilities and who otherwise are at risk of leaving or failing school, be given the opportunity to learn and use self-determination skills while in school. Beneficial life outcomes can be anticipated for students who participate in managing (i.e., being self-determined) their own school program before graduating from high school. Educators can develop students' self-advocacy and skills for planning for the future by engaging students with IEPs in leading their own IEP planning meetings.

What Are Rationales for Student-Led IEPs?

From 10 to 15 percent of students in any classroom have an Individual Education Program (IEP) to help them achieve their educational goals. In fact, advocacy efforts spearheaded by individuals with disabilities led to the incorporation of self-determination in our federal special education legislation, IDEIA, by having students, at age eighteen, sign their own IEP plans and, by age sixteen, participate to develop an Individualized Transition Plan that charts the course of activities during their school years to help them achieve their goals for post-school life.

Student-led IEPs not only actively and meaningfully engage students with IEPs in the development of their IEP goals, but they enable students to explicitly learn and exhibit self-determination skills (e.g., Hammer, 2004; Mason, McGahee-Kovac, & Johnson, 2004). Outcomes reveal that students who learn to lead their own IEPs become more confident in advocating for themselves as they negotiate their life paths. Mason and colleagues (2002) also found students who led their own IEPs were more inclined to meet their goals. The IEP plan becomes a dynamic vehicle for students to secure a future that realizes their full potential rather than a static document.

Who Can Conduct a Student-Led IEP?

Who can lead his or her own IEP meeting? Students of elementary, middle, and high school age have successfully been supported to direct their own IEP meetings (e.g., Barrie & McDonald, 2002; Hapner & Imel, 2002; Konrad & Test, 2004; Schumaker, 2006; Test, Browder, Karvonen, Wood, & Algozzine, 2002) as have students with all types and degrees of learning and behavioral challenges. Students with moderate and severe disabilities can and have taken leading roles in directing their own IEPs, with the support of their classmates' voices and ideas, teacher coaching, and alternatives to verbal direction of a meeting (i.e., PowerPoint presentation of photos, icons or words about a student) (e.g., Barton, 2003; Brown & Dean, 2009).

How Can Educators Support Students to Lead Their Own IEPs?

In a comprehensive approach (e.g., McGahee-Kovac, 2002), students learn about their strengths and own disability and its impact on their learning, the regulations and safeguards that regulate their IEP under IDEIA, the components of an IEP, and the steps of an IEP meeting. Students also learn how to determine their present levels of performance in academic and social domains, identify their needs, set goals, monitor their own progress, practice skills to communicate effectively (e.g., active listening, volume, clarity and pacing of speech, giving and receiving positive and constructive negative feedback) and run an effective meeting.

Table 8.7 shows an abbreviated version of a *Checklist for Student-Led Individual Education Program Plan Meeting* developed by Erica Dean to assist high school students direct their IEP meeting (Brown & Dean, 2009). The student agenda is identical to any IEP agenda, except for the prompts (e.g., Thank team members for coming.) or prompt questions (e.g., What transition activities do I need to reach my life goals?) for the student at each step of the agenda. Rehearsal for the actual IEP meeting is a key pre-IEP meeting activity. Patricia Brown developed a simplified agenda for her middle-level students with more intensive support needs who are planning for transition to high school. After introductions, students present (or display via PowerPoint slides) "A Little About Me," "Successes This Year," "What I Liked About School This Year," "What I've Learned," "Things I Do Well," "Things I Need Help With," "What I Need to be Successful at High School," "My Current Goals and Progress on Goals," and "My Future When I Finish School."

Supporting students to be self-determined by leading their own IEPs can take time. So, (a) start early in a student's life (elementary school is not too early), (b) devote time weekly to some aspect of the process, (c) be flexible and appreciate students will be comfortable and become proficient with different levels of participation and leadership; and (d) never ever underestimate students' capabilities.

What Do Students Say About Leading Their Own IEP?

What do students say about student-led IEPs? In Tolleson, Arizona, where Hapner and Imel (2002) long ago spearheaded student-led IEPs, middle level and high school students were quite vocal about their taking charge of their educational programs and never underestimating students' capabilities. Jason, an 18-year-old with learning disabilities noted, "I used to think IEP meetings weren't needed. . . . Now I just can't wait to have them. I'm telling what I need, not my teachers." Raul, a student with language challenges, stated, with a smile, "Teachers started to listen and show respect." Juan added, "I graduated eighth grade feeling proud of myself for working hard on how I can improve" (Hapner & Imel, 2002, p. 126).

REFLECTION

Think about students with IEPs planning and leading their own IEP meetings. In what ways might leading one's own IEP affect a student's motivation as well as self-determination? How might you change the way you teach to solicit and listen to what your students want to learn? Or, in what ways might you advocate for students as leaders in their classrooms or schools? What possibilities exist for students in classrooms or schools if all students are expected to explain how they want to plan their education for their own futures?

_____

_____

_____

_____

Table 8.7 Checklist for Student-Led Individual Education Program Planning Meeting

_____ Introductions of People Present
_____ Meeting Agenda

- Review **IEP Front Page**

  Is the information about me correct?

  What is my identified "disability?"

  Why do I qualify for special education services?

- Review **Present Levels of Performance**

  How am I doing? What do my teachers say about my achievement?

- Review **Assessment Data/Special Factors**

  What are my test scores? Do I need any special supports?

- Review **Goals**

  What do I need to do to be successful in classes and move toward my future goals? What do I need to graduate?

- Review **Accommodations/Modifications**

  What helps me in classes? How and where will I take my state standardized tests? Will tests have accommodations or modifications?

- Review **Services** and **Educational Setting**

  What special education services do I receive?

  Where and how often do I get these services?

  What does my entire educational program look like?

- Review (if sixteen or older) **Transition Services and Individualized Transition Plan**

  What am I doing inside and outside of school to prepare for adulthood? What transition activities do I need to reach my life goals?

  What am I doing to work toward passing the high school exit exam?

  What classes do I need to receive a diploma?

_____ Take questions and feedback from team members.

_____ Note "parent concerns."

Now that my parents have heard all about my plans and achievement, is there anything else they want addressed?

_____ Propose class schedule for next semester or next year.

_____ Read meeting notes and have teachers and parents review the notes.

  Make any needed additions or modifications.

_____ Get signatures and approval from IEP team members.

_____ Thank team members for coming.

_____ Pat myself on the back! I did a great job!

ADVOCATING FOR CHANGE IN SCHOOL AND DISTRICT POLICIES AND PRACTICES

In the previous section, the authors suggested what some might consider a radical policy and practice change of extending the self-determination opportunities afforded students leading their own IEPs. We now go even further by engaging every student in developing a personal learning plan (PLP). Advocating that every student develop a PLP is intended to challenge the negative assumption and stereotype regarding disabilities—the only people "in need" should have or can benefit from individualized educational goals and plans.

To equip readers with additional knowledge and tools to understand and engage in the content of the next chapter on institutionalization of change, we conclude this chapter with an overview of the elements of and strategies for organization change.

Advocating for Personal Learning Plans for All

As a culturally proficient member of an inclusive learning community, one action for change in school practice might be to advocate for school-wide or district-wide development for any and all students. PLPs expand the practice of having an Individualized Education Program for students eligible for special education to having an individualized plan for learning for *all* students. This idea emerged in Vermont (Fox, 1995) in the late 1990s, when that state lead the nation in Inclusive Education—the practice of welcoming, valuing, and educating all students, including students with significant learning challenges, into the general education programs and demographics. PLPs now are reemerging as a tool for fostering responsibility and self-determination for all students (Joe Wiseman, principal of Monarch School, November 4, 2016). PLPs are intended to build upon already excellent classroom strategies that support diverse learners (e.g., cooperative learning, integrated curriculum projects, authentic assessment, class meetings that emphasize collaboration, discipline models that emphasize personal responsibility and social skills instruction). PLPs also are intended to bring the school, community, and home together to ignite a student's interests in a coordinated fashion.

What Is a Personal Learning Plan? How Is It Developed? A PLP, when developed by a student, gives the student a stake in his or her education, gives the student's family increased opportunities to be involved in their child's education, and creates a "contract" by which a student takes responsibility for engaging in and documenting his or her own learning. The process of developing a PLP involves collaborating with a student to identify

1. strengths and interests (using person-centered planning processes such as the MAPs process featured in Chapter 5),

2. high-priority skills or knowledge to be addressed during the school year,

3. projects and learning activities through which the student can address his or her priorities that build on strengths and capitalize upon interests,

4. supports (e.g., teacher, peer, parent, community connections) the student needs to benefit from the plan and opportunities for family involvement, and

5. methods to assess progress in completing the activities set forth in the plan.

Figure 8.1 offers the Monarch Student Growth Plan personal learning plan template developed by the leadership team of Monarch School, a K–12 school in downtown San Diego for students and families impacted by homelessness. As with any PLP, the Monarch Student Growth Plan is designed to channel a student's strengths and personal learning priorities into directed goals that lead to personal development in ways selected by the student, supported by the student's teachers and family, and connected to the core curriculum.

The Monarch Student Growth Plan is based upon the four school-wide learning outcomes or *pillars* of student social, emotional, life skill, and academic transformation described in Figure 8.2.

Students choose specific personal *learning targets* for social growth (e.g., leadership, perseverance), emotional growth (e.g., empowered choices, practice of particular positive behaviors), life skill growth (e.g., personal responsibility, time management and planning), and academic growth (e.g., deep thinking, use of evidence to defend a claim, agency over learning) by answering the question, "What are your learning targets in each pillar to promote growth?" They then identify activities or *opportunities* that operationalize each goal by answering the question, "What will you do to meet your growth targets?" Finally, students are guided to identify measureable transformation *success criteria* by answer the two questions, "What is the evidence that you met your growth targets?" and "What is the deadline to meet this growth target?

Using the Monarch Student Growth Plan template, Dadisi, a sophomore interested in becoming a teacher, identified as a social pillar *learning target* "to build positive relations with peers, adults, and my Monarch community." The two corresponding *opportunities* he identified were to "mentor a younger student at least weekly" and "sit next to someone

Figure 8.1   The Monarch School's Personal Growth Plan Template

Student Name: Grade: Advisor: Meeting Dates:	Social	Emotional	Life Skills	Academic
LEARNING *What are your learning targets in each pillar to grow as a learner?*				
OPPORTUNITY *What will you do to meet your growth targets?*				
TRANSFORMATION *What evidence will show that you met your growth target; and what is the deadline to meet this growth target?* (Success Criteria)				

Source: Joe Wiseman, Principal of Monarch School, www.monarchschools.org

eating alone at lunch." His selected methods for *evidencing success* were to "log mentor hours in my Volunteer Log" and "journal about acts of kindness in my Growth Plan Journal."

Advantages of Personal Learning Plans. An essential element of self-determination is personal responsibility. How compelling is Dadisi's example in illustrating how educators can support students to develop personal responsibility? Clearly, PLPs provide opportunities for students to exercise personal responsibility for and invest in targeted areas of their own education. Because PLPs lay out experiences tailored to students' strengths and interests, students know that some aspect of the

Figure 8.2 The Four Pillars: Monarch's School-Wide Learning Outcomes

SOCIAL	EMOTIONAL	LIFE SKILLS	ACADEMIC
We will learn to discover the leader within, express ourselves in empowering ways and recognize our inherent value.	We will learn to be aware of our emotions, understand our response to those emotions, and practice positive behaviors.	We will learn to set achievable goals, gather resources to support those goals and execute a plan to accomplish those goals.	We will learn to be creative, collaborative and resourceful problem solvers who think critically and apply what we learn in school to all aspects of our lives.

education. opportunity. transformation

Source: Joe Wiseman, Principal of Monarch School, www.monarchschools.org

school day is intended to be personally meaningful and even exciting. The process of developing, implementing, and assessing progress in a PLP provides a vehicle for students (with teachers' and parents' guidance) to learn and practice numerous communication, collaboration, and problem-solving skills as well as the skill of setting and evaluating goals associated with core curriculum standards. PLPs also represent a vehicle for readily adding supports for a student, if that support is needed. If the student's individual needs become more complicated or intensive, a student's support team can be expanded from the student's teacher(s) and family to include additional school and community support persons (e.g., counselor, psychologist, special educator, community service providers).

Variables for Change and Strategies for Advocating for Change

Most of us are great with change, as long as it was our idea.

But change imposed from the outside can send some people into a tailspin.

Louise Penny (*Still Life*, 2005, p. 139)

For many people, change can be a scary and unwelcomed proposition. People experiencing change may often feel uncomfortable and even incompetent as they learn about where the change is leading, their role in the new order, and how they will be supported or where they might fit in. Change does not just happen; it requires people to understand that things could be better, to feel and generate a sense of urgency to make things better, and commit to taking action for the better. Change requires commitment and perseverance. Why? Despite every effort to deliberately plan a change, including change to Inclusive Schooling, it is never certain (a) how long change may take, (b) what exact steps will need to be taken along the way, (c) precisely how things will finally look, and (d) what will need to be adjusted and readjusted throughout the change process.

A Framework for Facilitating Change. Having stated these caveats, individuals and schools advocating for Inclusive Education cannot make the mistake that some have in not planning. Richard Villa and Jacqueline Thousand (2017) have found success with a framework for advocating and planning for change, which is comprised of five variables—vision, skills, incentives, resources, and action planning. To orchestrate change and progress in education, district and building-level leadership personnel must attend to all five of these variables by

- building a *vision* of inclusive schooling within a community;
- developing educators' *skills* and confidence to be inclusive educators;
- creating meaningful *incentives* for people to take the risk to embark on an inclusive schooling journey;
- reorganizing and expanding human and other *resources* for teaching for and to diversity; and
- planning for and taking *actions* to develop vision, skills, incentives, and resources.

Culturally Proficient Guiding Principles for Action Planning. Whatever process a school adopts to attend to these five variables, the process must yield regular, observable and measurable outcomes so that people in schools see and get excited about a new big picture. Further, applying the following seven guiding principles can facilitate success in planning, advocating, and acting for change.

- *Look outside.* Don't plan in a vacuum. Instead, educate yourself on social, political, cultural, and economic trends external to the world of school. Show the community that the change initiative, Inclusive Schooling, is relevant and contemporary by connecting it to this external information. Develop outside partnerships (e.g., state department, institutions of higher education, other schools with an Inclusive Schooling vision) to maximize needed human, political, and fiscal resources and momentum.

- *Look inside too.* Schools and school systems already have resources and strengths as well as Barriers to successful Inclusive Schooling. Carefully examine and discover the current internal strengths and the non-strengths of school policies, practices, organizational structures, and personnel.

- *Walk the talk and be inclusive.* Be proactive and ensure all relevant stakeholder and cultural groups inside and outside of the school, including students, are represented in the change process and communicated with regularly. People are at the core of change; we cause or impede it.

- *Believe in people.* Innovators and change leaders already exist within most school organization. Search for them and nurture them to allow their leadership skills to develop. Remember that students, families, and community members are potential change leaders.

- *Monitor the change.* Change is dynamic. People and forces driving and restraining change shift over time. Therefore, meet regularly to review progress, revise and modify plans, disband groups that have accomplished their tasks, and create new ad hoc teams to address new or additional needed strategies.

- *Revisit the vision often.* An inclusive vision can get lost or distorted over time, as new people come into the school and community who are unaware of or misunderstand the vision. Periodically reexamine the vision and use the media (e.g., newspaper articles, TV spots, the district website) to educate the community.

- *Put things in writing.* People do best if their decisions are put into a systematic written format (an action plan) that specifies in detail who will do what, by when, and to what criterion. Be sure to also memorialize in writing both success and setbacks. Organizations benefit from knowing their story. The story can (a) be shared with new people to educate them about their cultural journey, (b) help people to remember and learn from past mistakes, and (c) be used to celebrate what otherwise might be forgotten milestones.

Culturally Proficient Assumptions for Action Planning. In addition to attending to the five change variables and seven guiding principles just described, people in culturally proficient systems who engage in action planning for change both *examine* their unconscious assumptions (as described in Chapter 5) and *adopt* healthy assumptions about change. Fullan and Stiegelbauer (1991) advise people in the midst of change to healthfully assume that (1) their version of the change is not necessarily the one that will or should result; (2) no amount of knowledge ever clarifies which action is the "correct" one to take; (3) manageability is achieved by thinking big and starting small; (4) lack of participation or commitment is not necessarily a rejection of the vision—other factors (e.g., insufficient skills, incentives, or resources) may be the cause; (5) changing culture, not installing an innovation, is the real agenda; and (6) any action plan must be based on the five previous assumptions.

CASE STORY

Let's return to the Lakeside Union School District and one of the four middle schools in the district, Lincoln Middle School.

Part 1: A Very Special School Dance

Lincoln Middle School is located in the center of Lakeside School District. It is one of the oldest schools in the district and was renamed Lincoln Middle School in the mid-1980s following a community-led movement, changing the name from Walter E. Potter School to align with the "presidential naming of the local schools." Lincoln Middle School (LMS) reflects the demographics of the district with one exception. At the time, the district's central office administration located at LMS a special class for middle-school aged students identified as having moderate and severe disabilities, another for students identified as deaf and hard of hearing, and yet another for students who were blind or had significant visual impairments. In addition, the school served its own students identified as having specific learning disabilities, speech and language impairments, and other disabilities considered "mild" disabilities. This made LMS the district school with the greatest proportion of its students having IEPs and receiving special education services. Depending upon the year, students with IEPs represented between 20 and 25 percent of the student body.

On the annual school calendar is the *LMS spring dance* for eighth-grade students. This activity is sponsored by the Student Government Association (SGA) and is the equivalent of a high school senior prom. Students dress in semiformal attire, decorate the multipurpose room with a new theme each year, and hire a band to perform. Administrators and teachers are assigned to attend the event. The following week another annual event is held for eight graders. The difference in the two events is that the second event is called *A Night to Remember* and is held for and attended only by students eligible for special education. This event was established in the 1980s when the special classes were initially located at this site and continued, out of tradition and habit, through the decades. However, within the past few years most students eligible for special education are being served more inclusively through co-teaching arrangements between general educators and the various specialists and supports (e.g., special educators, speech pathologists, sign language interpreters). Members of the SGA volunteer to decorate the multipurpose room, assist students who attend the event, help serve the meal, and provide prerecorded playlist music for the students. School administrators and volunteer teachers and parents may attend the evening with their students.

When the new school year opens, Ashley Palacios, an eighth-grade student, is elected the new president of the SGA. She was elected on her platform of LMS being a school that prepares "global-ready" students who question what is happening at home and in the world, understand different perspectives, engage in respectful conversations, and take responsible action. At the first meeting of the SGA, Ashley presents an idea to the leadership team and their advisor, Paul Ornelas. She questions why there are two spring dances at MLS, tying it to her election platform, and suggests they host one eighth-grade spring dance event this year and eliminate the *Night to Remember* event. She expressed her strong conviction that the LMS spring dance should be what its name represents, a spring dance for LMS students, ALL LMS students. Some of the team members are stunned at her proposal. Mr. Ornelas is not sure about the implications of having one event that would include students with disabilities, who have "always" had their own event. He invites Alyce LaPlant, the new LUSD special education and pupil personnel services director to attend the next leadership team meeting. Attending the meeting with Mr. Ornelas and Ms. LaPlant's are Ashley Palacios, the SGA president; Daniel Miller, the SGA vice president; Samantha Lightfoot, the SGA secretary; Ansh Johar, the SGA treasurer; and Sara Bower, the SGA member-at-large. The meeting begins with Mr. Ornelas making an opening statement.

Paul Ornelas, SGA Advisor	*Good morning everyone, and thanks for coming to this early Monday morning meeting. Enjoy the juice and snacks. Please meet Ms. Alyce LaPlant. She is our new district special education and pupil personnel services director. I wanted her to meet you and attend our meeting this morning because of the importance of the topic we are discussing today. Ms. LaPlant, please meet our leadership team. They will introduce themselves and explain their stance on this topic. Ashley, let's start with you.*
Ashley Palacios, SGA President	*Thanks Mr. O. Hi Ms. LaPlant, and thanks for being here today. The topic we are discussing is having only one spring dance this year rather than a separate one for our special ed kids like we have had in the past. I feel strongly that we should include everyone at the same event. Special ed kids shouldn't be*

	separate from the rest of us. They are with us in classes, so they should be with us for the eighth-grade dance. That's what I think, anyway.
Daniel Miller, SGA Vice President	*Good morning, I'm Daniel, the SGA vice president. Well I don't feel as strongly about this issue as Ashley does. I know a few special ed kids, and I really don't think it matters to most. But one kid said something like, "Oh yeah, you mean the night they won't let us go with you 'normal' kids." I felt really bad when he said that. I didn't know it felt like that.*
Ansh Johar, SGA Treasurer	*Well, I hadn't really thought about this until Ashley brought it up. This will be a big change for this school. This could upset a lot of people who don't like changing things. I remember when my family first moved to the United States and Lakeside. People really had a hard time accepting us. Now things are all good. Change takes time. Do we have enough time to do this right?*
Samantha Lightfoot, SGA Secretary	*Well, uh, like no! Oh, sorry. I'm Sam. I don't think now is the time to change things. Let next year's class make the big change. I wanted to be a volunteer to help at the* Night to Remember *dance this year. I think it is so cool for them to have their special night…You know, so they won't be embarrassed when we are all dancing and stuff.*
Ashley Palacios, SGA President	*See what I mean, Ms. LaPlant? We aren't suppose to feel sorry for classmates; we need to support one another, no matter what!*
Sara Bower, SGA Member-at-Large	*Well, wait. I haven't spoken. I'm Sara. I was elected to be a member-at-large. I don't really know what that means, but I'm just happy to be on the team. I'm interested in what we decide, because I don't want to go to the special dance in the spring. I'm sure you can tell I get special help, because I'm deaf and I wear cochlear implants so I can hear. I want to go to the LMS spring dance just like the rest of you. My brother in the ninth grade told me I'd have to go to the special party for special kids like me. Are we gonna fix this?*

REFLECTION

Using the Essential Element of *Adapting to Diversity* and the suggestions for inclusive action from Table 8.1 as your frame, what do you notice happening in the case story? What do you predict might be some deeper issues that may surface as the story continues? In what ways might Paul Ornelas and Alyce LaPlant intervene and guide the conversation in a culturally proficient inclusive manner?

_____

_____

_____

_____

Part 2: Dancing the Night Away

Paul Ornelas, SGA Advisor	*OK, everybody. Hang on, now. I can tell that each of you has strong feelings about this topic. Let's hear from Ms. LaPlant now.*
Alyce LaPlant, Special Education and Pupil Personnel Services (SEPPS) Director	*Thanks, Mr. Ornelas, or as your students call you, Mr. O! And thank you for the invitation to be here today. I appreciated hearing from each of you and learning how you feel about this topic and this event. You are taking on a traditional event and thinking about changing it to become a more inclusive opportunity for all students who want to attend. And by the way, as the district director of special education and other support services, I have a responsibility to set out ground rules regarding language we use when referring to people with disabilities. Disability rights organizations and individuals with disabilities have loudly voiced the preference for the use of "person-first language"—referring to someone as a person first and making reference to a disability, second. For example, I might say "a student receiving special education services" rather than "a special ed kid." You might refer to me as "Alyce who has a disability" rather than "that disabled lady." Person-first language honors the fact that a person with a disability is first and foremost a person not a disability or someone who is defective. How about we try practicing this for the rest of this meeting. What do you say? (SGA members nod "yes")*
Ashley Palacios, SGA President	*Ms. LaPlant, what a good way to summarize the issue—changing the dance to be a "more inclusive opportunity" for any student. And Sara, uh, uh, ok . . . as someone who gets special education help, thank you for speaking up about your preference. By the way, I never heard about "person-first" language before. It makes sense, though—everyone is a person first.*
Daniel Miller, SGA Vice President	*Sara, you can come to the LMS spring dance because, you know, you are like, well, regular. But, some sped kids—oops, I mean, some students—just wouldn't feel comfortable being together with everyone.*

Alyce LaPlant, SEPPS Director	*Daniel, one of the things to keep in mind is that this leadership team, SGA, was elected by all of the students to represent all students. That, in itself, is an inclusive activity. Sara represents students who want to be included in the school dance rather than be excluded by having a separate activity because of a difference, in this case, their eligibility for services that help them to succeed.*
Ansh Johar, SGA Treasurer	*I know about how that feels—different, I mean. I want to be appreciated for who I am, but I don't want to be excluded because of who I am. Is that what you mean, Ms. LaPlant?*
Alyce LaPlant, SEPPS Director	*Yes, indeed, Ansh, that's exactly what I mean.*
Samantha Lightfoot, SGA Secretary	*Let's not get in a hurry, here. I can see your point here, Ms. LaPlant. You work with kids like Sara all the time. And because of the way our school is organized, we are all mixed together in most of our classes. In many of my classes, we have two teachers, like a math teacher and an education specialist or whatever, who help them . . . well, actually, every student. I just don't want to change the school dance, if it's gonna embarrass them or cause them to stay at home. So, what do we do now? Are we moving too fast?*
Paul Ornelas, SGA Advisor	*Well, we aren't ready to make the decision today. We have more thinking and more planning to do. What might be other questions or concerns that you have? You are advocating for yourselves and all of the students you now represent.*
Ashley Palacio, SGA President	*Well, if some of you are still trying to decide about this issue, I just want you to think about our history courses and things we have read about here at LMS. Would we sponsor a dance and then ask students who are black to have a separate dance? Or ask kids who are Hispanic or Jewish to have a separate dance?*
Daniel Miller, SGA Vice President	*Wait, Ashley, that's cold. Of course, we wouldn't. That would be so wrong and even illegal! We would never do that. This is so different.*
Samantha Lightfoot, SGA Secretary	*Wait! This is not discrimination, is it? This is about kindness.*
Alyce LaPlant, SEPPS Director	*OK, think about Ashley's questions and your responses. In what ways is excluding anyone from the dance different from what she described?*

Ansh Johar, SGA Treasurer	*Well, since you put it that way, there is no difference. I don't think the student leaders and teachers in the past meant to discriminate against students who get special education. But the outcome is certainly just that. Now, it's our responsibility to do something about this.* *Mr. O and Mrs. LaPlant, could you help us move forward with changing this activity? We need your guidance.*
Paul Ornelas, SGA Advisor	*We certainly will guide you through making this change. First, we need to know where everyone else is on this issue. Daniel? Sara? Samantha?*
Daniel Miller, SGA Vice President	*Well, I feel differently now than when we first started talking. Thanks, Mrs. LaPlant, Ashley, and Sara. I think we can work together on this project.*
Sara Bower, SGA Member- at-Large	*I can hardly wait to get others involved. Some students and parents will not like to change, just like in our meeting this morning. But if we work together to be inclusive, we can be successful.*
Samantha Lightfoot, SGA Secretary	*This has been hard for me. I didn't realize I was getting in the way of something so important. I was confusing kindness for separateness. I'm on board now.*
Alyce LaPlant, SEPPS Director	*Again, thank you for inviting me to be with you this morning. I am impressed with how you just lived out Ashely's SGA platform—questioning what is happening at home, listening to different perspectives, engaging in respectful conversations, and taking responsible action. You have truly exercised "global" leadership skills. I can see why you were elected to your SGA roles. Change isn't easy. But when you show willingness to adapt to the needs of others, as you have, and turn it into an action plan, you are well on your way to success. Congratulations!*

REFLECTION

Using the Essential Element of Adapting to Diversity and the suggestions for inclusive action from Table 7.1 as your frame, what do you notice happening now in this part of the case story? In what ways did Paul Ornelas and Alyce LaPlant guide the conversation for the students? What similar issues or activities are serving as Barriers to inclusion at your school or district? In what ways might this case story for Adapting to Diversity inform your conversations and actions for culturally proficient inclusive classrooms and schools?

_____

_____

_____

_____

DIALOGIC ACTIVITY

Change.

It has the power to uplift, to heal, to stimulate, surprise, open new doors, bring fresh experience and create excitement in life.

Certainly it is worth the risk.

Leo Buscaglia (n.d.)

As the above Leo Buscaglia quote suggests, change can uplift, open doors, and create excitement. In a culturally proficient learning community, the change is for opening doors and generating excitement to take action for diversity and Inclusive Schooling. Now that you have read this chapter, take a moment and think about ways in which you, your colleagues, and students might actively and continuously learn about and use the experiences and backgrounds of members of other cultures. With your grade-level team, your department group, and your faculty and paraprofessionals, engage in a dialogue using the following prompts:

- What is our shared understanding of Adapting to Diversity?
- What evidence do we have that Adapting to Diversity is a shared priority for all educators within our school?
- In what ways might we change the way we teach to more deliberately use the principles of universal design to uplift, open doors, and create learning excitement for all learners?
- In what ways might we tap the voice, diversity, and leadership potentials of our students *Adapting* to *Diversity* by using self-determination and self-advocacy skills described in this chapter?
- What changes in vision and mission statements and school and district policies would be your priorities for stimulating progress toward making Inclusive Schooling a reality?

_____

_____

_____

_____

PREVIEW OF CHAPTER 9

In this chapter, we examined the Essential Element of Adapting to Diversity and advocacy for and adoption of practices and policies to eliminate inequities and facilitate Inclusive Schooling. We introduced frameworks for understanding students, enhancing the relevance of instruction through the Universal Design for Learning process, and activating student self-determination.

Chapter 9 examines the Essential Element of Institutionalizing Cultural Knowledge and describes ways for driving changes in dispositions, practices, and policies into the multiple systems of a school and school district so that it sustains. The content of Chapter 9 is so important, because it helps us to avoid one of the most harmful Barriers to institutionalizing and sustaining any change; namely, complacency—thinking and acting as if you have "arrived" and do not need to tend to a change effort. Complacency can stifle the maintenance of an inclusive schooling vision and quality inclusive practices. Creating and maintaining inclusive environments is a long-term commitment that requires eternal vigilance. Change agents, no matter what the initiative, must articulate the vision for new staff every year they come on board, provide continuous quality professional learning, maintain incentives (e.g., celebrating innovators), provide human and other resource allocations, and engage educators in ongoing planning for and assessment of the quality of Inclusive Education experiences for everyone.

9 Institutionalizing Cultural Change

Learning and innovation go hand in hand. The arrogance of success is to think that what you did yesterday will be sufficient for tomorrow.

William Pollard
(as cited at http://www.azquotes.com/quote/234109)

GETTING CENTERED

Have you ever engaged in a school community where you immediately felt your role was already defined by the unspoken culture? In what ways did you feel valued and appreciated for the assets you brought to this school community? What environmental policies, practices, and human connections contributed to those feelings? In what ways are you personally invested in the vision, mission, practices, and policies of the school and/or district? Compare and contrast two school cultures: one where you felt welcomed and valued and another where the culture was all business and low energy. Now, think about how the schools' mission and vision were similar or different. In what ways did the actions and behaviors of the group members align with the espoused vision of the organization?

_____

_____

_____

_____

Institutionalizing Cultural Change: An Overview

The purpose of this chapter is to provide the reader with pathways to move from change resistors to change agents. The outcome of institutionalizing cultural change is to create an educational community culture that is understanding and accepting of the change process and embraces the culture as innovative and socially responsible for all. Organizations are made up of people organizing. Sounds simple enough. As people grow and change, so do organizations. Change is a natural process of organizations growing; positive, healthy change initiatives can occur when partnerships are welcomed and encouraged and cultural differences are honored. Change must be nurtured and institutionalized as natural and normal. The partnerships involved in institutionalizing cultural change include but are not limited to the following: the superintendent, principals, school board, teachers (general and special education), specialists, secretaries, janitors, the community, parents, and students. As we pointed out at the conclusion of the previous chapter, creating and maintaining Inclusive Schools is a long-term commitment that requires eternal vigilance. Change agents must articulate the vision for new staff every year as new members join the organization, provide on-going quality professional learning experiences, engage in on-going planning for and assessment of the quality of inclusive education experiences and practices for everyone, and detect and use teachable moments to model and be the change we want to see.

Following the same structure of the previous chapters, we present actions for this Essential Element in Table 9.1. The table presents three columns of information. The first column displays a brief definition of the first Essential Element of Cultural Proficiency of *Institutionalizing Cultural Knowledge*. The second column offers five actions that culturally proficient members of an inclusive learning community may take. The third column identifies systems, practices, strategies, and tools that are featured in this chapter to achieve each of the five actions.

REFLECTION

Take a moment and carefully read each of the five assessment actions of culturally proficient members of an inclusive learning community represented in column two of Table 9.1. What are actions you could take to become aware of the five dimensions of knowledge described? What partnerships may be more challenging than others in institutionalizing change? What are actions you have seen others take? How could expanding your knowledge of yourself, your school, your students, and your community benefit students with Individual Education Plans (IEPs) and students with other perceived differences or difficulties? What are some

Table 9.1 Systems, Practices, Strategies, and Tools That Facilitate the Actions of Institutionalizing Cultural Knowledge

Cultural Proficiency Essential Element #5	Actions of a culturally proficient member of an inclusive learning community	Specific systems, practices, strategies, and tools featured in this chapter
Institutionalizing Cultural Knowledge Driving the changes into the systems of the organization	I/we . . . • Work to influence the *vision, mission, policies*, and *practices* of the school and district to be aligned with the Guiding Principles of Cultural Proficiency • Advocate for learning about underserved and marginalized cultural groups as a major focus of the school and district's *professional learning* • Make learning about underserved and marginalized cultural groups within the school and community an integral part of my/our *ongoing learning* • Create opportunities for and take advantage of *teachable moments* for diverse groups to learn about each other and engage in ways that both honor who they are and challenge them to be even better • Am/are the change we want to see!	I/we . . . • Design and implement data-driven action plans focused on closing education gaps • Collaborate and host leadership institutes on *Culturally Proficient Inclusive Education* leading to site-based action planning for transformation • "Peel back the wallpaper" to examine data (e.g., MTSS Tier 1, 2, and 3 student data) to discover over-representation of or bias toward groups by characteristics such as race, gender, primary language, and efficacy of instruction • Support students to learn about and appreciating one another through the use of cooperative group learning and other inclusive instructional strategies • Actualize the vision and mission of success for all students by applying MTSS as the default proactive procedure and practice for detecting and honoring students' learning differences

professional learning experiences you have had or that you are aware of that would impact your disposition as a culturally proficient educator?

_____

_____

_____

_____

FIVE ACTIONS FOR INSTITUTIONALIZING CULTURAL KNOWLEDGE

Descriptions of systems, practices, strategies, and tools for engaging in the five assessment actions are identified in column two of Table 9.1. The five actions can be considered steps of assessment. Therefore, each of the next five sections is identified as Action 1 through 5. As you read each step and the examples provided, please remember that the examples are just that, examples. Take into consideration the personal and professional intersections that impact your interpretation. Use the inside-out approach described throughout the book to help guide your analytical thinking.

Action 1: Work to influence the *vision, mission, policies*, and *practices* of the school and district to be aligned with the Guiding Principles of Cultural Proficiency by designing and implementing data-driven action plans focused on closing education gaps.

In penning the Declaration of Independence, Thomas Jefferson articulated the American dream; namely, that "We hold these truths to be self-evident, that all men are created equal, that they are endowed by their Creator with certain unalienable Rights, that among these are Life, Liberty and the Pursuit of Happiness" (Jefferson, 1776). America's founding fathers had a clear vision of what it means to have the freedom to pursue personal happiness. In Chapter 8, we explained how to build a vision as a part of the framework for facilitating change as well as developing individualized personal plans. Now we will go further and discuss how a district can drive an action plan to support institutionalizing cultural change.

The vision is ground zero for establishing a common understanding for institutionalizing cultural change. The vision exemplifies the passion for the pursuit to impact ALL students and the dreams and ultimate celebrations of student learning. To strive towards the vision, members of school systems must use an organizational model or a variation or combination of models to be transparent and systematic. The Cultural Proficiency Essential Element: *Institutionalizing Cultural Knowledge* is the cornerstone and starting point of this pursuit where we begin to drive changes into the system of the organization.

Before delving into three organizational systems to guide the creation of an organizational action plan, let's first discuss the benefits of partnerships while planning and the challenges when working with those who are not invested in change.

Benefits of Involvement and Partnerships While Planning for Change

The partnerships established in a systemic approach include district administration and personnel, all school building staff, parents, and the community. In this chapter, we delve into the intricate partnerships of the school site community that are needed to build sustainability of inclusive educational best practices with specific attention to students who have or are receiving supports through an IEP or 504 plan. Voices from principals, parents, teachers, and students will provide context of real scenarios.

School community partnerships that foster equitable learning environments must have leadership that supports structures and space for conversations that are centered around the assets of all to develop a shared understanding of what we mean by inclusive educational opportunities (Lindsey, Terrell, Nuri-Robins, & Lindsey, 2012). When the conversations leading to action planning are centered around the school, community, and family assets, cultural barriers begin to break down, allowing for a shared vision to be created.

Engaging people in action planning is important for at least two reasons. First, participatory planning promotes individuals' personal ownership of the coming changes. Second, it helps prepare people for change by getting them to believe that change really will occur. Planning is the alarm signalling to everyone that things will no longer be the same. For the planning phase to accomplish this, administrators need to be up-front and effective communicators who can articulate the desired future and get people to see clearly how it can be achieved and what part each person will play.

An integral part of action planning is regular and continuous evaluation. One question to ask is, *What is worthy of evaluation?* Clearly, we want to know whether students and staff benefit from organizational and instructional arrangements. We also want to know about affective and process variables, such as educators' feelings at various points during the change process. Both outcome and affective process evaluations provide change agents the information needed to adjust the action plan or undertake new actions to deal with concerns, failures, and successes (Villa, Thousand, & Nevin, 2013).

Working With Those Not Yet Invested in the Challenge

Obviously, a best-case scenario is when school personnel *choose* to collaborate in action planning for change rather than do it simply because they're required to. However, this is not always possible. Collaboration in planning and teaching cannot be viewed as a voluntary activity. For educators to think that they have a choice as to whether or not to collaborate is similar to a team of health care professionals perceiving that they have a choice as to whether or not to collaborate in performing an operation, following the patient's progress, and providing follow-up care. Students and families have a right to expect educators to collaborate in planning and teaching, and educators have a professional, legal, and ethical responsibility to do so. As Villa et al. (2013) point out, there are personal benefits to collaborating with others, including the following:

> Although we get together on the basis of our similarity, we grow because of our differences. As in a successful marriage, once partners figure out and understand each other's perspectives, they are no longer just two individuals, but a union that is fundamentally different from each person alone. Furthermore, because of their differing perspectives, experiences, and skills, they create a synergy that is greater than either of their individual strengths. (p. 23)

Organizational Systems to Create Action Plans

Various models, systems, tools, and strategies exist to guide action planning for change. We offer three for your consideration, knowing full well that there is no "one size fits all" approach for facilitating change or perfectly suited unique culture of a particular community. These three models or approaches share processes to engage in a journey of shared decision making and equitable distribution of power that are aligned with the principles of Cultural Proficiency (CampbellJones, CampbellJones, & Lindsey, 2010). The three organizational change approaches are (1) Villa and Thousand's *Action Planning for Complex Change* approach, (2) Dilts's *Nested Logic Level* approach, and (3) Conzemius and O'Neill's *Framework for Shared Responsibility*.

Action Planning for Complex Change

We know that effective school organizations can be crafted, and they are crafted by individuals—individuals who choose to ensure the success of all students by being courageous and engaged in a school community during the change process.

Villa, Thousand, & Nevin (2013, p. 133)

Action Planning for Complex Change is an action planning approach successfully used by Richard Villa and Jacqueline Thousand (Villa & Thousand, 2017; Villa et al., 2013) to assist educators, administrators, and community members to consider the five dimensions of complex

change—vision, skills, incentive, resources, and action pl
articulate actions for change to and with those who are involved
ing and executing a change plan. People do best if their decisions are
into some systematic written format (action plan) that specifies in some
detail who will do what, by when, and to what criterion. Therefore, we
encourage administrators to work with general education teachers, cate-
gorical support personnel, paraprofessionals, and others to develop a written plan that delineates actions that will be taken to (1) build support for
the *vision* of Inclusive Schooling within a community; (2) develop educators' *skills* and confidence to be inclusive educators; (3) create meaningful
incentives for people to take the risk of embarking on an inclusive schooling journey; (4) reorganize, schedule, and expand human and other
resources for teaching diverse learners, and (5) *plan* concrete actions to
motivate and move educators, students, and the community to become
excited about the new vision.

Figure 9.1 shows a completed one-year action plan for Lakeside
Unified School District, which addresses the vision, skills, incentives, and
resources of this complex change model. The action plan was developed
after the district leaders recognized the need for and dedicated its professional resources to establishing co-teaching as a district-wide practice for
melding the expertise of general educators and educational specialists
(e.g., special educators, speech language pathologist, English language
development specialist) to Differentiated Instruction for all students (Villa
et al., 2013). Notice how each activity is delineated with timeline and success measures and accountability for monitoring implementation by
noting the actual outcomes and date of achievement. A variation of this
Action Planning for Complex Change model is used in Chapter 10 to
guide you and your school team to build a Culturally Proficient Inclusive
Schooling Action Plan that is based upon your study of and reflections
regarding the five Essential Elements described in this chapter and the
previous Chapters 5 through 8. We highly recommend that culturally
proficient educators and leaders who initiate any change use this or a
similar planning format to inform and hold accountable those engaged in
the change process.

As you read and reflect on the action plan, identify the cultural proficiency elements and shifts in perspective within the plan.

The *Nested Logic Level* Approach

Create a world to which people want to belong.

John Dilts
(from his 1996 book title, *Visionary Leadership Skills:
Creating a World in Which People Want to Belong*)

Figure 9.1 Lakeside USC Co-teaching for MTSS Year-Long Action Plan

	Actions • List major activities chronologically • Include preparation (e.g., funding) and implementation actions	Success Measure(s) "We will know we are successful if . . ." • What is measured? • Who will measure? • When to measure?	Responsible Person(s)	Date by Which to be Achieved	Actual Outcome
Building Consensus for a Vision of Co-Teaching	At the beginning of the new school year, tell teachers that the district will implement a co-teaching approach at each site in one year's time. Explain this year the approach will be piloted with volunteers at each site starting second semester.	Message communicated at August in-service	Dr. Alvarado (Superintendent)	August 23	Message communicated verbally and in writing at August 23 meeting
Skill Development	Provide district-wide, in-service on rationales for and approaches to co-teaching for all administrator, general and special educators; guidance, related services, and other support program personnel; and paraeducators.	Presenter hired	Ms. LaPlant (special education and pupil personnel services director)	Hire speaker by July 1	Speaker hired July 1
		Training occurs		August 23	Four-hour in-service on co-teaching
	Purchase co-teaching books for pilot teams.	Books purchased	Dr. Alvarado	July 15	Purchased June 15 and arrived July 1
	Set up book study groups in each building.	Book study groups established at each site	Building principals	Sept. 15	Groups set up by target date in all fourteen sites by September 30

Category	Activity	Indicator	Person Responsible	Timeline	Result
Incentives	Arrange for visitation to neighboring schools to see examples of co-teaching.	Visitations occur	Building principals and Dr. Alvarado (superintendent)	September, October, November	Each site sent teams to observe veteran teams; fifteen visits over three months
	Arrange for substitute coverage once a month to allow piloting co-teachers to plan during the school day.	Substitutes hired, and teachers meet	Building principals and pilot co-teaching teams at each building site	Monthly, October through June	Substitute coverage provided monthly for teams
	Co-teachers recreate co-taught lessons for faculty colleagues to participate in as if they were students in these classes.	Co-teachers teach lessons to colleagues	Dr. Alvarado, Ms. LaPlant, building principals, and pilot co-teaching teams	March 15–31 (one day per school site for 14 sites)	Occurred at every school site on one day between March 15 and March 31
Resources	Identify pilot co-teachers for first year of implementation.	A minimum of five co-teaching teams recruited at each building	Building principals	Sept. 15	Five teams recruited at all but two sites, where four were recruited
	Develop a master schedule that allows for common planning and teaching time for the pilot co-teaching partnerships.	Master schedule completed	Building principals, Ms. LaPlant, and guidance counselors	Dec. 10	Target met
	Identify new co-teachers for second year of implementation.	A minimum of five additional co-teaching teams recruited at each site	Building principals and Ms. LaPlant	March 20	Target achieved at all campus sites

Robert Dilts (1996, 2014) offers a *"nested logic level"* approach to behavioral and organizational change. Table 9.2 displays the hierarchy of the interconnected levels from bottom (i.e., environmental) to top (i.e., identity), defines each logic level, and identifies the *W* question or questions that are relevant and useful to use at each level (Garmston & Wellman, 1999) to transform mindsets and systems. The premise of the nested logic level approach is that all five logic levels are interconnected, with higher levels impacting levels below but not the reverse. See the descriptions of each level for an explanation of the hierarchical influences. Dilt's nested logic level approach can be used personally or within an organization and delivers the most significant change when all levels are addressed (Lindsey, Kearney, Estrada, Terrell, & Lindsey, 2015). Action plans that target lower nested levels (i.e., particular environments, individual behaviors) fall short of impacting long-term change. Action plans that target top-logic levels (e.g., examining our own identifies, values, and beliefs) have the greater chance of impacting systemic change at lower levels (e.g., the classroom environment and people's capabilities and behaviors). Like Cultural Proficiency, Dilts's "inside-out" approach focuses upon upper-level identity and belief systems to ensure equity considerations in developing and executing an action plan for transforming behaviors and environments (Lindsey, 2012). As Table 9.3 suggests, when members of an organization examine who they are (identity) and for whose purpose they exist (vision), they have a greater chance of developing people's capabilities to address behaviors and environments within the organization and share responsibility in developing resources to support agreed-upon initiatives.

The Dilts approach can be applied at the personal level to help change ones perspective about a problem through questioning at the various logic levels. Imagine a teacher who has a student who seems to be constantly off task during whole group instruction and who believes she has tried everything to help manage the behaviors that still persists. Questions that may help the teacher include the following:

- Why do you think this student is unable to attend during whole group instruction?
  (beliefs and values level)
- How might you respond differently?
  (behavior level and capability level)
- Do you think this student might be trying to assert a sense of who she is?
  (identity level)

With Table 9.2 in mind, consider why and how each question might help shift a teacher's perspective to see a viable solution?

Table 9.2 Nested Logic Levels With Definitions and Relevant Questions at Each Level

Logical Levels	Definition	Question(s) Relevant to This Level
Top and 5th Level: Identity	*Identity* is my sense of who I am, which organizes my beliefs, capabilities, and behaviors and my perception of myself in relation to larger systems of which I am a part, determining my role, purpose, and mission.	Who?
Level 4: Values and Beliefs	My *values and beliefs* determine my judgments about myself, others, and the world external to myself. My values and beliefs determine how an event has meaning for me, what motivates me, and what capacities and behaviors I will develop and use.	Why?
Level 3: Capabilities	*Capabilities* are my inner mental strategies, maps, and plans I develop and use to guide my behaviors and actions. At the capabilities level, I select, alter, and adapt my behavior to know how to do something in a wide variety of contexts. Behavior without any inner strategy, map or plan as a guide is a habit, ritual, or uncontrolled reaction.	How?
Level 2: Behaviors	*Behaviors* are my specific actions and reactions (including the words I speak) through which I interact with the people and environment around me. My behaviors include my non-reflexive conscious movements and actions controlled by my psychomotor system and my reflexive movements.	What?
Bottom 1st Level: Environment	A particular *environment* is comprised of many factors from physical setting and weather conditions, to noise level and the smell and taste of food, to the individuals and groups in the environment. I uses my senses to perceive a particular environment and make conscious and unconscious adjustments to maintain balance, respond to changes, and be safe, comfortable, and/or engaged	Where? When?

Framework for Shared Responsibility

Focus, reflection, and collaboration =

Leadership with shared responsibility =

Continuously improving results

Anne Conzemius and Jan O'Neill (2001) offer yet another framework for action planning represented by the above change formula. Their

Framework for Shared Responsibility is designed to create structures, systems, processes, and policies wherein every participant and stakeholder can contribute his or her knowledge, experience, and skill for the overarching purpose of continuously improving student learning. The framework is driven by three interdependent elements—focus, reflection, and collaboration—defined in Table 9.3.

The overarching goal in applying the framework is that when asked, "Who is responsible for student?" every response will be, "I am." The framework provides structures for developing action plans, SMART goals (described in detail in the next chapter), professional learning, district strategic plans, and self-assessments. The framework aligns with the Cultural Proficiency Principles, Essential Elements, and actions described in this book in that, its stance is: responsibility for student learning must be an inside-out process that relies upon a community of stakeholders mutually invested in learning, adapting, and innovating rather than an "outside-in" accountability process.

Table 9.3   Focus, Reflection, and Collaboration Defined

Focus

Focus involves attending to the need for creating a clear and compelling shared vision and mission as well as shared values and expectations of improving student results and leading students to new levels of performance.

Reflection

Conzemius and O'Neill (2001) view reflection as both a mindset and process for learning from past actions to better accomplish goals in the future. They describe reflection as "a way of thinking about the world and one's relationship to it . . . a willingness to change because of what the data reveal and the skill to know what to do with the data collected" (p. 15). Reflection involves making it a priority that members of the school community intentionally evaluate current performance, using data whenever possible. Questions for promoting reflection include, "'Where are we now?' 'How are we doing compared to what we want to accomplish?' and 'What are we learning?'" (p. 14).

Collaboration

Because collaboration involves developing interdependent relationships, it is a process, and the process involves getting members of the community together to share their knowledge and ideas, focus upon their shared purpose(s), set measureable and achievable goals, and rely upon each other to achieve the goals. Collaboration harnesses the "two heads are better than one" synergistic effect—meaning a team's effectiveness exceeds what individuals accomplish on their own. It is during this phase of the shared responsibility model that shared goals, collaborative and collective responsibilities, and professional inquiry are put into action.

SUMMARY

The three approaches for promoting organizational change just featured share, as a goal, the striving pursuit for sustainability through a community of members who are all invested in a common vision and mission. They share the presumption that people within a system learn together and share responsibilities only when involved in the goal setting, planning, and decision making at all levels. All three approaches are intended to be adaptive, flexible, and responsive in order to continuously improve educational practices and student learning. They share an underlying premise that change is an on-going process that takes commitment, time, motivation, data, courage, collaboration, and conversations to move student learning forward. Each approaches offers a structure that allows for fluid, synergistic energy and promotes a culture of community building to enhance student learning.

REFLECTION

The organizational change leader Peter Senge (1990) observed that, "when there is a genuine vision (as opposed to the all-too-familiar 'vision statement'), people excel and learn, not because they are told to, but because they want to" (www.wisdomquotes.com/quote/peter-senge-2.html). Creating an educational community culture that is accepting of the change process and embraces the culture as innovative and socially responsible for all is at the heart of organizational change. As you reflect on the three organizational change processes, think about how they embed cultural proficient practices that will lead to culturally proficient learning communities that can facilitate change.

_____

_____

_____

_____

Action 2: Advocate for learning about underserved and marginalized cultural groups as a major focus of the school and district's _professional learning_ by collaborating and hosting leadership institutes on _Culturally Proficient Inclusive Education_ leading to site-based action planning for transformation.

"If you build it, they will come."

(from the 1989 *Field of Dreams* American film)

Teachers' commitment to an innovation only comes after they have acquired initial competence in the new skills necessary to implement the innovation (McLaughlin, 1991), making professional learning a central practice to installing and driving Inclusive Education into the systems of a school organization. In what ways might we advocate for and collaborate with others to make learning about best practices and our students efficient and effective?

Using Every Student Succeeds Act as an Opportunity. The Every Student Succeeds Act (ESSA), the most recent reauthorization of the federal Elementary and Secondary Education Act, was signed into law in December of 2015 by the then U.S. president, Barack Obama. This general education legislation and its accompanying regulations replace the previous No Child Left Behind (NCLB) regulations and federal sanctions and afford flexibility and leverage to states and districts that NCLB did not. Even though ESSA is more holistic in determining if schools are struggling or succeeding, it still holds struggling schools highly accountable for the professional learning of its staff. For instance, the bottom 5 percent of Title I schools are required to develop and implement an action plan of job-embedded professional learning for improvement of all teachers (Sparks, 2016). Although implementation of ESSA may be unclear, equity issues will continue to be addressed by state and local educators.

The latitude ESSA provides can be used as a catalyst for institutionalized support for professional learning that enhances educators' skills and understanding of what really works as interventions for students. ESSA emphasizes the use of evidence-based interventions, with an on-going cycle of evaluation to see where and with whom interventions work and where and with whom they do not work (Sparks, 2016). Through this emphasis, ESSA is creating opportunities for the focus of a school and district to be on what does and does not work for its own students with IEPs and students in Tier 1, 2, and 3 levels of a school's Multi-Tiered System of Support.

ESSA and MTSS can work together as a catalyst for systems change that focuses professional learning on expanding educator expertise with best practices in teaching and learning described in this chapter and Chapter 7. As educators, we have an opportunity to be seized! We can mold and personalize professional learning to support our colleagues in all roles to learn about underserved and marginalized cultural groups. Now is the time to take the organizational change processes described in Action 1 and carefully craft action plans for educators to have continuous professional learning with meaningful impact and clearly defined student outcomes.

Crossing Boundaries for Shared Professional Learning. Hesselbein, Goldsmith, and Beckhard (1997) promote removing boundaries of job titles and hierarchy and boundaries of district lines and, instead, sharing of experts, expertise, and follow-up coaching. Why not be efficient and advocate for and create regional opportunities where schools and districts identify and pool professional assets and expertise? One of the authors of this book has supported districts and state departments of education across the country to do just this, organizing annual summer leadership institutes to tap the expertise of local, regional, and national talent in larger-scale events and venues that allows for cross-pollination of information, stories, success experiences, and strategies for overcoming challenges.

Being Our Own Professional Developers and Learners. Teachers sharing examples of their use of best practices can develop teacher skills and help members get to better know and value one another's various areas of expertise. Tapping into district or local educator expertise, instead of bringing in the one-time "expert," will help create ownership and sustainability for an action plan aligned with a vision for all students experiencing success. This internal leadership development leverages talent from within and allows for on-going, thoughtful inquiry conversations within the educational organization and the building of a culture of care with community members invested in nurturing one another to impact student achievement (Piowlski & Kamphoff, 2017).

REFLECTION

William Pollard is noted for observing that "[w]ithout change there is no innovation, creativity, or incentive for improvement" (www.brainyquote .com/quotes/authors/w/william_pollard.html).

Take a moment to examine the Figure 9.1 action plan. In what ways might ESSA be a catalyst for professional learning in schools and districts? How can educators advocate for continued professional learning that enhances their abilities to be socially responsive to the needs of all students? How might you and other educators collaborate to build culturally proficient inclusive practices within your site-based action planning for transformational change? What might this collaboration look like in your school setting? What practices are working that can be used as leverage upon which to build? Who are educators and potential partners who are doing amazing practices that emulate the mission and vision of the action plan? In what ways do you and your colleagues lift them up as educational experts?

_____

_____

_____

_____

Action 3: Make learning about underserved and marginalized cultural groups within the school and community an integral part of my/our _on-going learning_ by "pealing back the wallpaper" to examine data (e.g., MTSS Tier 1, 2, and 3 student data) to discover over-representation of or bias toward groups by characteristics such as race, gender, primary language, and efficacy of instruction.

Culturally proficient educators identify and develop Cultural Proficiency within themselves, and in turn, infuse that knowledge of self and students into an inclusive environment where equitable instructional strategies are practiced (Piowlski, 2013). Traits of culturally proficient educators (Nuri-Robins, Lindsey, Lindsey, &Terrell, 2012), which are identified in Table 9.4, enable educators to shift their perceptions about student achievement gaps and address its sociocultural and school-related origins (Nieto & Bode, 2012). Piowlski (2013) describes how culturally proficient teachers focus on what they and their students can learn and can do. They are being intentional in using what they are learning about their students to adjust instruction.

> [E]ducators must not dwell on what they do not have control over. Yet it is imperative that their instruction shifts to adjust to students' prior knowledge and experiences. They must acknowledge the sociocultural elements (family configuration, socioeconomic, ethnicity, race, parental education) and, within these context factors, frame lesson plans and differentiate instruction to meet learners' needs. School related factors are elements within a teacher's control. Teachers can increase student learning by using what they know and understand about a student's prior knowledge to guide instruction. (p. 10)

Nieto (2010) divides the achievement gap into "a resource gap and an expectation gap" (p. 47). By performing a gap analysis for both dimensions, teachers can begin to peel back the layers that both restrict and promote student engagement and learning and use student differences as assets rather than deficits.

Table 9.4 Traits of Culturally Proficient Educators

• Having a mindset that guides instructors and builds confidence and competence
• Using specific tools for effectively describing, responding to, and planning for issues and opportunities that emerge in diverse environments
• Becoming and growing as an educator
• Valuing the learner as thinker and doer
• Honoring and respecting the cultural identities of all learners
• Designing experiences that build on prior knowledge and experiences of the learner
• Understanding assessment bias
• Holding high expectations for each learner
• Presenting rigorous, standards-based content
• Selecting materials and resources that reflect multicultural perspectives
• Managing the dynamics of difference
• Valuing diversity and inclusion

Cultural Proficiency requires us to be more than outside observers. It requires us to take an inside-out approach of looking below the surface to uncover disparities in practices and policies that might not be transparent or that might be distorted by assumptions. Then we can craft action plans, as described above for Action 1, using "real up-close and personal" data. In *Peeling Back the Wallpaper* (Avelar LaSalle & Johnson, 2016), the authors describe the actions of stakeholders in a school district that did just that. District stakeholders were concerned that their district's Latino and African American students attended four-year colleges at a much lower rate that Caucasian and Asian students. In order help educators understand the need to look below the surface to uncover the truth about how formal and informal policies and practices impact marginalized cultural groups within the school, they coined an investigation to understand the gap in achievement patterns that led to this disparity "The Wallpaper Effect." Four layers were peeled back. The first layer of district-level data showed overall gains in student proficiency levels, English language mastery, graduation rates, and students being college ready. On the surface, this data suggested the district seemed to be doing well.

Peeling back second layer, the investigative team looked to identify the students who were considered successful, which turned out to be students who participated in student government. They then asked, "Why such low number of Latino or African American students in student government? They found that, contrary to their initial assumptions (e.g., students are interested in spending time outside of class with peers of the same ethnicity, have jobs or are in sports, or do not have grades to qualify to serve), the unintentional barrier to participation was the way in which new members were recruited (i.e., a lunchtime booth of current members who were primarily Caucasian and Asian). This finding serves is an example of how systemic practices that go unexamined can directly marginalize specific groups of students.

The team continued a third layer of "peeling back the wallpaper," by asking the question, "Why are advanced placement (AP) classes populated by Caucasian and Asian students?" This examination revealed a set of district practices that discouraged enrollment of AP courses to those who did not, on the surface, meet placement criteria. With this new knowledge and understanding, active recruiting of the underrepresented became a priority, and changes were made to intentionally counsel and place students who met some of but not all of placement criteria.

The fourth layer of examination explored why most Latino and African American students did not go on to college, beginning with finding out how school counselors provided college information to students. Findings unearthed unintentionally biased information dissemination practices that, then, were corrected.

This case study of peeling back the wallpaper illustrates how underlying assumptions about underserved or marginalized groups must be examined to ensure practices and policies provide opportunity access to all student groups. It is also illustrates how being intentional about ongoing learning about groups within the school community through examination of policies, practices, and student data (e.g., MTSS Tier 1, 2, and 3 data) can detect intentional or unintentional bias toward groups, which can lead to action planning to create a more caring and effective learning community.

REFLECTION

Senge, Hamilton, and Kania make the following observation about how "[c]hange often starts with conditions that are undesirable, but artful system leaders help people move beyond just reacting to these problems to building positive visions for the future" (2015, p. 29).

With this observation and the previous Action 3 content in mind, what are some red flags in your educational community indicating that your school may need to experience the "wallpaper effect" and systematically peel back layers of data and engage in inside-out inquiry with groups in the learning community to discover and debunk untrue assumptions and discover the real formal and informal policies, procedures, and practices that are sources of inequity?

Examine and disaggregate Tier I achievement data, Tier II and III intervention results, and progress for students with an Individual Education Program to determine over-representation by ethnicity, race, gender, language, perceived ability, or other demographic distinctions. As you and your colleagues examine this data, what are underlying assumptions about why certain students or groups are or are not progressing? How can you test these assumptions? How can you peel back to layers of the wallpaper to find out what is really going on?

_____

_____

_____

_____

Action 4: Support students to learn about and appreciate one another through the use of cooperative group learning and other inclusive instructional strategies.

Can teachers both create opportunities for student learning in instructional arrangements that embrace and thrive on difference and individual uniqueness and maintain relevance and rigor of teaching? Fortunately, the answer is "yes." Teachers who possess culturally proficient dispositions and seek knowledge of each student's lived experiences and prior academic knowledge will be able to create learning structures that promote inquiry, curiosity, student wonderings about their learning, and positive and supportive peer relations. One particularly powerful instructional arrangement for supporting students to learn about and appreciate one another is cooperative group learning. A historical focus on ability grouping rather than diversity grouping has limited the possibilities of creating learning experiences where student explore and express their diverse perspectives and focus upon social and emotional development as much as academic knowledge and skill acquisition. Cooperative group learning changes all of that.

Cooperative group learning has been practiced and researched for decades, with many conceptualizations and definitions. Among the definitions is Chartock's (2010), which defines cooperative group learning as a "teaching strategy in which small groups (a) use a variety of learning activities to improve their understanding of subject matter, (b) interact in responsible ways, and (c) develop social skills through sharing of common goals" (p. 45). As we note in Chapter 6, cooperative group learning is among the nine most powerful instructional strategies to increase student performance regardless of perceived ability or disability, culture, race, gender, primary language, and other dimensions of student difference (Marzano, Pickering, & Pollock, 2001). We explain that we are most attracted to David and Roger Johnson's Learning Together approach because it is the one approach where students are directly taught and held accountable for using the very social skills (e.g., encouraging others, questioning for clarification, giving positive feedback) that equip them to appreciate one another's diversity and be successful in human relations (Johnson & Johnson, 1999; 2009; Johnson, Johnson, & Smith, 1998).

It can be argued that for students with learning and language challenges, cooperative learning is a must. For students from culturally and linguistically diverse communities, (i.e., African American, Latino) cooperative or communal learning may be preferred over individualistic or competitive structures. Kagan, Kyle, & Scott (2004) make this argument.

> Cooperative learning is the single most effective educational approach for meeting the needs of all students in inclusive classrooms. Attempts at inclusion without cooperative learning often backfire, resulting in students with special needs feeling isolated and segregated . . . If we are to follow the law, if we are to create least restrictive learning environments, and if we are to integrate students with special needs into regular classrooms, it is mandatory that our instruction includes frequent cooperative learning that includes teambuilding, class-building, and social skill development. Placing students in regular education classrooms is not inclusion; inclusion depends on effective cooperative learning. (Ch. 17, p. 16)

Organizing and planning for cooperative groups is your opportunity to engage students in a variety of groupings that are centered not only upon academics but also upon social-emotional learning and interpersonal growth. So, group to maximize not only academic heterogeneity but diversity along cultural, interest-based, learning style, personality, and any other dimension where students can complement and learn about one another's differences.

REFLECTION

What is your understanding of cooperative grouping strategies? As you think about the diverse needs of students in your classrooms and schools, what might be some reasons to include cooperative groupings as instructional strategies? In what ways might these inclusion strategies inform your work as an educator? Who else might you include as partners in cooperative grouping as a teaching/learning approach?

_____

_____

_____

_____

Action 5: I/we am/are the change we want to see! Actualize the vision and mission of success for all students by applying MTSS as the default proactive procedure and practice for detecting and honoring students' learning differences.

In Chapter 1, we shared with you the assumptions that we held as we wrote this book. One of the assumptions is that the work of leading a change toward Inclusive Education is *NOT* the work of someone else but rather *our* work. Being the change we want to see takes many forms. I/we can model Inclusive Education through our own actions. I/we can locate, create, and showcase and publicize Inclusive Schools. I/we can get into positions of authority (e.g., running for the school board, becoming an officer of the teacher's union, volunteering for local, regional, and statewide committees and taskforces) with influence in reforming school policy or practice. I/we can take any of the actions described in this and the previous four chapters concerning the Essential Elements of Cultural Proficiency.

In Chapter 4, we propose a Multi-Tiered System of Supports or MTSS as the overarching systems approach to creating Inclusive Schools, by activating district-wide (rather than school-by-school) resources and external (e.g., social services agencies, continuing education) resources and partnerships to provide "high-quality first instruction, supports, and interventions in academics and behavior for all students, regardless of whether they are struggling or have advanced learning needs" (California Services for Technical Assistance and Training, 2015, p. 2). To achieve the highest performance of every student, a MTSS approach requires educators to learn and use principles, processes, and strategies described in this and Chapters 5 through 8.

Action 5 is about walking the talk—not just committing to, but taking leadership in applying MTSS as the default proactive procedure and practice for detecting and honoring students' learning differences. With this cultural mindset, teachers can look beneath the surface of students and view their differences as an asset rather than a deficit to influence student learning (Nieto, 2010).

REFLECTION

Action 5 is about taking bold steps. Now that you know what you know, what actions are you willing to take? What are some important learnings you know now that you didn't know prior to reading this chapter? As you think about your role as educator, what key questions come to mind for you as you design an inclusive classroom/school?

_____

_____

_____

_____

CASE STORY

This last Case Story illustrates how one Lakeside school team, the Student Study Team (SST) at John Adams Elementary School, consciously and conscientiously takes Action 5 and applies the principles and practices of the MTSS, which the district had adopted to catch students before they failed and to avoid special education referral. The student who is the focus of the SST's conversations and work is Diana, a first grader who recently arrived in the United States as an unaccompanied minor. How are they attempting to be the change they want to see? What are their challenges, solutions, learnings, and wonderings?

Part 1: SST Meeting 1

John Adams is one of the eight elementary schools in the Lakeside Unified School District (LUSD). As we learned in Chapter 5, the school reflects the diversity of the district; however, the teaching staff is primarily Caucasian and female. Because of the school's large number of Spanish-speaking children learning English, at least one Spanish English dual emersion class is available at each grade level. In Chapter 5, we met the principal, Adam Watson, and special educator, Angela Teague, and followed their work with Pegah's family and Pegah's first-grade teacher to resolve a conflict over Pegah's use of an iPad in the classroom.

This story begins the summer before the opening of the same school year. Until June of that year Diana, six years old, lived with her mother, father, and eleven- and thirteen-year-old brothers in Honduras. Her father was seasonally employed in the pineapple fields and had very limited resources. About four months prior to Diana's immigration, two young girls from her village disappeared. Diana's mother, Maria, became very fearful for her daughter's safety and found a way to send her to the United States to live with her aunt Marisol Rodriquez, a Lakeside resident. In June, Diana arrived at the U.S. border with a group of unaccompanied minor children. She then came to her aunt's home after spending several weeks in a Citizenship and Immigration Services (CIS) facility for undocumented children. Diana stated that on the day she left Honduras, her mother had given her the doll she carries to school each day. She has not spoken with her family since leaving Honduras in early June.

Diana's aunt, Ms. Rodriquez, had been a nurse in Honduras and currently works as a certified nurse assistant (CNA) in a skilled nursing facility in Lakeside. Ms. Rodriquez came to the school in August to register Diana and provided the principal, Mr. Watson, with some limited information about her niece's background. She indicates that Diana, who had a few months of part-time schooling before arriving in the United States, would turn seven in September. To the best of her knowledge, Diana has had a relatively safe and happy early childhood, despite the family's economic situation. Diana's Aunt Rodriquez tells the principal that Diana has had no English instruction and has only occasionally heard English since arriving, as the family exclusively speaks Spanish in the home.

Mr. Watson, in consultation with the site's primary-grade English language development (ELD) teacher, Sol Garza, and the district's new social worker assigned to the school, Sophia Nguyen, decided it best to place Diana in Efron Bautista's first-grade dual-immersion classroom. In Mr. Bautista's classroom, she receives literacy and social studies instruction in Spanish in the morning and math and science instruction in English in the afternoon. Diana is also placed in a support group with other new arrivers, where she receives forty-five minutes of intensive language development instruction from a skilled paraeducator supervised by the school's ELD teacher.

Four weeks into the school year, Mr. Bautista notes that Diana has fallen behind her peers in a number of ways. She has difficulty following directions in both English and Spanish. He notes that she struggles with phonemic awareness and recognizing sight words in both languages. She is also behind in math. She rarely speaks in class or social situations, plays alone, and seems disengaged much of the time. As a concerned and competent teacher, Mr. Bautista has decided to complete a request for a pre-referral meeting with the school's Student Success Team (SST). The SST is the school's Tier 1 pre-referral general education problem-solving team comprised of the referring teacher, the parent/guardian(s) of the child of concern, three general education grade-level (i.e., K/1, 2/3, 4/5) representatives, an ELD teacher, and when deemed appropriate and necessary, the principal, the site's social worker, a special educator, and/or a psychologist. For this SST meeting, because of Diana's immigration experiences, in addition to Mr. Bautista and Diana's aunt, the principal and social worker are in attendance. Ms. Rodriquez was offered an interpreter but declined, as she has been in the United States for many years working as a CNA. She is quite proficient in day-to-day English as well as medical terminology.

Adam Watson, Principal	*Thank you all for coming to one of our first SST meetings of the year. Ms. Rodriquez, you have met everyone in the room, except Ms. Teague, who was invited because of her expertise as a special educator in teaching reading and math. We want you to know, first and foremost, as Diana's caretaker and family member, we value your knowledge, opinions, ideas, and concerns.*
Marisol Rodriquez, Diana's Aunt	*Since Ms. Nguyen came to our house and talked with me about Diana's family and her history getting here, I have learned so much about what she calls trauma and reactions to stress that Diana seems to show. Mr. Bautista communicates with me most every day, and I know we share the same concerns about learning math and her understanding sounds and words, following directions, not playing with classmates, talking, and being a part of her first-grade class.*
Efron Bautista, Diana's First-Grade Dual-Emersion Teacher	*Yes, Ms. Rodriquez, you have been so open to sharing what you see at home as well as recognizing our concerns about Diana's social and academic progress. I believe all children benefit from learning two languages. Using Spanish at home, as you do, and English and Spanish here at school is a great way to build a solid foundation in her first language, Spanish, while learning English, a language which will serve her well as her second language.*
Sol Garza, English Language Development (ELD) Teacher	*And it is a strength that she is in THIS school, with resources for increasing language development, such as Mr. Bautista's dual-emersion classroom and the newcomer reading group, where she can develop friendships with other Spanish-speaking English learners. I have the good fortune of working in his class for an hour each day and have seen the same behaviors you two have talked about.*

Sophia Nguyen, Social Worker	*Diana is "safe" now, but we know that what she may have witnessed traveling here and the loss of her family through separation may have left her fearful for herself and her family for a long time, making it difficult for her to concentrate and learn. It is such a strength for Diana that she is with you, Ms. Rodriquez, someone who can be in contact with her family and who has the love and resources to support her transition. You and I have both seen trauma symptoms, including anxious and sad moods and even withdrawal. And when I visited, you reported she has having nightmares and difficulty sleeping through the night. This, combined with her lack of attention and low school performance, suggests she could really benefit from what we here at school call TF-CBT, which is short for trauma-focused cognitive behavior therapy, with a Spanish-speaking child trauma specialist. I have connections with several good ones and can make a referral for the twelve-week intervention, if that is something you would want and agree to. It will not cost you anything; we just have to figure out with you how and when to get her to the specialist.*
Marisol Rodriquez, Diana's Aunt	*Wow, I had no idea there was this kind of support for children like Diana. Si, si, si! Let's figure out how to get this going. I can transport her as long as it is after 3 p.m., when my work shift ends. What else do I need to know?*
Amy Wong, Second-Grade Teacher and SST Chair	*Good question, Mrs. Rodriquez. Mr. Bautista, could you tell the rest of us on the team who have not been in your classroom a little bit more about what you have seen with Diana? We want to be as supportive in our suggestions as possible, so the more details the better!*
Efron Bautista, Diana's First-Grade Dual-Emersion Teacher	*Sure, of course. I see low attention during reading and math instruction while Diana's classmates are actively engaged. Her work samples show that she has consistent errors in addition and subtraction, even when using manipulatives. She counts from one to twenty in English, yet does not seem to have "number sense" beyond five. She has learned most of the letter names in Spanish but does not match them to the letter sounds. When asked questions or given directions in Spanish and English, she does not respond and averts eye gaze downward. She has yet to play or talk with other children in the classroom or on the playground. When other children try to include her in play, she goes off to play alone with her dolly. Ms. Rodriquez, you and I have talked about these things, and you say you have seen the same, yes?*

Marisol Rodriquez, Diana's Aunt	*Sí, es verdad! (Yes, it is true.) I am so worried and will do anything to help Diana be happy and learn. I also am trying to set up an account at my bank with a branch near her family to transfer money every month, so they can buy a cell phone and minutes each month. It is very cheap there—about twenty dollars for a flip phone and ten dollars for enough minutes for Diana to talk with her family for a few minutes each week. I would get them on Facebook to use Messenger or Skype, but that requires a smart phone and Internet service on a computer, and that is just beyond their means, at least for now.*
Adam Watson, Principal	*You are a fantastic advocate for Diana and a creative thinker. Thanks for letting us know all this. May I ask you if Diana has had a vision and hearing screening yet? If she hasn't, this is routine for all of our students. This information will tell us if vision and hearing issue are the source of or contributing to her attention and learning difficulties. It might give me more information to answer the question, "At this time, should she learn in Spanish only?" There is no right or wrong answer. All pathways can lead to higher academics and better understanding and thinking.*
Marisol Rodriquez, Diana's Aunt	*Diana has not had these screenings, so please, please, do these tests!*
Amy Wong, Second-Grade Teacher and SST Chair	*I know that we have adopted and are in full swing with our MTSS support systems. Ms. Rodriquez, I will explain MTSS to you after the meeting in more details. In short, it is a lot of fancy letters, an acronym, for giving students what they need right away, so they can experience success. How about we do what we are doing with all of our students this year—use data to determine what they will be doing in our school-wide literacy and math intervention block? During this block, Diana could join the Tier 2 reading intervention group of students focusing on letter-sound correspondence. We will access her every two weeks to see how she is progressing in the reading intervention. For math, Diana could join the Tier 2 math intervention group with students who need the same skill development as she. Ms. Rodriquez, we generally do not get the special educator involved at this point, as we want to try the interventions we already have in place. But, we would have the speech pathologist, who has specialized expertise regarding language development, visit Mr. Bautista's class and observe Diana during both the Spanish and English periods of the class to assess her language use and understanding.*

Marisol Rodriquez, Diana's Aunt	*This all sounds good to me. You are the teachers and know best.*
Amy Wong, Second-Grade Teacher and SST Chair	*As the chair of this group, may I summarize what we have suggested for Diana for the next weeks until we meet again? First, we will get those vision and hearing screenings done in the next week and pass this information on to Ms. Rodriquez. Then, Ms. Nguyen will arrange for the TF-CBT twelve-week sessions with a Spanish-speaking therapist and work out transportation with you, Ms. Rodriquez. I am very familiar with the first- and second-grade Tier 2 interventions used during our school-wide math and literacy blocks. So, during the literacy block, Diana will join the more intensive Interventions for Reading Success literacy group of five to six students that meets four days per week for twenty minutes. She also will join the On Cloud 9 Math intervention group of five to six students that meets Mondays, Wednesdays, and Fridays for twenty minutes. Mr. Bautista, we could get Diana in these groups right away on Monday, if that works for you. And we will ask the speech pathologist to observe Diana within the next couple of weeks and join us for our follow-up meeting. How's that?*
Efron Bautista, Diana's First-Grade Dual-Emersion Teacher	*This sounds like a great plan. I know that we have agreed that students should be in an intervention program for at least six to eight weeks before we reconvene with the family and the SST team. Would it make sense to schedule our follow up SST meeting around December 1? Ms. Rodriquez, would that work for you?*
Marisol Rodriquez, Diana's Aunt	*I will make it work. I will still be working the 7 a.m. to 3 p.m. shift in December. Could we make the meeting after 3 p.m.?*
Amy Wong, Second-Grade Teacher and SST Chair	*How about 3:30 p.m.? Students are released from classes at 3 p.m., and Diana can stay in our afterschool program while we meet. Does that work for everyone?*
Marisol Rodriquez, Diana's Aunt	*Yes, that sounds perfect. Thank you.*
Adam Watson, Principal	*Let me thank the team for really using the Multi-Tiered System of Supports we worked so hard to put into place last year to benefit Diana. And thanks, everyone, for your focused, thoughtful, and efficient solution finding! I am so proud of our John Adams team! Ms. Rodriquez, thank you for being here today.*

REFLECTION

As you reflect on this initial conversation, what might be some of the major issues facing the team? In what ways might you use the five Essential Elements to manage the process of the next SST? What are some values, beliefs, and assumptions that are in place that need to be surfaced as the conversation moves forward?

As noted in Table 9.1, an action culturally proficient members of an inclusive learning community can take is to facilitate the institutionalization of cultural knowledge by aligning school *practices* with the Cultural Proficiency Guiding Principles. In what ways do you detect this occurring among any of the members of this group? Who and how?

_____

_____

_____

_____

Part 2: SST Meetings 2

Literacy and math interventions were implemented starting the week following the SST meeting. Within two weeks of the SST meeting, the TF-CBT intervention with a Spanish-speaking therapist also was initiated at the local mental health center. Hearing and vision assessments revealed no vision or hearing difficulties. On December 1, the SST reconvened and now included the speech and language pathologist. Data from the MTSS interventions were reported. In careful consideration of the data, members of the SST team asked themselves: *What do the data tell us about Diana's progress? What should we do next for Diana?* Let's drop in on some of the conversation that occurred during this second SST meeting.

Efron Bautista, Dual-Emersion First-Grade Teacher	*Ms. Rodriquez, as I have just shown you and the team, mathematics intervention data show that Diana is making steady progress. Math appears to be a relative academic strength area. Diana just has not had the opportunity to learn math, since she wasn't in school before attending John Adams here in Lakeside. I suggest we keep her in this intervention group and continue to track her progress.*
Marisol Rodriquez, Diana's Aunt	*Bien, bien! This is so good to hear. How is she doing with her classmates?*

Efron Bautista, Dual-Emersion First-Grade Teacher	*I have seen more social interactions with classmates in both the classroom and on the playground. She seems to be developing friendships with a couple of the girls and one in particular, who is in her math intervention group. She particularly seems to like games where the kids cooperate, such as jump rope.*
Sol Garza, English Language Development Teacher	*Let's look at this graph that shows Diana's scores in reading at the end of each week. See that she goes up a bit and then back down; the goal is for Diana to reach this end-of-year target by her scores going up to match the line on the graph that connects her starting score over here on the left to this score on the right. Make sense?*
Marisol Rodriquez, Diana's Aunt	*Oh yes, I see. So what is going on? She is doing OK in math but not in reading.*
Lori Hesser, Bilingual Speech Language Pathologist	*May I chime in? The intervention she gets is designed for students to respond a lot, so they can get teacher feedback. What I noticed, despite the intervention, the teacher's enthusiasm, and frequent attempts to pull Diana in, Diana rarely responded unless directly called upon. And then she says just a word or two.*
Adam Watson, Principal	*In our MTSS approach to support all students, when one level of support, which we call Tier 2, does not seem to be enough, we increase that support to what we call Tier 3. For Diana, a Tier 3 intervention approach could look like the group size being reduced to two students, the intervention period lengthening from twenty to thirty minutes, and the frequency of sessions increased from four to five days per week.*
Amy Wong, Second-Grade Teacher and SST Team Chair	*Yes, this allows for increased opportunity for Diana to respond and get teacher feedback. It's hard not to respond in a group of two! In a group of five, Diana had only a fifth of twenty minutes—four minutes—of potential time to engage. In other words, she could hide easier when others responded and filled the time.*
Sol Garza, ELD Teacher	*The teacher can have more personalized "in the moment" adjustments in a group of two. And a thirty-minute, five-day-a-week intervention translates into seventy more minutes—over an hour—of personalized instruction a week, as compared to what she is getting now at Tier 2. The extra minutes can help Diana to pick up, remember, and use her reading skills in the classroom, at home, and wherever she is.*

Jamie Tate, Third-Grade SST Team Member	*I am both a third-grade teacher and a Tier 3 reading intervention teacher during the school-wide intervention block. I am so enthusiastic about the progress students have been making when they get Tier 3 support. And I also realize that Tier 3 interventions, which have such low teachers/student ratios and extended personalized time, take considerably more human resources, so we try to move back to less intensive supports if progress substantially increased with Tier 3 intervention. So, I say, let's design Tier 3 support, as Sol has described, for Diana.*
Adam Watson, Principal	*Jamie, thanks for reminding the group that students often make great progress in Tier 3 interventions, which is exactly what we want to happen for Diana. Thank you also for reminding us that Tier 3 interventions generally are meant to be shorter term in order to make up and accelerate growth. Ms. Rodriquez, if Diana is in the Tier 3 reading intervention for several months and is still not moving forward, we will want to dig deeper to see if she may be experiencing some specific learning difficulty and would benefit from additional, specialized academic instruction.*
Marisol Rodriquez, Diana's Aunt	*This is reassuring to know. I'd like to learn more about this "additional specialized academic instruction."*
Lori Hesser, Bilingual Speech and Language Pathologist	*I would be happy to talk with you about it after the meeting or when it works for you. I am so pleased to finally get to meet you. As you know, I have observed Diana, listening to her use of language, and am happy to report that Diana is beginning to speak in Spanish during the Spanish period of class. I did notice some mistakes in the words she chose to use and in her sentence structure. Has that been anything you have noticed?*
Marisol Rodriquez, Diana's Aunt	*Yes, now that she is speaking up more, I have noticed that, too. Her Spanish is not perfect, but we are working on that at home.*
Lori Hesser, Speech and Language Pathologist	*Ah, that is good to know. During the English period of Mr. Bautista's class, Diana seems to understand the social conversations her classmates are having by watching what they are doing and following the lead of others. If it is OK with you and the team, I suggested that, over the next couple of months, I continue to periodically visit Mr. Bautista to observe Diana's language development and use in both languages.*

Sophia Nguyen, Social Worker	*Ms. Rodriquez and I would like to catch you up on the TF-CBT intervention. Diana and her aunt are seven weeks into the TF-CBT intervention. I would like to continue to meet with Diana weekly, and we will continue with the TF-CBT intervention for another five weeks, to get to the twelve-week minimum meetings. How is the TF-CBT going, in your opinion, Ms. Rodriquez?*
Marisol Rodriquez, Diana's Aunt	*There is so much to learn, but it really is helping me not only with Diana but the families that I work with at the skilled care facility. For example, I learned that Diana can feel love for and worry about her family while developing a love for me and her new community. For many of my patients at work, I become like a family member, and that is OK. There is enough love to go around. Also, I want you to know that, with the money I figured out how to send to Diana's family, they were able to get a little "non-smart" phone and are able to buy enough air time to call and speak with Diana and me for fifteen to twenty minutes a week, which they plan to do on Sunday afternoons after church. They don't have Internet access, so this was our alternative. Now, Diana is sleeping through the night more often, and her nightmares happen less often. She still worries, but she so looks forward to Sundays.*

The SST meeting wrapped up with the SST chair, Amy Wong, summarizing and checking for agreement that the Tier 3 intervention plan suggested in the meeting would start within the next few days and that the other agreements we heard in the above conversation would continue to occur. Because of the unusually long winter holiday break and the President's Day holidays, both of which interrupted Tier 3 interventions, the team wanted to give the Tier 3 literacy intervention adequate time (i.e., a full eight weeks) before determining its impact. The team set the next meeting, the third SST meeting, for March 1. Diana's aunt would still have on-going communication with Diana's teacher, Mr. Bautista, and the social worker, Ms. Nguyen.

REFLECTION

As you reflect on this stage of the conversation, what might be some of the major issues facing the team? In what ways might you use the five Essential Elements to manage the process of the next SST? What are some values, beliefs, and assumptions that are in place that need to be surfaced as the conversation moves forward?

One action culturally proficient members of an inclusive learning community can take to facilitate the institutionalization of cultural knowledge identified in Table 9.1 is to create opportunities for and take advantage of *teachable moments* for diverse groups to learn about one another and engage in ways that both honor who they are and challenge them to be even better. What might be some teachable moments in the dialogue that just occurred? In what ways do they inform members of this group about each other? In what ways are you learning about self and others as you read this section?

_____

_____

_____

_____

Part 3: SST Meetings 3

The Tier 2 math interventions continued with Diana making steady progress toward grade-level performance. The TF-CBT intervention concluded after twelve weeks, with the therapist assessing no need for more sessions unless monitoring by Diana's social worker, Ms. Nguyen, determined a need. On March 1, the SST reconvened. Data from the MTSS interventions were reported. In careful consideration of the data, members of the SST team again asked themselves: *What do the data tell us about Diana's progress? What should we do next for Diana?* Let's once again drop in and listen to some of the conversation that occurred during this third SST meeting.

Sophia Nguyen, Social Worker	*It has been ten months now since Diana left her family in Honduras to journey north and arrive here. My conversations with Diana and Ms. Rodriquez suggest that, with the weekly phone conversations and her increasing circle of grade-level friends, Diana is feeling safer and is more able to attend to her schooling. She has told me that she loves her teacher, Mr. Bautista, and her classmates. Diana is by no means "over" her trauma, and she continues to live with sadness about her family in Honduras. Too often children seem to stabilize and supports are phased out too early. I suggest that my support continues, particularly through the summer and the anniversary of her transition here. I will work with Ms. Rodriquez to search for summer experiences for Diana, since she will not have her daily schooling routine. What are your thoughts, Ms. Rodriquez?*

Marisol Rodriquez, Diana's Aunt	*I would like that very much. I was beginning to think about summer as well. I, too, see Diana laughing and smiling more. We have found a couple of her classmates, too, who are learning English like Diana, and one English-speaking classmate, who lives in the same complex. Diana plays with her after school and on the weekends. This has been terrific for her, and I welcome any ideas for summer learning and play opportunities that are free or inexpensive. We have a limited budget, as I am single and the sole breadwinner.*
Lori Hesser, Bilingual Speech and Language Pathologist	*Since we returned from winter break, I have had a chance to regularly observe and interact with Diana, as I have several students in Mr. Bautista's classroom who receive speech and language support from me. We have worked out an arrangement where, on Mondays, Wednesdays, and Fridays, I co-teach with Mr. Bautista for forty-five minutes of the ninety-minute literacy block. We have created four to five language development and literacy development stations through which all students rotate. I get to observe and listen to all of the students at my language station and take informal language samples in both Spanish and English from not only the students who are learning Spanish or need speech and language services but every student in the class. It has been great fun and has opened my eyes to the power of providing speech and language services in general education rather than pulling students out into small groups. I get to support the language development of every student, including Diana. What I have been able to observe is her rapid development in actually speaking up and conversing with peers as well as comprehending and following teacher directions, daily routines, and academic language in Spanish. She still has some errors in grammar, so I will keep track of this through continuing to informally sample her language use in Spanish and English, compare her language patterns in both languages, and work with her and the other students on common errors through our center and station rotation system. In English, Diana's comprehension is greatly improved. She now is attempting to communicate in English rather than Spanish both during the Spanish and English segments of the day. She clearly is having fun with learning this second language. Her musical intelligence is strong, she retains most anything that she sings or rhymes. So, we have also built this into at least one station activity for her day. Mr. Garza, Mr. Bautista, both see Diana every day. What are your observations?*

Sol Garza, English Language Development Teacher	*Lori, it is so exciting that you have started co-teaching with Efron. As you know, this is our district's initiative this year and our fearless principal, Adam, is bound and determined that we figure out how to schedule this to be the default way for all specialists to serve students if not by next fall, as soon after that as possible. ELD teachers have been delivering our language development services through co-teaching in general education classroom for some time. Wow, we have seen language development accelerate for newcomers through our co-teaching and co-thinking, as Mr. Bautista put it. Teachers continue to use the strategies we model during co-teaching throughout the day, when we are not with them. We are sold on co-teaching for Diana and all students. Since I also am in Mr. Bautista's classroom co-teaching during the social studies block, I too see Diana and can confirm that she is rapidly picking up vocabulary and showing that she is learning the differences and similarities in Spanish and English sentence structure and more!*
Efron Bautista, Dual-Emersion First-Grade Teacher	*It has been great having both Ms. Hesser and Mr. Garza co-teaching with me at different times of the day. Their expertise is so welcomed, as I am a third-year teacher and have so much to learn from them. This year, my students are grasping content faster than in my first two years of teaching. I have others to co-think and plan with. I truly am learning how to differentiate instruction. That's why we co-teach, after all, right? I also keep close track of my students who are receiving Tier 2 and 3 intervention support. Diana continues to make steady progress and gains in her math intervention. Her math intervention teacher and I agree that Diana should continue getting this support through the year. We think she will be up to grade level by June. That is our target, and we believe we can reach it. How is Diana doing in her Tier 3 reading intervention? I have her graph right here. So, let's take a look. As you see, she had a bit of a drop in her scores after the long winter break. But she recouped and doubled her rate of progress to actually exceed the projected rate in this more intensive intervention. Her Tier 3 intervention teacher, who happens to be our very own Jamie Tate, and I talked about next steps. Since Diana is making such great progress in the Tier 3 intervention, we agree it is smart to move her to a Tier 2 intervention level to see if progress can be maintained, especially without large gaps in intervention, such as occurred during the winter breaks.*

Jamie Tate, Third-Grade SST Team Member	*Ms. Rodriquez, I am so proud of Diana and how hard she works. What a lover of learning! With the support she is getting in Mr. Bautista's class, she is ready to move back to less-intensive supports. As I said at the last SST meeting, Tier 3 interventions, which have such low teachers/student ratios and extended personalized time, take considerably more human resources, so we try to move back to less-intensive supports if progress substantially increases with Tier 3 intervention.*
Adam Watson, Principal	*Jamie, once again, thanks for reminding the group that students often make great progress in Tier 3 interventions, which is exactly what happened for Diana. Ms. Rodriquez, I was glad Lori Hesser and you had a chance to talk after the last meeting about special education and the additional specialized academic instruction that it could provide. Dropping to Tier 2 allows us to see if she can thrive with less support. It also lets us see if there is a decline in progress, which would suggest a very high level of support is needed to maintain progress. Most student supports teams would judge that if a student like Diana did not make progress in the less-intensive Tier 2, a referral for assessment for a suspected disability would be considered valid and not premature. Ms. Rodriquez, how does this plan sound to you? What are your thoughts, feelings, and ideas?*
Ms. Rodriquez, Diana's Aunt	*Ms. Hesser explained all of this to me and gave me some materials in English and Spanish on what the special education process looks like and why it can be helpful and also my rights as Diana's guardian. I really do understand why moving back to less support in reading is important. I am so impressed by how you all have joined forces to wrap your teaching arms around Diana and the other students, as well. I trust your suggestions.*
Amy Wong, Second-Grade Teacher SST Team Chair	*As the chair of this team, I will do as I did in the previous two meetings. I'll summarize what I think we have agreed upon for Diana. First, Ms. Nguyen will continue social work supports with Diana, and Ms. Rodriquez will focus on summer learning and recreation opportunities. Second, Tier II math services will continue. Third, Tier III reading services will drop to the less intensive Tier II level that Diana had this fall. We will make this adjustment by next week, if that is O.K. with everyone. Fourth, Mr. Garza and Ms. Hesser will continue to co-teach with Mr. Bautista, supporting him to differentiate instruction and monitor Diana's language and literacy development. Shall we meet again in eight weeks, let's say on May Day, May 1?*

| Ms. Rodriquez, Diana's Aunt | *I like those steps. If we again could make our meeting at 3:30, I would appreciate it. I want to thank Mr. Bautista for his daily communication and Ms. Nguyen for being there for me anytime I have a doubt or question. Diana is lucky to go to John Adams.* |
| Adam Watson, Principal | *We are the lucky ones—lucky to have Diana as such an eager student and you as her loving advocate and guardian.* |

REFLECTION

As you reflect on this stage of the conversation, what might be some of the major issues facing the team? In what ways might you use the five Essential Elements to manage the process of the next SST? What are some values, beliefs, and assumptions that are in place that need to be surfaced as the conversation moves forward?

What might be actions that culturally proficient members of an inclusive learning community can take to facilitate the institutionalization of cultural knowledge identified in Table 9.1, which create opportunities for and take advantage of *teachable moments* for diverse groups to learn about each other and engage in ways that both honor who they are and challenge them to be even better. In what ways do they help members of this group learn about each other?

_____

_____

_____

_____

Part 4: The Rest of the Story

The SST group reconvened for a fourth time to look at Diana's progress data. Ms. Nguyen and Ms. Rodriquez reported that they found a nearby community recreation program that two of Diana's friends will attend, and the families are figuring out how to share transportation and child care responsibilities before and after the program hours. Summer Science in the Park is a key program featuring learning experiences. Mr. Bautista reports that Tier 2 math intervention data suggests that by June Diana will achieve or at least get close to end-of-first-grade skill performance and likely not need math intervention in second grade, particularly with the summer experiences Diana will have. Reducing the intensity of reading intervention to a Tier 2 did not adversely affect Diana's learning rate; her progress continued on an upward slope. The team agreed that Diana stay in Tier 2 literacy intervention through the end of the school year and as with math, assess her performance in the fall to determine if Tier 2 intervention is warranted. The team reminded Ms. Rodriquez of her option, at any time, to request an assessment for eligibility for special education but reassured her that this was not what they saw as necessary at this time. The MTSS they had wrapped around Diana had done its job and had furthered these team members' commitment to expanding their collaboration through co-teaching. Let's eavesdrop on one last conversation that occurred immediately after the May 1 SST meeting.

Adam Watson, Principal	*Team, would you be willing to take a few minutes to reflect on our SST and MTSS work this year? Because of your SST leadership and involvement with students who have received Tier 2 and Tier 3 instruction, you have more intimate knowledge of how things have been working than some of the other faculty. I am curious to know how you think this year went, with the implementation of our district's MTSS process and the co-teaching action plan developed by the district Professional Learning Planning Committee? I want to hear from everyone, and I will start with my reflections. For one thing, I am pleased with how we were able to integrate the SST process, which we have had for years to problem solve for individual students, with the data-driven three-tiered "pyramid" approach to preventing student failure and quickly responding to students having difficulty making progress in the general education curriculum or managing their behavior. Jamie, what about your reflections?*
Jamie Tate, Third-Grade SST Team Member	*I have a confession to make. As you likely know, our third-grade team has been reluctant to embrace the MTSS intervention structure and processes. All that data collection and time talking about individual students just seemed "over the top" in terms of the extra time and energy it would take. As a matter of fact, I became an SST member and volunteered to apply my Reading Recovery training and experience as a Tier 3 interventionist during the intervention block because I wanted to keep a close eye on how this new process was rolled out. At the beginning of the year, I felt just like my third-grade team— suspicious that MTSS was just designed to make the special education referral process more difficult so the district could trim the budget and save money on hiring specialists or some other budget-related motive. You have to realize that our team had gotten accustomed to referring students who were a couple years behind for special education assessment. Using the old "IQ-achievement discrepancy model" of determining eligibility for a learning disability, it usually took until third grade for a*

student to have a big enough gap to be referred and qualify. Now, Response to Intervention, where we must document a student's failure to respond to increasingly intensified intervention, is replacing the discrepancy approach. We resented being placed under the microscope, being held accountable for documenting what we were doing to use "evidence-based methods" to boost achievement, and having to produce data before Tier 2 and 3 supports kicked in. Why couldn't we just refer for testing? All of these extra steps—we were grouchy and annoyed.

*But, I have seen the light. (Everyone laughs.) Seriously, this experience with Diana, tiered interventions, and our social worker, who has educated us on trauma-informed interpretations of behavior and support strategies, changed my mind totally. I am a little ashamed for my stubborn attempt to cling to past ways of doing things. But, thanks to you all and this experience, I want to become and **be** the change that we want to see! And I have one other third-grade teacher whose thinking has shifted. We just chatted yesterday, and we would like to be the classrooms where students with IEPs get specialized academic instruction through co-teaching with Angela Teague, our primary-grade special educator, and you, Lori, our speech pathologist. What you and Efron have done in the first grade is how I want to transform my classroom. I now see how two or more people sharing responsibility for planning and teaching allows for differentiation and personalized instruction to help students achieve College and Career Readiness Standards. How about that for a "true confession?" Can you tell I have developed some trust in this team?*

Amy Wong,
Second-Grade
Teacher SST
Team Chair

Wow, Jamie. "Be the change that we want to see"—that needs to be our new school vision or motto. Wadda you think, Adam? I too am all in on being one of the second grade teachers to co-teach with Lori, Sol, Angela, Sophia . . . whomever. And Adam, if you would consider placing Diana in my classroom for next year and work with Lori to schedule into my classroom students who she can provide speech and language services through co-teaching, it would be fabulous. I would love for us to set up a station teaching rotation similar to what Efron and Lori have done in first grade. Lori, if you are in my class, you also can follow Diana's language progress and more authentically assess if she is experiencing any particular difficulties in both or either language.

Lori Hesser, Bilingual Speech and Language Pathologist

Great idea, Amy. If we can make it work, let's get our team and Angela together to do some serious scheduling for the fall before the school year is out. You all know what my caseload is like. But if we think strategically and "hand schedule" students with IEPs, Angela and I and our primary-grade paraeducators can maximize our co-teaching opportunities. And we don't have to just co-teach during language arts. As you know, Sol, our English language development expert co-teaches during social studies, science, and math, depending on when his time can be scheduled into a classroom. At the co-teaching training that the district put on for speech and language pathologists, I saw a video of a middle-level math class where the speech and language pathologist was supporting students' use of academic language and assessing student language development when working in small groups. I had never thought of using the language-rich problem-solving math environment as an ideal place to teach and have students generalize the language skills on their IEPs. So how about we expand our thinking on not only who can co-teach but what content areas are ripe for co-teaching! At the workshop, one of the trainer's statements that really stuck with me was "Four well-planned co-taught lessons are infinitely better than five unplanned lessons taught on the fly." That observation is what prompted Efron and me to agree on a Monday, Wednesday, and Friday partnership. We have carved out some live and virtual time to plan, using our Google Classroom platform and a really easy lesson plan template we created at the workshop. Finally, I just want to let you know that Alyce LaPlant, our special education coordinator, passed on to me a few articles that she read when she went through her University of Vermont (UVM) education administration masters' program. One article was by a UVM speech and language professor, Patricia Prelock, who she got to know in her interdisciplinary leadership course. Lauren Bland and Prelock found students who received speech and language intervention through collaborating in general education had more complete and intelligible utterances than those who received pull-out services. That was in 1995. Throneburg and colleagues found the same for vocabulary development in 2000. In 1999, Farber and Klein found that doing something very much like what Efron and I are doing resulted in better student performance in listening, writing, and vocabulary and concept understanding than a one-teacher only model. It's crazy that these findings have been around for a couple decades. It's time we did something to intensify our collaboration to intensify services for our Lakeside students.

Efron Bautista, Dual-Emersion First-Grade Teacher	*Good for you, Lori, for making us part of that Farber and Klein research study. I hope we get similar results; and I think we will. I do have to tell all of you that I was a bit overwhelmed with the thought of having not just one but two different experienced "experts" in language development and difference in my class. As a still relatively "green" teacher, it was just a little intimidating, at first. But that changed quickly, and today I would say, "Give me a co-teacher in each of my four curriculum blocks!" I know that is impossible. However, if we could figure out how to get additional support during the math block, it would be great. Hey Lori, you could try out doing what you saw in the video—come on in and "language up" math. Then, maybe Angela, our primary-grade special educator, could provide support three times a week during literacy to continue out literacy station rotation system that is humming! I am just brainstorming!*
Sol Garza, English Language Development Teacher	*I'd like to share that what really helped us ELD teachers to understand co-teaching and its variations and how each variation allows for differentiation, which was a year-long book study. We decided to start a breakfast club study group before school every two weeks. Our lead ELD teacher convinced the department to purchase for each school site, the 2013 third edition of Villa, Thousand, and Nevin's A Guide to Co-Teaching: New Lessons and Strategies to Facilitate Student Learning. Every two weeks we would meet up at a different school for an hour, and the host teacher would provide coffee and breakfast goodies. Starting with Chapter 1, we all read one chapter per meeting and, with a structured agenda, summarized key learnings, identified how we could apply the learnings with educators and administrators at our sites, and shared positivos regarding co-teaching actions we had taken since the last breakfast club meeting. Among what we learned was how to work with school administrators to schedule for co-teaching. I don't know why we weren't smart enough to ask our special education and speech and language counterparts to join us or open it to any teacher who wanted to come. But we could learn from that error and do this as a school-wide book study, if we wanted. Right?*
Adam Watson, Principal	*These are all amazing ideas, which we could actually put in place if we really are the change that we want to be. For one of the non-instructional work days at the end of the year, let's set aside a work day where we invite everyone of the LUSD Visionizers group who can make it to spend as much of the day with us as they can to share district-wide learnings and insights. True co-teaching is the piece of the puzzle we have been missing to create a genuinely inclusive John Adams for students, teachers, and families. I am jazzed! We can showcase success stories and examine MTSS data; anyone who has been*

co-teaching can describe their journey and thoughts for the future. I will be calling upon you to talk this up and help me think through how best to use the principles and Tools of Cultural Proficiency to explore the possibilities in ways that feel safe, invite and honor everyone's voices, and spark creativity!

REFLECTION

As you reflect on this final stage conversation, what might be some of the major concerns and opportunities facing the team? In what ways might you use the five Essential Elements to manage the process of the next SST? What are some values, beliefs, and assumptions that are in place that need to be surfaced as the conversation moves forward?

_____

_____

_____

_____

DIALOGIC ACTIVITY

Reengineering educational practices is a complex proposition. Yet an increasing number of educational communities are choosing to do so. The good news is that we now know ways to facilitate change. We know we must engage the community in action planning to build consensus for the vision, help staff members acquire skills, provide meaningful incentives, and allocate the necessary resources in order to institutionalize and drive a change into the system. With your grade-level team, your department group, your faculty, and paraprofessionals, engage in a dialogue about what action you might take collectively using the following prompts:

- What is our shared understanding of Institutionalizing Cultural Knowledge?
- What evidence do we have that Institutionalizing Cultural Knowledge is a shared priority for all educators within our school?
- In what ways might we work to influence the *vision, mission, policies,* and *practices* of the school and district to be aligned with the Guiding Principles of Cultural Proficiency?
- In what ways might we make learning about out students our professional learning focus?
- In what ways might we "peel back the wallpaper" to discover bias toward groups of students?

PREVIEW OF CHAPTER 10

In this chapter, we examined the Cultural Proficiency Essential Element of *Institutionalizing Cultural Knowledge* by identifying and analyzing five action steps. The next chapter, Chapter 10, instructs us on how to develop an action plan for institutionalizing change toward Inclusive Education. It is time to take action!

10 Engaging in Action: When All Means ALL!

Vision without action is merely a dream.
Action without vision just passes the time.
Vision with action can change the world.

Joel Barker, Futurist and Author
(as cited at www.joelbarker.com/perfect-quotes/)

GETTING CENTERED

What is your reaction to this very well known quote by the futurist, Joel Barker? What actions could you take to actualize and sustain a vision of culturally proficient Inclusive Education for all children? What actions are you willing to take to move toward changing the world by doing something differently to serve students as a culturally proficient educator and leader?

_____

_____

_____

_____

THE INSIDE-OUT PROCESS: YOU, YOUR SCHOOL, AND YOUR COMMUNITY

This chapter is designed for you to develop a collaborative, school- or district-wide action plan to live the vision of all students being served in inclusive learning communities. Up to this point in the book, you have had the opportunity to

- reflect on your "inside-out" process for learning about your own culture, the culture of your school, and the culture of the community you serve;
- engage in conversations with your colleagues about current policies and practices involving students receiving special education services;
- consider the Tools of Cultural Proficiency and the inclusive practices described in the previous chapters as a framework for teaching, so that all students experience success at levels higher than even before;
- reflect on your thinking and your practice; and
- examine case stories from the Lakeside Unified School District as models for learning about and applying the lens of Cultural Proficiency and MTSS to actualize the inclusive *"vision and practice of welcoming, valuing, empowering, and supporting the diverse academic, social/emotional, language and communication learning of all students in shared environments and experiences"* (Villa & Thousand, 2016, p. 18).

Now, we invite you to first review and summarize your learning and then design an action plan for how you want to function as a culturally proficient educator and organization. This is a three-step process to bring your learning forward from Chapters 5 through 9 and plan for future actions.

Chapter 5: Assessing Cultural Knowledge Through Authentic and Differentiated Strategies

As an initial step in designing an action plan, we guide you through a three-step process of summarizing your learning about the Essential Element of Assessing Cultural Knowledge and its relationship to your educational role as educator, administrator, counselor, related services provider, district office administrator, or parent.

Step 1: Inside-Outside Process. We invite you to take a few moments to reexamine Chapter 5, paying particular attention to your inside-out *Reflection* learning responses. Review your entries and synthesize at least two reflections that represent your inside-out learnings relative to yourself, your school, and the community your school serves. Enter these synthesized learnings in the space below.

_____

_____

_____

_____

Step 2: Case Story and Illustrations. This time, browse Pegah's case story and the other stories illustrating the use of the strategies described in the chapter. Summarize one or two key ideas you glean from reading them again. Use the space below to summarize those key ideas.

_____

_____

_____

_____

Step 3: Getting Centered and Dialogic Activity. Read your responses to the opening (i.e., Getting Centered) and closing (Dialogic Activity) reflections in Chapter 5, paying particular attention to your reactions and your observations of self and others. Use the space below to summarize key learning and insights.

_____

_____

_____

_____

Chapter 6: Valuing Diversity Through Inclusiveness

This time we invite you to return to Chapter 6 and summarize your learning about the Essential Element of Valuing Diversity and its relationship to your educational role as educator, administrator, counselor, related services provider, district office administrator, or parent.

Step 1: Inside-Outside Process. Revisit Chapter 6, paying particular attention to your inside-out *Reflection* learning responses. Review your recordings and synthesize at least two reflections that represent your inside-out learnings relative to yourself, your school, and the community your school serves. The space below is provided for you to summarize your learnings.

_____

_____

_____

_____

Step 2: Case Story and Illustrations. This time browse the Zen's "Dramatic Dilemma" and "Zen's Gifts" case story and the other stories illustrating the use of the strategies described in the chapter. Summarize one or two key ideas you glean from reading the story and illustrations again. Use the space below to summarize those key ideas.

_____

_____

_____

_____

Step 3: Getting Centered and Dialogic Activity. Read your Chapter 6 opening (Getting Centered) and closing (Dialogic Activity) reflections. As you read, take note of feelings and thoughts that surface for you and your observations of self and others. Use the space below to summarize key learning and insights.

_____

_____

_____

_____

Chapter 7: Managing the Dynamics of Diversity Through Collaboration, Creative Problem Solving, and Conflict Management

To progress in constructing knowledge to develop a personal and district action plan, repeat the three-step review and summary process for the Essential Element of Managing the Dynamics of Diversity explored in Chapter 7. Be intentional in following the prompts and mindful of thoughts and reactions that arise.

Step 1: Inside-Outside Process. Review Chapter 7, paying particular attention to your *Reflection* learning responses. Synthesize these responses into two summary reflections that represent the inside-out process relative to you, your school, and the community your school serves. Use the space below to memorialize the two summary reflections.

_____

_____

_____

_____

Step 2: Case Story and Illustrations. Now take a moment to browse through the Chapter 7 Kaitlin "Too Close for Comfort" and "Managing Our Differences" case stories and the other stories illustrating the use of the strategies described in the chapter (e.g., the SODAS IF application; the "quick brainstorm with kids" CPS variation). Summarize one or two key ideas you take from the stories. Use the space below to summarize those key ideas.

_____

_____

_____

_____

Step 3: Getting Centered and Dialogic Activity. Your Chapter 7 opening (Getting Centered) and closing (Dialogic Activity) reflections may evoke reactions and observations about yourself and others. Use the space below to summarize your reactions, observations, learning, and insights.

_____

_____

_____

_____

Chapter 8: Adapting to Diversity Through Advocacy and Universal Design for Learning

You now are familiar with the three-step review and summary process provided to support you in designing your action plan. Enjoy your journey of continuous self-discovery by reviewing the Essential Element of Adapting to Diversity described in Chapter 8.

Step 1: Inside-Outside Process. Take another look at Chapter 8, carefully reexamining your *Reflection* learning responses. Now construct two reflections prompted by this reexamination that represent the inside-out process relative to you, your school, and/or the community your school serves. Summarize your learning in the space below.

_____

_____

_____

_____

Step 2: Case Story and Illustrations. Browse through the Chapter 8 "A Very Special School Dance" and "Dancing the Night Away" case stories and the other stories illustrating the use of the strategies described in the chapter. What do you notice about your responses? Summarize one or two key ideas you take from the vignettes. Use the space below to summarize those key ideas.

_____

_____

_____

_____

Step 3: Getting Centered and Dialogic Activity. Please reread your Chapter 8 opening (Getting Centered) and closing (Dialogic Activity) reflections. Take note of your reactions and observations of self and others. The space below is provided for you to summarize your reactions, observations, learning, and insights.

Chapter 9: Institutionalizing Cultural Change

This final three-step review is to summarize learning about the Essential Element of Institutionalizing Cultural Knowledge and its relationship to you and your role as a member of an educational community. This process will help you design your action plan and make commitments for yourself and the students you serve.

Step 1: Inside-Outside Process. Look once again at Chapter 9, carefully reexamining your *Reflection* learning responses. Review your entries and synthesize two reflections that represent the inside-out process relative to you, your school, and/or the community your school serves. Enter these two reflections in the space below.

_____

_____

_____

_____

_____

_____

Step 2: Case Story and Illustrations. Browse through the Chapter 9 Diana MTSS case story and the other stories illustrating the use of the strategies described in the chapter one more time. What do you notice about your responses? Summarize one or two key ideas you gathered from rereading the stories. Use the space below to summarize those key ideas.

_____

_____

_____

_____

Step 3: Getting Centered and Dialogic Activity. Read your Chapter 9 opening (Getting Centered) and closing (Dialogic Activity) reflections. What do you notice as you review your reactions and observations of self and others? The space below is provided for you to summarize key reactions, observations, learning, and insights.

_____

_____

_____

_____

MOVING FROM WORDS TO ACTION: SIX STEPS TO INCLUSIVE EDUCATION

Now, read through your summaries and reactions in the three-step review process of the five chapters on the Essential Elements. Use the space below to summarize your reactions/feelings to the reading and reflective activities. Your summary may be key words or you may choose a longer, expository approach.

_____

_____

_____

_____

As you read and analyze what you have written, what insights do you have about yourself as a teacher, administrator, counselor, district office administrator, paraprofessional, or parent working in a diverse setting to provide access and equitable opportunity to all students?

_____

_____

_____

_____

1. In what ways does the inside-out approach of Cultural Proficiency and Inclusive Education contribute to learning about yourself?

_____

_____

_____

_____

2. In what ways does the inside-out approach contribute to learning about the culture of your school?

_____

_____

_____

_____

3. In what ways does the inside-out approach contribute to learning about the community your school/district serves?

_____

_____

_____

_____

4. Now that you know what you know, what three commitments are you willing to make to be an advocate for equity and Inclusive Education in your school?

_____

_____

_____

_____

5. In what ways will you, in whatever role you play, support equity and inclusion in your school? What three bold steps are you willing to take within the next three to six months to demonstrate your commitments?

_____

_____

_____

_____

Schools of this twenty-first century are charged with serving all students well. The laws are clear that all students are to receive an appropriate education in the least restrictive environment. So, we educators are facing an urgency to examine our policies and practices in ways we have not done before. It is up to us to craft sustainable action steps for actualizing Culturally Proficient Inclusive Schooling environments for ourselves and our students. We educators must ensure that _all truly does mean all_ and includes students with the full range of learning preferences and differences, especially students with Individual Education Program (IEP) plans. Schools and educators are still figuring out how best to achieve the vision of genuinely inclusive classrooms. Figuring this out through a lens of Cultural Proficiency is one approach to get to this vision quicker. Now, each of us must move toward action in our schools and communities. Now that you are aware of the urgency in your community and your school, to what actions are you willing to commit?

YOUR TURN

Chapter 9 presented several approaches to action planning for change. In this chapter, we offer a variation of one of the approaches, the Complex Change Action Planning approach (Villa & Thousand, 2017; Villa, Thousand, & Nevin, 2013), to assist you as you integrate what you learned and committed to in the previous section of this chapter with the variables of complex change to craft a personal and organizational action plan for creating and sustaining a culturally proficient inclusive schooling environment.

We offer the Culturally Proficient Inclusive Schooling Action Plan (CPISAP) shown in Figure 10.1 as a template to help you along your journey. Each of Chapters 5 through 9 provides you with culturally proficient inclusive actions in the text and in Tables 5.1, 6.1, 7.1, 8.1, and 9.1. The CPISAP guides you to consider these actions as you plan to address four variables that must be considered for a complex change toward Inclusive Schooling to occur and be sustained. The variables involve

- building a *vision* of Inclusive Schooling within a community,
- developing educators' *skills* and confidence to be inclusive educators,
- providing meaningful *incentives* for people to take the risk to embark on an inclusive schooling journey, and
- reorganizing and expanding human and other *resources* for teaching for and to diversity.

School plans are only as good as the actions of the people who design and carry out the plans. Often great accreditation, evaluation, and strategic plans end up on shelves never consulted again until the next evaluation or planning cycle arrives. This action plan is different, because students' educational lives are at stake.

Once the plan is developed, it must become public and launched into action. Through a process of gap analysis (Fisher, Frey, & Pumpian, 2012), the plan is constantly monitored and assessed for gaps between what you intended to accomplish (i.e., the goals and culturally proficient actions) and the actual outcomes. This process of benchmarking holds those who have taken responsibility for taking action accountable. Making the action plan public gives educators and community members ownership of the goals and expectations as well as the actions necessary to reach those goals.

Components of a *Culturally Proficient Inclusive Schooling Action Plan*

The Culturally Proficient Inclusive Schooling Action Plan (CPISAP) includes the following components.

- **School Vision and Mission Statements**—The goals and actions outlined in the CPISAP should align with the school's shared vision and mission. Therefore, for each goal, community members developing the CPISAP must ask the question, "To what extent does this goal align with the current vision and mission statements?" If it is determined that the goal and the vision and mission statements align, all is well and the next steps of determining actions to achieve the goal are generated. What if it is desired that a proposed goal to forward Culturally Proficient Inclusive Education does not appear to align with the vision or mission? The goal may be reconsidered or reshaped. Or a different question may be asked; namely, "Do the school's vision and mission statements need to be reexamined and updated to reflect cultural changes and advancements in best educational practice?" As times and culture change, so must school vision and mission statements. Culturally proficient learning communities revisit vision and mission statements on a regular basis and if necessary, revise and refine the statements to align with the contemporary values of the community.

- **Goals**—The CPISAP is designed to grow and support educators to consider and implement new strategies for ensuring equity and inclusive learning opportunities for all students. The planning team determines outcomes needed to address the complex change variables (i.e., vision, skills, incentives, and resources) and translates the outcomes into observable and measurable goals for which concrete action steps can be formulated. As shown in Figure 10.1, team members are prompted to answer the question, "What goals do we need to reach this outcome?" for the outcomes of

  ○ instilling and installing a *vision* of Inclusive Schooling and a Multi-Tiered System of Supports (MTSS);
  ○ building *skills* and capacity for Cultural Proficiency, Inclusive Schooling, and MTSS;
  ○ providing *incentives* to engage community members in Culturally Proficient Inclusive Schooling and MTSS practices; and
  ○ orchestrating technical, material, organizational, and human *resources* for Inclusive Schooling and MTSS.

We recommend CPISAP planners compose SMART goals. SMART is an acronym for the following five attributes of a quality goal.

Specific = The goal identifies the who, what, when, where, which, and why of the goal.

Measurable = The goal includes concrete criteria (e.g., how much, how many, how we will know) for measuring success.

Attainable = The goal considers what is needed (e.g., development of people's knowledge, skills, attitudes, and resources) to make the goal achievable.

Realistic = The crafters of the goal answer "yes" to two questions: Is the goal high enough? and Are we willing to work hard enough to reach it?

Timely and Tangible = The crafters of the goal answer "yes" to the following questions: Do we have a sense of urgency? Do we have a timeline with short- and long-term actions to achieve the goal? Can we picture the outcome? Do we know when we have reached the goal?

- **Culturally Proficient Actions**—In our Figure 10.1 CPISAP, culturally proficient actions are listed in the second column. Action steps are carefully planned, chronologically ordered behaviors that help move a team toward achieving its goals in each of the complex change dimensions of vision, skills, incentives, and resources. Both preparation and implementation actions should be included in an action sequence. Planned actions are built on the five Essential Elements of Cultural Proficiency (noted at the top of the second column) and best practices for organizational transformation along the dimensions of complex change. For demonstrated concrete actions for building vision, skills, incentives, and resources, see Villa and Thousand (2017) and Villa, Thousand, and Nevin (2013). The action steps are the heart of the success of the CPISAP.
- **Accountability and Measures of Success**—Goals need to be measurable so you and your team can benchmark (measure how you are doing at any point in time) your actions for points of success or stuckness. Benchmarking is a leadership action that helps a team move forward based upon data rather than by wondering how they are doing or by assuming the results are good or bad. In the third column of the Figure 10.1 action plan, see the starter phrase, "*We will know we are successful if/when . . .*" This is the phrase you and your teammates must next contemplate, discuss, and agree upon, remembering that success measures, data, and benchmarks must be observable and measureable. *What* is measured? What *are* the measures? What data will you collect? What are benchmarking questions for tracking progress toward achieving the SMART goals (identified in the plan's first column) and implementing the *actions* (identified in the plan's second column). *Who* will be responsible for collecting and examining data and benchmarks? *When* or how often will data and benchmarks be examined to assess progress? The results of analyzing these data are fed back into the plan in ways to support continuous learning. The plan itself may be revised as your team analyzes data. The fourth and fifth columns of Figure 10.1 identify *who* will provide oversight of actions and goals and the *date* by which a goal or action is to be accomplished.
- **Actual Outcomes**—The last and sixth column of our Figure 10.1 CPISAP provides a place to note *actual outcome*s. Planned outcomes are not always what people think they will be. Sometimes outcomes

fall short of what was hoped for; sometimes they surprise and exceed expectations; and sometimes they just are different than what was expected, but just as good or even better!

Review Figure 10.1 and think about how it applies to your school and district. In what ways might this action plan template support your planning for a culturally proficient inclusive education environment?

REFLECTION

Take a few minutes and write your new thinking about the importance of developing an action plan. In what ways does this CPISAP template inform your work? How do the five Essential Elements of Cultural Proficiency inspire or enhance concrete action steps for you?

_____

_____

_____

_____

DEEPEN YOUR ACTIONS IN A CULTURALLY PROFICIENT WAY

As you reflect on the content of this book, what comes to mind for you? The following questions intentionally use the personal pronoun "I" and the personal, plural pronoun, "we," so you might use these questions to guide your thinking, planning, and actions:

Of what am I most intentional about in my teaching, learning, leading, and parenting?

_____

_____

Who am I, in relation to my colleagues?

_____

_____

Who am I, in relation to my students?

_____

_____

Figure 10.1 Culturally Proficient Inclusive Schooling Action Plan

School Community: _____

Our School Vision:

Our School Mission:

Goals by Change Variable	Culturally Proficient Actions	Success Measure(s) "We will know we are successful if/when…" Include:	Person(s) Responsible	Date by Which to be Achieved	Actual Outcomes

• What goals do we need to achieve the outcome of each change variable?
 • Is the goal written using SMART criteria?
 • To what extent does the goal align with current vision and mission statements? Do the vision and/or mission statements need to be revisited or revised to better align with Culturally Proficient Inclusive Schooling values?
	• List actions chronologically
	 • Include preparation (e.g., funding) and implementation actions
	 • Include actions for:
	  ○ assessing cultural knowledge and the current reality
	  ○ valuing diversity
	  ○ managing the dynamics of diversity
	  ○ adapting to diversity
	  ○ institutionalizing cultural knowledge
		• what is measured
		 • who will measure
		 • when to measure			

VISION: Instill and Install a Vision of Inclusive Schooling and a Multi-Tiered System of Supports
What goals do we need to reach this outcome?

Goal One:	Actions to Achieve Goal One:	Success Measure(s):	Person(s) Responsible:	Date:	Outcomes:
Goal Two:	Actions to Achieve Goal Two:	Success Measure(s):	Person(s) Responsible:	Date:	Outcomes:

252

SKILLS: Build Skills and Capacity for Cultural Proficiency, Inclusive Schooling, and MTSS

What goals do we need to reach this outcome?

	Actions to Achieve	Success Measure(s)	Person(s) Responsible	Date	Outcomes
Goal One:	Actions to Achieve Goal One:	Success Measure(s):	Person(s) Responsible:	Date:	Outcomes:
Goal Two:	Actions to Achieve Goal Two:	Success Measure(s):	Person(s) Responsible:	Date:	Outcomes:

INCENTIVES: Provide Incentives to Engage People in Culturally Proficient Inclusive Schooling and MTSS Practices

What goals do we need to reach this outcome?

	Actions to Achieve	Success Measure(s)	Person(s) Responsible	Date	Outcomes
Goal One:	Actions to Achieve Goal One:	Success Measure(s):	Person(s) Responsible:	Date:	Outcomes:
Goal Two:	Actions to Achieve Goal Two:	Success Measure(s):	Person(s) Responsible:	Date:	Outcomes:

RESOURCES: Orchestrate Technical, Material, Organizational, and Human Resources for Inclusive Schooling and MTSS

What goals do we need to reach this outcome?

	Actions to Achieve	Success Measure(s)	Person(s) Responsible	Date	Outcomes
Goal One:	Actions to Achieve Goal One:	Success Measure(s):	Person(s) Responsible:	Date:	Outcomes:
Goal Two:	Actions to Achieve Goal Two:	Success Measure(s):	Person(s) Responsible:	Date:	Outcomes:

SMART Goals:

Specific = Who, what, when, where, which, why?

Measurable = Concrete criteria for measuring success: How much, how many, how will we know?

Attainable = What do we need to be successful? What knowledge, skills, attitudes, and/or resources do we need to develop to attain the goal?

Realistic = Is our goal high enough and are we willing to work hard enough to reach it?

Timely & Tangible = What is our sense of urgency? Do we have a timeline with short- and long-term actions to achieve the goal? Can we picture the outcome? Do we know when we have reached the goal?

Who are we as a professional community?

_____

_____

What are we learning that will ensure equity through inclusive schooling experiences and the implementation of a Multi-Tiered System of Supports for all students?

_____

_____

What are we doing with what we are learning about Cultural Proficiency and Inclusive Schooling practices?

_____

_____

Who else do we need to include in our community about implementing the Cultural Proficiency as a lens for Inclusive Schooling?

_____

_____

What (additional) data would be helpful as we develop our Culturally Proficient Inclusive Schooling Action Plan?

_____

_____

The final words of this book will be yours. Space is provided below for you to personally commit to actions steps. These final questions are designed to help you focus on your future actions and commitment to yourself and your learning community.

- In what ways am I willing to commit _myself_ to use Cultural Proficiency and Inclusive Education as the lenses through which I examine and design or redesign my current work focused on serving all students?
- In what ways am I willing to commit _my professional communities_ to use Cultural Proficiency and Inclusive Education as the lenses through which we examine and design or redesign our current work focused on serving all students?

- What are my short- and long-term *goals*? What will I accomplish with my commitment to these goals?
- What are the first steps I will take? What are my second steps? What is my *personal* culturally proficient *action plan* to forward Inclusive Education?

Use this space to record your responses and your commitments:

_____

_____

_____

_____

_____

DIALOGIC ACTIVITY

Engage in dialogues with your colleagues to continue your shared understanding of *a school culture in support of all learners being welcomed, valued, empowered, and supported in shared inclusive educational environments and experiences*. In what ways does the action plan you have formulated inform your implementation of inclusive practices and a Multi-Tiered System of Supports for all students? What currently is in place in your school and district that supports implementation? Are you ready to write, expand, or modify your action plan? Continue the dialogue throughout small learning communities in your school district. Once shared understanding is reached, what steps might you take to fully implement your action plan for every learner?

_____

_____

_____

_____

OUR INVITATION AND COMMITMENT TO YOU

We are partners with you in this journey toward culturally proficient inclusive educational practices. We invite you to share with us your experiences as you grow and develop in your profession. We want to hear your stories, questions, and commitments to this work. And we encourage you to share with us and others your actions, strategies, materials, and learning as you ensure equity through inclusive educational practice. We look forward to our dialogue with you.

Contact us!

Delores is at dblindsey@aol.com

Jacqueline is at jthousan@csusm.edu

Cindy is at cjew@callutheran.edu

Lori is at lori.piowlski@mnsu.edu

Resource A: Book Study Guide

Culturally Proficient Inclusive School: All Means ALL!

Delores B. Lindsey, Jacqueline S. Thousand,
Cindy L. Jew, Lori R. Piowlski
Corwin, 2018

CHAPTER 1: WHAT ARE THE EQUITY AND ACCESS GAPS AND WHY DO THEY PERSIST?

Content Questions to Consider

- In what ways do you describe equity?
- What are equity gaps?
- What do the co-authors mean by the misalignment of vision and mission statements pertaining to "all" students?
- As you examine your vision statement, ask:
  - Vision: Who are we?
  - Alignment: Are we who we say we are?
- What do you understand the purpose of this book to be?

Personal Reaction Questions to Consider

- What is your reaction to the intent of this book?
- What is your reaction to examining and discussing equity, access, and achievement/equity gaps in your school/classroom/district/ organization?

- If you are unsure of the statistical gaps, where can you go find out? Some suggestions are state and district websites, National Center for Educational Statistics at https://nces.ed.gov/ (Item Maps), or *Kids Count Data* at http://datacenter.kidscount.org
- In what ways might you describe the current access/achievement gaps within your context? What examples exist?

CHAPTER 2: USING THE TOOLS OF CULTURAL PROFICIENCY AND THE VISION AND PRACTICES OF INCLUSIVE EDUCATION AS A CONCEPTUAL FRAMEWORK

Content Questions to Consider

- How do you describe the four Tools?
- In what ways do you describe the *inside-out process*?
- In what ways are the Guiding Principles as core values consistent with how you view yourself and your school?
- In what ways will the Essential Elements provide you with "action" steps on your journey toward Cultural Proficiency?
- How do you describe Inclusive Education?
- In what ways do Table 2.1 and Table 2.2 inform your work about Culturally Proficient Inclusive Schools?
- What question do you have about the Conceptual Framework?

Personal Reaction Questions to Consider

- How would you describe where you are with Inclusive Education NOW?
- How would you describe where you need to go?
- How might you either begin or deepen a consideration of equitable practices in your school or district?

CHAPTER 3: BARRIERS TO CULTURALLY PROFICIENT INCLUSIVE EDUCATION

Content Questions to Consider (Use Table 3.1 for reference)

- Describe the Barriers to Culturally Proficient Inclusive Education
- What might be some Barriers that you recognize in your classroom, school, or district?

- Describe how and why culture and other student attributes are embraced as assets to overcome these Barriers to Cultural Proficiency.
- Explain how the Guiding Principles serve to counter the Barriers to Cultural Proficiency.

Personal Reaction Questions to Consider

- What is your reaction to the Barriers section? To the Guiding Principles as core values?
  - Describe the manner in which the Essential Elements are informed and supported by the Guiding Principles.
  - In what ways do the Essential Elements serve as standards for personal, professional behavior?
- What is your reaction, personally or professionally, as you become acquainted with the Tools?
- What more do you want to know/learn about Cultural Proficiency?
- What are the Barriers that exist in your context, and how can you shift the focus on the need to adapt and change?

CHAPTER 4: OVERCOMING BARRIERS AND CREATING OPPORTUNITIES FOR LEARNING

Content Questions to Consider

- Describe what the Guiding Principles, as examined in the nine questions, are guiding you to examine?
- What are the Barrier busting paradigms identified in the chapter?

Personal Reaction Questions to Consider

- When answering the nine questions in the Guiding Principles, how might you summarize your findings in developing your core values that are intended to serve the diversity in your community?
- What are some actions you identified as Barrier busters in your context?

CHAPTER 5: ASSESSING CULTURAL KNOWLEDGE THROUGH AUTHENTIC AND DIFFERENTIATED STRATEGIES

Content Questions to Consider

- What do you understand the Essential Element *Assessing Cultural Knowledge* to be?

- In what ways do you describe the "authentic and differentiated strategies?"
- What might you anticipate as possible advantages for using Assessing Cultural Knowledge to develop more authentic instructional strategies?
- What might be some opportunities for you and your colleagues to assess cultural knowledge?
- In what ways does Table 5.1 inform your work?
- What connections were you able to make to Pegah's story?

Personal Reaction Questions to Consider

- What is your reaction to this chapter?
- What have you identified as your own inside-out learning process?
- To what extent do you know your cultural background and the impact/influence it might have on your relationship with your students?
- What are some questions you have about the cultural backgrounds and experiences of your students?
- What actions might you take to get to know your students' assets?
- What questions do you have and what do you need to learn about disabilities and the IEP process?
- Reflect on students you know who have disabilities and how or why they are marginalized in your context (i.e., name them, claim them, and then commit to confront the underlying view of diversity and disability).
- What might be some opportunities ahead for professional learning involving topics in this chapter?

CHAPTER 6: VALUING DIVERSITY THROUGH INCLUSIVENESS

Content Questions to Consider

- Describe the Essential Element *Valuing Diversity*.
- In what ways does Valuing Diversity enhance inclusion in the classroom and schools?
- What evidence might you and your colleagues collect to demonstrate the value the school holds for diversity and difference?
- Examine family and school-community collaborations that now exist; in what ways, might you adopt and apply a *valuing* perspective?
- In what ways does Table 6.1 inform your work?

Personal Reaction Questions to Consider

- What is your reaction to this chapter?
- In what ways do you want to develop as leader? Co-teacher? Co-learner?
- In what ways are values for social justice evident in your teaching, learning, and leading style and behaviors?
- In what ways do you include cooperative learning within your classroom/school?
- How might retrofit approaches to differentiated instruction be used in your setting? What are your mismatches?
- What connections were you able to make to the illustrations about Ms. Swanson and Ms. Tac and the case story about Zen and the "Dramatic Dilemma?"

CHAPTER 7: MANAGING THE DYNAMICS OF DIVERSITY THROUGH COLLABORATION, CREATIVE PROBLEM SOLVING, AND CONFLICT MANAGEMENT

Content Questions to Consider

- How might you describe *Managing the Dynamics of Difference*?
- In what ways might you illustrate collaboration using the Essential Element of Managing the Dynamics of Difference?
- How might creative problem solving enhance the teaching and learning environment? How do you interact to understand and appreciate sources of conflict in your context?
- In what ways might any or all of the three CPS variations for helping adults and students problem solve and resolve conflict be helpful in your context?
- In what ways does Table 7.1 inform your work?

Personal Reaction Questions to Consider

- How do you view your own professional learning with regard to your school and the community it serves?
- How do you react to professional learning as a general educator or a special educator?
- In what ways might you reach out to others who seem to be stuck in their profession?
- What connections were you able to make to Katlyn's case story, "Too Close for Comfort?"

CHAPTER 8: ADAPTING TO DIVERSITY THROUGH ADVOCACY AND UNIVERSAL DESIGN FOR LEARNING

Content Questions to Consider

- Please describe the Essential Element, *Adapting to Diversity*.
- In what ways do evidence-based approaches align with adapting to the community one serves?
- In what ways does Table 8.1 inform your work? How might MI and UDL be utilized in your context?
- What connections were you able to make about the case story, "A Very Special School Dance?"

Personal Reaction Questions to Consider

- In what ways is Cultural Proficiency a *journey*?
- How do you describe your understanding of *Adapting to Diversity*?
- Reflect on potential leadership of colleagues and students; what are some potential possibilities?
- How might personal learning plans (PLP's) be used as a vehicle to support diverse learners in your context?
- In what ways can you and your school use the information from this chapter?

CHAPTER 9: INSTITUTIONALIZING CULTURAL CHANGE

Content Questions to Consider

- How do you describe the Essential Element, *Institutionalizing Cultural Knowledge*?
- You have been reading the phrase *inside-out* process throughout this book. What does it mean to you now? What has been added to your knowledge? In what ways does it apply to schools?
- What is the *institutionalizing* issue in the case story about Diana? Who needs help and why do you think it to be so?
- What might be some change issues your school and district are facing related to serving all learners?

Personal Reaction Questions to Consider

- What were your thoughts and personal reactions about the information in this chapter? In what ways do your reactions inform intentional use of support systems?

- In what ways might you use the information from Table 9.1 and other information from this chapter?
- Which pathway provides you the knowledge to shift from change resistors to becoming change agents?
- Reflecting on the five actions for Institutionalizing Cultural Knowledge, where are you within the five actions? Where are the gaps on which you can focus to develop an action plan?
- What connections were you able to make to the case story, "Diana's Story?"

CHAPTER 10: ENGAGING IN ACTION: WHEN ALL MEANS ALL!

Content Questions to Consider

- In what ways do the Essential Elements serve as standards for professional learning?
- How might the Essential Elements be useful for you and your school?
- In what ways do SMART goals support the work of Culturally Proficient Inclusive Schooling?
- Why do conversations matter?
- Now that you know what you know, to what *professional* actions are you willing to commit?

Personal Reaction Questions to Consider

- What were your thoughts and personal reactions about the information in this chapter?
- In what ways do your reactions inform your future choices for working in your school?
- In what ways can you and your school use the information from this chapter?
- Now that you know what you know, to what *personal* actions are you willing to commit?

Resource B: Cultural Proficiency and Inclusive Schooling Books' Essential Questions

Corwin Cultural Proficiency Books	Authors	Focus and Essential Questions
Cultural Proficiency: A Manual for School Leaders, 3rd ed., 2009	Randall B. Lindsey Kikanza Nuri-Robins Raymond D. Terrell	This book is an introduction to Cultural Proficiency. The book provides readers with extended discussion of each of the tools and the historical framework for diversity work. • What is Cultural Proficiency? How does Cultural Proficiency differ from other responses to diversity? • In what ways do I incorporate the Tools of Cultural Proficiency into my practice? • How do I use the resources and activities to support professional learning? • How do I identify Barriers to student learning? • How do the Guiding Principles and Essential Elements support better education for students? • What does the *inside-out* process mean for me as an educator? • How do I foster challenging conversations with colleagues? • How do I extend my own learning?

(Continued)

(Continued)

Corwin Cultural Proficiency Books	Authors	Focus and Essential Questions
Culturally Proficient Instruction: A Guide for People Who Teach, 3rd ed., 2012	Kikanza Nuri-Robins Randall B. Lindsey Delores B. Lindsey Raymond D. Terrell	This book focuses on the five Essential Elements and can be helpful to anyone in an instructional role. This book can be used as a workbook for a study group. • What does it mean to be a culturally proficient instructor? • How do I incorporate Cultural Proficiency into a school's learning community processes? • How do we move from "mindset" or "mental model" to a set of practices in our school? • How does my "cultural story" support being effective as an educator with my students? • In what ways might we apply the "Maple View Story" to our learning community? • In what ways can I integrate the Guiding Principles of Cultural Proficiency with my own values about learning and learners? • In what ways do the Essential Elements as standards inform and support our work with the Common Core Standards? • How do I foster challenging conversations with colleagues? • How do I extend my own learning?
The Culturally Proficient School: An Implementation Guide for School Leaders, 2nd ed., 2013	Randall B. Lindsey Laraine M. Roberts Franklin CampbellJones	This book guides the reader to examine their school as a cultural organization and to design and implement approaches to dialogue and inquiry. • In what ways do Cultural Proficiency and school leadership help me close achievement gaps? • What are the communication skills I need to master to support my colleagues when focusing on achievement gap topics? • How do "transactional" and "transformational" changes differ and inform closing achievement gaps in my school/district? • How do I foster challenging conversations with colleagues? • How do I extend my own learning?

Corwin Cultural Proficiency Books	Authors	Focus and Essential Questions
Culturally Proficient Coaching: Supporting Educators to Create Equitable Schools, 2007	Delores B. Lindsey Richard S. Martinez Randall B. Lindsey	This book aligns the Essential Elements with Costa and Garmston's Cognitive Coaching model. The book provides coaches, teachers, and administrators a personal guidebook with protocols and maps for conducting conversations that shift thinking in support of all students achieving at levels higher than ever before. • What are the coaching skills I need in working with diverse student populations? • In what ways do the Tools of Cultural Proficiency and Cognitive Coaching's States of Mind support my addressing achievement issues in my school? • How do I foster shifting conversations with colleagues? • How do I extend my own learning?
Culturally Proficient Inquiry: A Lens for Identifying and Examining Educational Gaps, 2008	Randall B. Lindsey Stephanie M. Graham R. Chris Westphal Jr. Cynthia L. Jew	This book uses protocols for gathering and analyzing student achievement and access data. Rubrics for gathering and analyzing data about educator practices are also presented. A CD accompanies the book for easy downloading and use of the data protocols. • How do we move from the "will" to educate all children to actually developing our "skills" and doing so? • In what ways do we use the various forms of student achievement data to inform educator practice? • In what ways do we use access data (e.g., suspensions, absences, enrollment in special education or gifted classes) to inform school-wide practices? • How do we use the four rubrics to inform educator professional learning? • How do I foster changing conversations with colleagues? • How do I extend my own learning?
Culturally Proficient Leadership: The Personal Journey Begins Within, 2009	Raymond D. Terrell Randall B. Lindsey	This book guides the reader through the development of a cultural autobiography as a means to becoming an increasingly effective leader in our diverse society. The book is an effective tool for use by leadership teams.

(Continued)

(Continued)

Corwin Cultural Proficiency Books	Authors	Focus and Essential Questions
		• How did I develop my attitudes about others' cultures? • When I engage in intentional cross-cultural communication, how can I use those experiences to heighten my effectiveness? • In what ways can I grow into being a culturally proficient leader? • How do I foster challenging conversations with colleagues? • How do I extend my own learning?
Culturally Proficient Learning Communities: Confronting Inequity Through Collaborative Curiosity, 2009	Delores B. Lindsey Linda D. Jungwirth Jarvis V. N. C. Pahl Randall B. Lindsey	This book provides readers a lens through which to examine the purpose, the intentions, and the progress of learning communities to which they belong or wish to develop. School and district leaders are provided protocols, activities, and rubrics to engage in actions focused on the intersection of race, ethnicity, gender, social-class, sexual orientation and identity, faith, and ableness with the disparities in student achievement. • What is necessary for a learning community to become a "culturally proficient learning community?" • What is organizational culture and how do I describe my school's culture in support of equity and access? • What are "curiosity" and "collaborative curiosity," and how do I foster them at my school/district? • How will "breakthrough questions" enhance my work as a learning community member and leader? • How do I foster challenging conversations with colleagues? • How do I extend my own learning?
The Culturally Proficiency Journey: Moving Beyond Ethical Barriers Toward Profound School Change, 2010	Franklin CampbellJones Brenda CampbellJones Randall B. Lindsey	This book explores Cultural Proficiency as an ethical construct. It makes transparent the connection between values, assumptions, and beliefs with observable behaviors, making change possible and sustainable. The book is appropriate for book study teams. • In what ways does "moral consciousness" inform and support my role as an educator? • How does a school's "core values" become reflected in assumptions held about students?

Corwin Cultural Proficiency Books	Authors	Focus and Essential Questions
		• What steps do I take to ensure that my school and I understand any low expectations we might have? • How do we recognize that our low expectations serve as ethical Barriers? • How do I foster challenging conversations with colleagues? • How do I extend my own learning?
Culturally Proficient Education: An Assets-Based Response to Conditions of Poverty, 2010	Randall B. Lindsey Michelle S. Karns Keith Myatt	This book is written for educators to learn how to identify and develop the strengths of students from low-income backgrounds. It is an effective learning community resource to promote reflection and dialogue. • What are "assets" that students bring to school? • How do we operate from an "assets-based" perspective? • What are my and my school's expectations about students from low-income and impoverished backgrounds? • How do I foster challenging conversations with colleagues? • How do I extend my own learning?
Culturally Proficient Collaboration: Use and Misuse of School Counselors, 2011	Diana L. Stephens Randall B. Lindsey	This book uses the lens of Cultural Proficiency to frame the American Association of School Counselor's performance standards and the Education Trust's Transforming School Counseling Initiative as means for addressing issues of access and equity in schools in collaborative school leadership teams. • How do counselors fit into achievement-related conversations with administrators and teachers? • What is the "new role" for counselors? • How does this "new role" differ from existing views of school counselor? • What is the role of site administrators in this new role of school counselor? • How do I foster challenging conversations with colleagues? • How do I extend my own learning?
A Culturally Proficient Society Begins in School: Leadership for Equity, 2011	Carmella S. Franco Maria G. Ott Darline P. Robles	This book frames the life stories of three superintendents through the lens of Cultural Proficiency. The reader is provided the opportunity to design or modify his or her own leadership for equity plan.

(Continued)

(Continued)

Corwin Cultural Proficiency Books	Authors	Focus and Essential Questions
		• In what ways is the role of school superintendent related to equity issues? • Why is this topic important to me as a superintendent or aspiring superintendent? • What are the leadership characteristics of a culturally proficient school superintendent? • How do I foster challenging conversations with colleagues? • How do I extend my own learning?
The Best of Corwin: Equity, 2012	Randall B. Lindsey, Ed.	This edited book provides a range of perspectives of published chapters from prominent authors on topics of equity, access, and diversity. It is designed for use by school study groups. • In what ways do these readings support our professional learning? • How might I use these readings to engage others in learning conversations to support all students learning and all educators educating all students?
Culturally Proficient Practice: Supporting Educators of English Learning Students Learners, 2012	Reyes L. Quezada Delores B. Lindsey Randall B. Lindsey	This book guides readers to apply the five Essential Elements of Cultural Competence to their individual practice and their school's approaches to equity. The book works well for school study groups. • In what ways do I foster support for the education of English learning students? • How can I use action research strategies to inform my practice with English learning students? • In what ways might this book support all educators in our district/school? • How do I foster challenging conversations with colleagues? • How do I extend my own learning?
A Cultural Proficient Response to LGBT Communities: A Guide for Educators, 2013	Randall B. Lindsey Richard Diaz Kikanza Nuri-Robins Raymond D. Terrell Delores B. Lindsey	This book guides the reader to understand sexual orientation in a way that provides for the educational needs of all students. The reader explores values, behaviors, policies, and practices that impact lesbian, gay, bisexual, and transgender (LGBT) students, educators, and parents/guardians. • How do I foster support for LGBT colleagues, students, and parents/guardians?

Corwin Cultural Proficiency Books	Authors	Focus and Essential Questions
		• In what ways does our school represent a value for LGBT members? • How can I create a safe environment for all students to learn? • To what extent is my school an environment where it is safe for the adults to be open about their sexual orientation? • How do I reconcile my attitudes toward religion and sexuality with my responsibilities as a PreK–12 educator? • How do I foster challenging conversations with colleagues? • How do I extend my own learning?
Culturally Proficient Response to the Common Core: Ensuring Equity Through Professional Learning, 2015	Delores B. Lindsey Karen M. Kearney Delia Estrada Raymond D. Terrell Randall B. Lindsey	This book guides the reader to view and use the Common Core State Standards as a vehicle for ensuring all demographic groups of students are fully prepared for college and careers. • In what ways do I use this book to deepen my learning about equity? • In what ways do I use this book to deepen my learning about CCSS? • In what ways do I use this book with colleagues to deepen our work on equity and on the CCSS? • How can I and we use the Action Planning guide as an overlay for our current school planning?
Culturally Proficient Inclusive Schools: All Means ALL! 2018	Delores B. Lindsey Jacqueline S. Thousand Cindy L. Jew Lori R. Piowlski	This book provides responses and applications of the four Tools of Cultural Proficiency for educators who desire to create and support classrooms and schools that are inclusive and designed intentionally to educate all learners. General educators and special educators will benefit from using the five Essential Elements and the tenets of Inclusive Schooling to create and sustain educational environments so that when we say *all* students, we truly mean *all*! students will achieve at levels higher than ever before. Essential questions: • What might be some ways general and special educators can work collaboratively to create conditions for all students to be successful?

(Continued)

(Continued)

Corwin Cultural Proficiency Books	Authors	Focus and Essential Questions
		• In what ways does this book address issues of equity and access for all students? • How do the four Tools of Cultural Proficiency inform the work of Inclusive Schooling? What's here for you? • In what ways does the Action Plan template offer opportunities for you and your colleagues? • For what are you waiting to help narrow and close equity gaps in your classroom and schools? • How do I foster challenging conversations about Inclusive Education with colleagues? • How do extend my own learning about ways in which to facilitate inclusive learning environments?
Corwin Inclusive Schooling Books and Resources	**Authors**	**Focus and Essential Questions**
Differentiating Instruction: Planning for Universal Design and Teaching for College and Career Readiness, 2nd ed., 2015	Jacqueline S. Thousand Richard A. Villa Ann I. Nevin	This book guides the reader to use two approaches—retrofit and Universal Design for Learning (UDL)—for differentiating instruction. The book provides sample differentiated lessons designed by elementary, middle, and high school co-teaching partners, who we follow as they merge their knowledge and skills and use evidence-based instructional strategies and technology to plan lessons that address College and Career Readiness standards. • In what ways do I use this book to deepen my understanding and use of the retrofit and UDL approaches for differentiating the content, product, and process of instruction to provide students access to the curriculum? • In what ways do I use the tools in this book to foster equity and Inclusive Education for all students? • In what ways do I use this book to deepen my learning about College and Career Readiness standards and how instruction can be adapted to allow any student to demonstrate these standards? • How do I foster challenging conversations with colleagues about differentiation instruction to provide access to general education to students with IEPs, English learners, and other students who would benefit from professional collaboration?

Corwin Cultural Proficiency Books	Authors	Focus and Essential Questions
A Guide to Co-Teaching: New Lessons and Strategies to Facilitate Student Learning, 3rd ed., 2013	Richard A. Villa Jacqueline S. Thousand Ann I. Nevin	This book guides the reader to learn about the four approaches to co-teaching; the origins and support for co-teaching; administrative actions that support co-teaching; and tools for establishing trust, improving communication, and planning. • In what ways do I use this book to deepen my learning about co-teaching as a structure for delivering inclusive special education services? • In what ways do I use this book with colleagues to deepen our work on equity and Inclusive Education? • How can I and we use the Action Planning template (Resource K) and the other tools to guide our school planning for collaborative planning and teaching for equity? • How do I foster challenging conversations about co-teaching with colleagues to ensure students with IEPs, English learners, and other students who would benefit from collaboration have access to the general education curriculum? • How can I and we use the Action Planning template (Resource K) and the other tools to guide our school planning for collaborative planning and teaching for equity?
PD Resource Center https://us.corwin.com/en-us/nam/a-guide-to-co-teaching-pd-resource-center This resource center supports the book, *A Guide to Co-Teaching: New Lessons and Strategies to Facilitate Student Learning,* 3rd ed., 2013	Richard A. Villa Jacqueline S. Thousand	Designed to support ***A Guide to Co-Teaching***, third edition, this center provides all the materials needed to lead professional learning to help teachers effectively collaborate and co-teach. The resource provides teachers with video examples, study guides, reflective questions, and practical application activities. It enables facilitators to lead professional learning on best practices in and organization support for co-teaching. • In what ways could this professional learning resource center support our school and district's professional learning about collaborative thinking, planning, and teaching? • How might I use this resource center to engage others in learning conversations about how better to support all students' learning and all educators' educating through collaborative and co-teaching arrangements? • How do I extend my own learning by using this resource center site to polish my own co-teaching understandings and skills?

(Continued)

(Continued)

Corwin Cultural Proficiency Books	Authors	Focus and Essential Questions
Collaborating With Students in Instruction and Decision Making: The Untapped Resource, 2010	Richard A. Villa Jacqueline S. Thousand Ann I. Nevin	This book guides the reader to learn how to effectively use the one resource schools will never take away from a teacher—the students themselves. Readers learn how to harness student creativity as decision makers, advocates, and instructors through cooperative learning, peer tutoring, co-teaching, peer mediation, and other methods of self-determination. • What are the "assets" that students bring to school that we have not yet tapped? • In addition to what is presented in this book, what are ways to tap into these assets? • What are my and my school's assumptions about students with disabilities and other learning differences that might lower expectations or disenfranchise students? • How do I foster challenging conversations with colleagues about how to turn instruction, advocacy, and decision making over to students using the concepts and methods describe in this book? • How do I extend my own learning about student self-determination and empowerment?
A Guide to Co-Teaching with Paraeducators: Practical Tips for K–12 Educators, 2009	Ann I. Nevin Jacqueline S. Thousand Richard A. Villa	This book focuses the reader's attention on the expanding role of paraeducators and provides practical guidelines for collaborating with paraeducators to give students with and without special education needs access to highly qualified instructors in the general education classroom and individualized attention that promotes learning for all students. • What is the "new role" for paraeducators? • How does this "new role" differ from existing views of paraeducators? • What is the role of special and general educators and site administrators in this new role of paraeducators? • In what ways might paraeducators contribute to achievement-related conversations with "professional" educators? • How do I foster challenging conversations about changing roles and responsibilities of paraeducators with colleagues?

Additional Inclusive Schooling Resources	Authors	Focus and Essential Questions
Leading an Inclusive School: Access and Success for All, 2017 Publisher: Association for Supervision and Curriculum Development, Alexandria, VA	Richard A. Villa Jacqueline S. Thousand	This book uses a *Schoolhouse Model* conceptual framework to explain how Multi-Tiered System of Supports, co-teaching, and differentiated instruction work together and build upon administrative leadership and creative and collaborative problem-solving processes to ensure access and success in general education for all students. • Why is leading Inclusive Schooling an important topic for teachers, administrators, students and their parents, and community members to examine? • What are the leadership characteristics and behaviors needed for leading systems change to Inclusive Education? • How might I use this book to engage others in my school and district in learning conversations to emulate the practices describe on each floor of the *Schoolhouse Model* to support all students learning and all educators educating all students? • How do I foster challenging conversations with colleagues about each floor of the *Schoolhouse Model* for Inclusive Schooling? • How do I extend my own learning about how to lead change toward Inclusive Schooling?
The Inclusive Education Checklist: A Self-Assessment of Best Practices, 2016 Publisher: National Professional Resources, Naples, FL	Richard A. Villa Jacqueline S. Thousand	This checklist assessment resource describes and provides best practice indicators for fifteen inclusive education best practices essential to quality Inclusive Education. The *Inclusive Education Checklist* is designed to assist schools, districts, administrators, policy makers, community members, and professionals interested in education as well as parents and youth to assess, develop, and implement inclusive services for student with disabilities. For each of the fifteen best practices, assessment results suggest where a school is performing (i.e., from "needs to start" and "needs considerable improvement" to "on our way" and "doing well") in its progress toward inclusive education excellence. These data can then be used to plan for continuous program improvement.

(Continued)

(Continued)

Additional Inclusive Schooling Resources	Authors	Focus and Essential Questions
		• How do I extend my own learning about best practices in Inclusive Education by reading about and honestly assessing my school and my district on the best practice indicators? • How might I engage our school or district to use this checklist to assess and engage in learning conversations about how well we are doing supporting all students' learning? • How might I engage my school and district colleagues to analyze the data generated from the checklist assessments to develop an action plan for initiating actions to improve our commitment and performance on one or more of the fifteen best practices included in this checklist assessment?
RTI: Co-Teaching and Differentiated Instruction—The Schoolhouse Model, 2011 Publisher: National Professional Resources, Port Chester, NY	Richard A. Villa Jacqueline S. Thousand	This laminated trifold provides the reader and educators involved in pre-service and in-service professional learning a quick and easy reference guide to the *Schoolhouse Model* conceptual framework described in more detail in the 2017 *Leading the Inclusive School: Access and Success for All* text. • How might I use and share this trifold to help others in my school and district understand and engage in learning conversations about the dimension of change on each floor of the Schoolhouse Model to support all students learning and all educators educating all students? • How do I foster challenging conversations with colleagues about each floor of the Schoolhouse Model for Inclusive Schooling? • How do I extend my own learning about each of the floors and dimensions of the Schoolhouse Model to prepare me to engage in and support school and district efforts to forward Inclusive Education?

References

ADA National Network. (2015). *Guidelines for writing about people with disabilities.* Retrieved from https://adata.org/factsheet/ADANN-writing

Adams, James. (2001). *Conceptual blockbusting: A guide to better ideas* (4th ed.). New York, NY: Basic Books.

Agran, Martin, & Hughes, Carolyn. (2008). Asking student input: Students' opinions regarding their individualized education program involvement. *Career Development for Exceptional Individuals, 31*(2), 69–76. doi: 10.1177/0885728808317657

Armstrong, Thomas. (1987). *In their own way.* Los Angeles, CA: Tarcher.

Armstrong, Thomas, (2009). *Multiple Intelligences in the classroom* (3rd ed.). Alexandria, VA: Association for Supervision and Curriculum Development.

Arndt, Sandra, Konrad, Moira, & Test, David W. (2006). Effects of the self-directed IEP on student participation in planning meetings. *Remedial & Special Education, 27*(4), 194–207. doi: 10.1177/07419325060270040101

Avelar La Salle, Robin, & Johnson, Ruth S. (2016). Peeling back the wallpaper. *Educational Leadership, 74*(3), 79–84.

Bacon, Jessica K. (2017). Navigating assessment: Understanding students through a disability studies lens. In Meghan Cosier & Christine Ashby (Eds.), *Enacting change from within: Disability studies meets teaching and teacher education* (pp. 39–59). New York: Peter Lang.

Baker, Edward T., Wang, Margaret C., & Wahlberg, & Herbert J. (1994). The effects of inclusion on learning. *Educational Leadership, 52*(4), 33–35.

Bambara, L. M., Koger, F., Burns, R., & Singley, D. (2016). Building skills for home and community. In F. Brown, J. M. McDonnell, & M. E. Snell (Eds.). *Educating students with severe disabilities* (8th ed., pp. 438–473. Boston: Pearson.

Barrie, Wendy, & McDonald, John. (2002). Administrative support for student-led individualized education programs. *Remedial and Special Education, 23*(2), 116–121.

Barton, Diane. (2003). *Helping students develop their IEPs: Making it accessible to every student.* Unpublished master's thesis, California State University San Marcos, San Marcos.

Benjamin, Steve. (1989). An ideascape for education: What futurists recommend. *Educational Leadership, 7*(1), 8–14.

Biklen, Doug, & Burke, Jamie. (2006) Presuming competence. *Equity and Excellence in Education, 39,* 166–176.

Blackorby, Jose, Wagner, Mary, Camero, Renée, Davies, Elizabeth, Levine, Phyllus, Newman, Lynn, Marder, Camille, & Sumi, Carl. (with Chorost, Michael, Garza, Nicolle, & Guzman, Anne-Marie). (2005). *Engagement, academics, social adjustments, and independence.* Palo Alto, CA: Stanford Research Institute. Retrieved from www.seels.net/designdocs/engagement/All_SEELS_out comes_10-04-05.pdf

Bland, Lauren E., & Prelock, Patricia A. (1995). Effects of collaboration on language performance. *Communication Disorders Quarterly, 17*(2), 31–37.

Brendtro, Larry K., Brokenleg, Martin, & Van Bockern, Steven. (1990). *Reclaiming youth at risk: Our hope for the future.* Bloomington, IN: National Education Services.

Brown, Patricia, & Dean, Erica. (2009, July). *Listen to the voice of students: Student-led IEPs and self-advocacy.* Paper presented at the 11th Annual San Diego Summer Leadership Institute, San Diego, CA.

Buscaglia, Leo. (n.d.). AZQuotes.com. Retrieved from www.azquotes.com/quote/565197

California Services for Technical Assistance and Training. (2015). A multitiered system of supports with response to intervention and universal design for learning: Putting it all together (Special insert). *The Special EDge, 28*(2), 1–4.

CampbellJones, Franklin, CampbellJones, Brenda, & Lindsey, Randall B. (2010). *The culturally proficient journey: Moving beyond ethical barriers toward profound change.* Thousand Oaks, CA: Corwin.

Chartock, Roselle, K. (2010). *Strategies and lessons for culturally responsive teaching.* Boston, MA: Allyn & Bacon.

Conzemius, Anne, & O'Neill, Jan. (2001). *Building shared responsibility for student learning.* Alexandria, VA: Association for Supervision and Curriculum Development.

Cosier, Meghan, & Ashby, Christine. (2016). Disability studies and the "work" of educators. In Meghan Cosier & Christine Ashby (Eds.), *Enacting change from within: Disability studies meets teaching and teacher education* (pp. 1–19). New York: Peter Lang.

Cross, Terry, L., Bazron, Barbara J., Dennis, Karl, . . . Isaacs, Mareasa R. (March, 1989). *Toward a culturally competent system of care: A monograph on effective services for minority children who are severely emotionally disturbed.* Washington, DC: Georgetown, University Child Development Program, Child and Adolescent Service System Program (CASSP) Technical Assistance Center.

Curwin, Richard L., Mendler, Allen N., & Mendler, Brian D. (2008). *Discipline with dignity: New challenges, new solutions* (3rd ed.). Alexandria, VA: Association for Supervision and Curriculum Development.

Davidson, Neal. (2002). Cooperative and collaborative learning: An integrative perspective. In Jacqueline S. Thousand, Richard A. Villa, & Ann I. Nevin (Eds.), *Creativity and collaborative learning: The practical guide to empowering students, teachers, and families* (2nd ed., pp. 181–195). Baltimore, MD: Paul H. Brookes.

Deal, Terrence E. (1987). The culture of schools. In Linda T. Shieve & Mariam B. Schoenheit (Eds.), *Leadership: Examining the elusive* (pp. 3–15). Alexandria, VA: Association for Supervision and Curriculum Development.

Deal, Terrence, & Kennedy, Allen A. (1982). *Corporate cultures: The rites and rituals of corporate life*. Reading, MA: Addison Wesley.

Deal, Terrence E., & Peterson, Kent D. (1990). *The principal's role in shaping school culture*. Washington, DC: U.S. Government Printing Office.

de Bono, Edward. (1985). *Six thinking hats*. Boston, MA: Little, Brown.

de Bono, Edward. (1992). *Serious creativity: Using the power of lateral thinking to create new ideas*. New York, NY: Harper Business.

Dilts, Robert B. (1996). *Visionary leadership skills: Creating a world in which people want to belong*. Capitola, CA: Meta Publications.

Dilts, Robert B. (2014). *A brief history of logical levels*. Retrieved from http://www.nlpu.com/Articles/LevelsSummary.htm

Donnellan, Anne M., & Leary, Martha R. (1984). *Movement differences and autism/mental retardation*. Madison, WI: DRI Press.

Donovan, M. Suzanne, & Bransford, John. D. (Eds.). (2005). *How students learn: History, mathematics, and science in the classroom*. Committee on How People Learn: A Targeted Report for Teachers. Division on Behavioral and Social Sciences and Education. Washington, DC: National Academies.

Dunn, Rita, & Dunn, Kenneth. (1987). Dispelling outmoded beliefs about student learning. *Educational Leadership, 44*(6), 55–61.

Easton, Lois B. (2008). From professional development to professional learning. *Phi Delta Kappa, 89*, 755–759.

Echevarria, Jana, Frey, Nancy, & Fisher, Doug. (2016). *How to reach the hard to teach: Excellent instruction for those who need it most*. Alexandria, VA: Association for Supervision and Curriculum Development.

Elementary and Middle School Technical Assistance Center. (n.d.). *Disproportionality: The disproportionate representation of racial and ethnical minorities in special education*. Retrieved at http://www.emstac.org/registered/topics/disproportionality/faqs.htm

Falvey, Mary, Blair, Mary, Dingle, Mary P., & Franklin, Nancy. (2000). Creating a community of learners with varied needs. In Richard A. Villa & Jacqueline S. Thousand (Eds.), *Restructuring for caring and effective education: An administrative guide to creating heterogeneous schools* (2nd ed., pp. 186–207). Baltimore, MD: Paul H. Brookes.

Falvey, Mary A., Forest, Marsha S., Pearpoint, Jack, & Rosenberg, Richard L. (2002). Building connections. In Jacqueline S. Thousand, Richard A. Villa & Ann I. Nevin (Eds.), *Creativity and collaborative learning: The practical guide to empowering students, teachers, and families* (2nd ed., pp. 29–54). Baltimore, MD: Paul H. Brookes.

Falvey, Mary A., Givner, Christine C., Villa, Richard A., & Thousand, Jacqueline, S. (2017). In Richard A. Villa & Jacqueline S. Thousand (Eds.), *Leading the inclusive school* (pp. 7–16). Alexandria, VA: Association for Supervision and Curriculum Development.

Farber, Judith G., & Klein, Evelyn R. (1999). Classroom-based assessment of collaborative intervention program with Kindergarten and first-grade students. *Language, Speech and Hearing Services in the Schools, 30*, 89–91.

Field, Sharon, Martin, Jim, Miller, Robert, Ward, Michael, & Wehmeyer, Michael. (1998). *A practical guide for teaching self-determination*. Reston, VA: Council for Exceptional Children.

Fisher, Douglas, Frey, Nancy, & Hattie, John (2016). *Visible learning for literacy: Implementing the practices that work best to accelerate student learning*. Thousand Oaks, CA: Corwin.

Fisher, Douglas, Frey, Nancy, & Pumpian, Ian. (2012). *How to create a culture of achievement in your school and classroom*. Alexandria, VA: Association of Supervision and Curriculum Development.

Fox, Timothy. (1995). *Student-centered education: Creating a collaborative school climate through Personal Learning Plans*. Progress report prepared for the Vermont Statewide Systems Change Project. Burlington, VT: University of Vermont.

Frattura, Elise M., & Capper, Colleen. A. (2007). *Leading for social justice: Transforming schools for all learners*. Thousand Oaks, CA: Corwin.

Freire, Paolo (1970). *Pedagogy of the oppressed*. New York: Continuum.

Fullan, Michael. (2001). *Leading in a culture of change*. New York: Wiley.

Fullan, Michael. (2008). *The six secrets of change: What the best leaders do to help their organizations survive and thrive*. San Francisco, CA: Jossey-Bass.

Fullan, Michael G., & Stiegelbauer, Suzanne. (1991). *The new meaning of educational change* (2nd ed.). San Francisco, CA: Jossey-Bass.

Gallagher, Beth, & Hinkleman, Kirk. (2012). *Intentional teaming: Shifting organizational culture*. Toronto, Ontario, Canada: Inclusion Press.

Gardner, Howard. (1983). *Frames of mind: The theory of Multiple Intelligences*. New York: Basic Books.

Gardner, Howard. (2011). *Frames of mind: The theory of Multiple Intelligences* (3rd ed.). New York: Basic Books.

Garmston, Robert J., & Wellman, Bruce M. (1999). *The adaptive school: A sourcebook for developing collaborative groups*. Norwood, MA: Christopher-Gordon.

Giangreco, Michael F., Cloninger, Chigee J., Dennis, Ruth E., & Edelman, Susan W. (2002). Problem-solving methods to facilitate inclusive education. In Jacqueline S. Thousand, Richard A. Villa, & Ann I. Nevin (Eds.), *Creativity and collaborative learning: The practical guide to empowering students, teachers, and families* (2nd ed., pp. 111–135). Baltimore, MD: Paul H. Brookes.

Glasser, William. (1986). *Control theory in the classroom*. New York, NY: HarperCollins.

Glasser, William. (1990). *The quality school: Managing students without coercion*. New York, NY: HarperCollins.

Gleason, Sonia Caus, & Gerzon, Nancy. (2013). *Growing into equity: Professional learning and personalization of high-achieving schools*. Thousand Oaks: CA: Corwin.

Goleman, Daniel, Kaufman, Paul, & Ray, Michael. (1993). *The creative spirit: Tie-in (PBS)*. New York: PLUME.

Gonzalez, Norma, Moll, Luis, & Amanti, Cathy. (2005). *Funds of knowledge: Theorizing practices in households, communities, and classrooms*. Mahwah, NJ: Lawrence Erlbaum.

Green, Maxine. (1985). The role of education in democracy, *Educational Horizons, 63*(Special Issue), 3–9.

Gregory, Gayle H., & Chapman, Carolyn. (2013). *Differentiated instructional strategies: One size does not fit all* (3rd ed.). Thousand Oaks, CA: Corwin.

Haager, Diane, Dimino, Joseph A., & Pearlman Windmueller, Michelle. (2014). *Interventions for reading success* (2nd ed.). Baltimore, MD: Paul H. Brookes.

Hall, Tracey, Strangman, Nicole, & Meyer, Anne. (2011, Winter) *Differentiated instruction and implications for UDL implementation*. Wakefield, MA: National Center on Accessing the General Curriculum.

Hammer, Michelle R. (2004). Using the self-advocacy strategy to increase student participation in IEP conferences. *Intervention in School and Clinic, 39*(5), 295–300.

Hapner, Athena, & Imel, Breck. (2002). The students' voices: "Teachers started to listen and show respect." *Remedial and Special Education, 23*(2), 116–121.

Harry, Beth. (2003). Trends and issues in serving culturally diverse families of children with disabilities. *Journal of Special Education, 36*, 131–138.

Hattie, John. (2009). *Visible learning: A synthesis of over 800 meta-analyses relating to achievement*. New York, NY: Routledge.

Hazel, J. Stephen, Schumaker, Jean Bragg, Sherman, James A., & Sheldon, Jan. (1995). *ASSET: A social skills program for adolescents*. Champaign, IL: Research Press.

Hehir, Thomas. (2005). Eliminating ableism in education. *Harvard Educational Review, 72*(1), 1–33.

Hesselbein, Francis, Goldsmith, Marshall, & Beckhard, Richard. (1997). *The leader of the future: New visions, strategies and practices for the new era*. New York, NY: The Drucker Foundation.

Higgins Averill, Oral, & Rinaldi, Claudia. (2011, May). *Research brief: Multi-tier system of supports (MTSS)*. Waltham, MA: Urban Special Education Leadership Collaborative. Retrieved from www.urbancollaborative.org/research-briefs

Howard, William L., Alber-Morgan, Sheila R., & Konrad, Moira. (2017). *Exceptional children: An introduction to special education* (11th ed.). Boston, MA: Pearson Education.

Individuals with Disabilities Education Improvement Act. (IDEIA) of 2004, PL 108-446, U.S.C. § 1400 *et seq.*

Jefferson, Thomas. (1776, July 4). *Charters of freedom*. Retrieved from http://www.archives.gov/exhibits/charters/declaration_transcript.html

Johnson, David W., & Johnson, Roger T. (1989). *Cooperation and competition: Theory and research*. Edina, MN: Interaction Book Company.

Johnson, David W., & Johnson, Roger T. (1991). *Teaching children to be peacemakers*. Edina, MN: Interaction Book Company.

Johnson, David W., & Johnson, Roger T. (1996a). Conflict resolution and peer mediation programs in elementary and secondary schools: A review of the research. *Review of Educational Research, 66*(4), 459–506.

Johnson, David W., & Johnson, Roger T. (1996b). Cooperative learning and traditional American values. *NASSP Bulletin, 80*(579), 11–18.

Johnson, David W., & Johnson, Roger T. (1999). *Learning together and alone: Cooperative, competitive, and individualistic learning* (5th ed.). Needham Heights, MA: Allyn & Bacon.

Johnson, David W., & Johnson, Roger T. (2002). Ensuring diversity is positive: Cooperative community, constructive conflict, and civic values. In Jacqueline

S. Thousand, Richard A. Villa & Ann I. Nevin (Eds.), *Creativity and collaborative learning: The practical guide to empowering students, teachers, and families* (2nd ed., pp. 197–208). Baltimore: Paul H. Brookes.

Johnson, David W., & Johnson, Roger T. (2009). An educational psychology success story: Social interdependence theory and cooperative learning. *Educational Researcher, 38*(5), 365–379.

Johnson, David W., Johnson, Roger T., & Smith, Karl A. (1998). Maximizing instruction through cooperative learning. *PRiSM: Journal of the American Society for Engineering Education, 7*(6), 24–29.

Jones, Stephani M., Bailey, Rebecca, Brion-Meisels, Gretchen, & Partee, Ann. (2016). Choosing to be positive. *Educational Leadership, 74*(1), 63–68.

Jorgensen, Cheryl. (2005). The least dangerous assumption: A challenge to create a new paradigm. *Disability Solutions, 6*(3), 1 & 5–8.

Kagan, Spencer, Kyle, Patricia, & Scott, Sally. (2004). *Win-win discipline: Strategies for all discipline problems.* San Clemente, CA: Kagan.

Kalambouka, Afroditi, Farrell, Peter, Dyson, Alan, & Kaplan, Ian. (2007). The impact of placing pupils with special education needs in mainstream schools on the achievement of their peers. *Educational Research, 49*(4), 365–382.

Kalyanpur, Maya, & Harry, Beth. (2012). *Cultural reciprocity in special education: Building family-professional relationships.* Baltimore, MD: Paul H. Brookes.

Kelly, Dottie. (1992). Introduction. In Thomas Neary, Ann Halvorsen, Robi Kronberg, & Dottie Kelly (Eds.), *Curricular adaptations for inclusive classrooms* (pp. 1–6). San Francisco: California Research Institute for the Integration of Students with Severe Disabilities, San Francisco State University.

King, Martin Luther. (n.d.). Retrieved from http://www.secretan.com/books-dvds/quotes-from-one/

Konrad, Moira, & Test, David. (2004). Teaching middle-school students with disabilities to use an IEP template. *Career Development for Exceptional Individuals, 27*(1), 101–124.

Kunc, Norman. (2000). Rediscovering the right to belong. In Richard A. Villa & Jacqueline S. Thousand (Eds.), *Restructuring for caring and effective education: Piecing the puzzle together* (2nd ed., pp. 77–92). Baltimore, MD: Paul H. Brookes.

Kunc, Norman, & Van der Klift, Emma. (1994). *Hell-bent on helping: Benevolence, friendship, and the politics of help.* Retrieved from http://www.broadreachtraining.com/articles/arhellbe.htm

Learning Forward. (2011). *Standards for professional learning.* Oxford, OH: Author. Retrieved from http://learningforward.org/standards-for-professional-learning

Lee, Harper. (1960). *To kill a mockingbird.* Philadelphia, PA: Lippincott.

Leff, Herbert L. (1984). *Playful perception: Choosing how to experience your world.* Burlington, VT: Waterfront Books.

Lindsey, Randall (Ed.). (2012). *The best of Corwin: Equity.* Thousand Oaks, CA: Corwin.

Lindsey, Delores B., Jungwirth, Linda D., Pahl, Jarvis V. N. C, & Lindsey, Randall B. (2009). *Culturally proficient learning communities: Confronting inequities through collaborative curiosity.* Thousand Oaks, CA: Corwin.

Lindsey, Delores B., Martinez, Richard S., & Lindsey, Randall B. (2007). *Culturally proficient coaching: Supporting educators to create equitable schools.* Thousand Oaks, CA: Corwin.

Lindsey, Delores B., Kearney, Karen M., Estrada, Delia, Terrell, Raymond, D., & Lindsey, Randall B. (2015). *A culturally proficient response to the common core: Ensuring equity through professional learning.* Thousand Oaks, CA: Corwin.

Lindsey, Delores B., Diaz, Richard, Nuri-Robins, Kikanza, & Lindsey, Randall B. (2010). Focus on assets, Overcome barriers. *Leadership, 39*(5), 12–15.

Lindsey, Randall B., Graham, Stephanie M., Westphal, R. Chris, Jr., & Jew, Cynthia L. (2008). *Culturally proficient inquiry: A lens for identifying and examining educational gaps.* Thousand Oaks, CA: Corwin.

Lindsey, Randall B., Karns, Michelle S., & Myatt, Keith. (2010). *Culturally proficient education: An assets-based response to conditions of poverty.* Thousand Oaks, CA: Corwin.

Lindsey, Randall B., Nuri-Robins, Kikanza, & Terrell, Raymond D. (2009). *Cultural proficiency: A manual for school leaders* (3rd ed.). Thousand Oaks, CA: Corwin.

Lindsey, Randall B., Roberts, Laraine M., & CampbellJones, Franklin. (2013). *The culturally proficient school: An implementation guide for school leaders* (2nd ed.). Thousand Oaks, CA: Corwin.

Linn, Diana, & Hemmer, Lynn (2011). English language learner disproportionality in special education: Implications for the scholar-practitioner. *Journal of Educational Research and Practice, 1*(1), 70–80.

Linton, Simi. (1998). *Claiming disability: Knowledge and identity.* New York: New York University Press.

Lipsky, Dorothy K., & Gartner, Alan (1989). *Beyond separate education: Quality education for all.* Baltimore, MD: Paul H. Brookes.

Lo, Lusa. (2012). Demystifying the IEP process for diverse parents of children with disabilities. *Teaching Exceptional Children, 44*(3), 14–20.

Lovitt, Thomas. (1991). *Preventing school dropout: Tactics for at-risk, remedial, and mildly handicapped adolescents.* Austin, TX: Pro-Ed.

Marzano, Robert J., Pickering, Debra J., & Pollack, Jane E. (2001). *Classroom instruction that works: Research-based strategies for increasing student achievement.* Alexandria, VA: Association for Supervision and Curriculum Development.

Mason, Christine Y., McGahee-Kovac, Marcy, & Johnson, Lora. (2004). How to help students lead their IEP meetings. *TEACHING Exceptional Children, 36*(3), 18–25.

McGahee-Kovac, Marcy. (2002). *A student's guide to the IEP.* Washington, DC: The National Information Center for Children and Youth with Disabilities. Retrieved from www.autismspeaks.org/docs/family_services_docs/Students Guide.pdf

McLaughlin, Margaret W. (1991). The Rand change agent study: 10 years later. In A. R. Odden (Ed.), *Education policy implementation* (pp. 143–156). Albany: State University of New York Press.

Mount, Beth. (1995). *Capacity works.* New York, NY: Graphic Futures.

Murray, Frank B. (2002). Why understanding the theoretical basis of cooperative learning enhances teaching success. In Jacqueline S. Thousand, Richard A. Villa, & Ann I. Nevin (Eds.), *Creativity and collaborative learning: The practical guide to empowering students, teachers, and families* (2nd ed., pp. 175–180). Baltimore: Paul H. Brookes.

Nagel, Greta. (1994). *The Tao of teaching: The special meaning of the Tao Te Ching as related to the art and pleasures of teaching.* New York, NY: Donald I. Fine.

National Alternate Assessment Center. (2006). *Designing from the ground floor: Alternate assessment on alternate standards. Part three: Theory of learning—What students with the most significant cognitive disabilities should know and be able to do . . .* (A publication of the U.S. Office of Special Education and Rehabilitative Services.) Retrieved from www.osepideasthatwork.org/toolkit/ground_floor_part_1e.asp

National Center for Educational Restructuring and Inclusion. (1995). *National study on inclusive education.* New York: City University of New York.

Nevin, Ann I., Harris, Kathy, & Correa, Viviene. (2001). Collaborative consultation, school reform, and diversity among regular and special educators. In Cheryl A. Utley & Festus E. Obviator (Eds.), *Special education, multicultural education, and school reform: Components of a quality education for students with mild disabilities* (pp. 173–187). Springfield, IL: Charles C Thomas.

Nevin, Ann I., Thousand, Jacqueline S., & Villa, Richard A. (2009). *A guide to co-teaching with paraeducators: Practical tips for K–12 educators.* Thousand Oaks, CA: Corwin.

Nieto, Sandra. (2010*). Language, culture, and teaching: Critical perspectives* (2nd ed.). New York, NY: Routledge.

Nieto, Sandra, & Bode, Patty. (2012). *Affirming diversity: The sociopolitical context of multicultural education* (6th ed.). Boston, MA: Pearson Education.

Noddings, Nel. (1992). *The challenge to care in school.* New York, NY: Teachers College Press.

Nuri-Robins, Kikanza J., & Bundy, Lewis (2016). *Fish out of water: Mentoring, managing, and self-monitoring people who don't fit in.* Thousand Oaks, CA: Corwin.

Nuri-Robins, Kikanza, Lindsey, Randall B., Lindsey, Delores B., & Terrell, Raymond D. (2012). *Culturally proficient instruction: A guide for people who teach* (3rd ed.). Thousand Oaks, CA: Corwin.

O'Brien, John, & Mount, Beth. (2005). *Make a difference: Guidebook for person-centered direct support.* Toronto, Ontario, Canada: Inclusion Press.

Office of Special Education and Rehabilitative Services. (2016). *38th annual report to Congress on the implementation of the Individuals with Disabilities Education Act.* Alexandria, VA: ED PUBS, Education Publications Center, U.S. Department of Education. Retrieved from http://www.ed.gov/about/reports/annual/osep

O'Neill, Robert E., & Jameson, Matt J. (2016). Designing and implementing individualized positive behavior support. In Fredda Brown, James McDonnell, & Martha E. Snell (Eds.), *Instruction of students with severe disabilities* (8th ed., 228–263). Boston, MA: Pearson.

Orsati, Fernanda. (2016). Humanistic practices to understand and support students' behaviors: A disability studies in education framework. In Meghan Cosier & Christine Ashby (Eds.), *Enacting change from within: Disability studies meets teaching and teacher education* (pp. 1–19). New York: Peter Lang.

Osborn, Alex F. (1993). *Applied imagination: Principles and procedures of creative problem-solving* (3rd ed.). Amherst, MA: Creative Education Foundation Press. (First edition published 1953)

Palincsar, A. S., & Brown, A. L. (1988). Teaching and practicing thinking skills to promote comprehension in the context of group problem solving. *Remedial and Special Education, 9*(1), 53–59.

Parnes, Sidney J. (1992). *Source book for creative problem-solving: A fifty year digest of proven innovation processes.* Amherst, MA: Creative Education Foundation Press.

Penny, Louise. (2005). *Still life.* New York, NY: St. Martin's Press.

Perie, Marianne, Moran, Rebecca, & Lutkus, Anthony D. (2005). *NAEP 2004 trends in academic progress: Three decades of performance in reading and mathematics (NCES 2005-464).* U.S. Department of Education, Institute of Education Sciences, National Center for Education Statistics. Washington, DC: U.S. Government Printing Office.

Piowlski, R. (2013). *Culturally proficient teachers.* (Doctoral dissertation). Retrieved from ETD collection for University of Nebraska, Lincoln. (Accession No. AAI3558753) Retrieved from http://digitalcommons.unl.edu/dissertations/

Piowlski, Lori R., & Kamphoff, Dan L. (2017). Building a sustainable university-school partnership on mutual assets. *School-University Partnerships: The Journal of the National Association for Professional Development Schools Journal, 12*(2).

Quezada, Reyes L., Lindsey, Delores B., & Lindsey, Randall B. (2012). *Culturally proficient practice: Supporting educators of English learning students.* Thousand Oaks, CA: Corwin.

Research and Training Center on Independent Living. (2013). *Guidelines: How to write and report about people with disabilities* (8th ed.). Lawrence: University of Kansas. Retrieved from www.rtcil.org/products/media/guidelines

Rios-Aguilar, Cecillia. (2010). Measuring funds of knowledge: Contributions to Latino/a students' academic and nonacademic outcomes. *Teachers College Record, 112*(8), 2209–2257.

Santana, Luz, Rothstein, Dan, & Bain, Agnes. (2016). *Partnering with parents to ask the right questions: A powerful strategy for strengthening school-family partnerships.* Alexandria, VA: Association for Supervision and Curriculum Development.

Sarason, Seymore B., Levine, Murray, Godenberg, I. Ira, Cherlin, Dennis L., & Bennet, Edward M. (1966). *Psychology in community settings: Clinical, educational, vocational and social aspects.* New York, NY: John Wiley & Sons.

Schein, Edgar. (1989). *Organizational culture and leadership: A dynamic view.* San Francisco, CA: Jossey-Bass.

Schrumpf, Fred. (1994). The role of students in resolving conflicts in schools. In Thousand, Jacqueline S., Villa, Richard A., & Nevin, Ann I. (Eds.), *Creativity and collaborative learning: A practical guide to empowering students and teachers* (pp. 275–291). Baltimore, MD: Paul H. Brookes.

Schumaker, Heather. (2006). *The student-led Individual Education Program (IEP) process: An approach to increasing confidence and self-advocacy in 8th grade students with special learning needs.* Unpublished master's thesis, California State University San Marcos, San Marcos.

Senge, Peter. (1990). www.wisdomquotes.com/quote/peter-senge-2.html

Senge, Peter M., Hamilton, Hal, & Kania, John. (2015, Winter). The dawn of system leadership. *Stanford Social Innovation Review, 27–33.*

Sennett, Frank. (2004). *400 quotable quotes from the world's leading educators.* Thousand Oaks, CA: Corwin.

Smith, Laura, Foley, Pamela, F., & Chaney, Michael P. (2008). Addressing classism, ableism, and heterosexism in counselor education. *Journal of Counseling and Development, 86,* 303–309.

Sparks, Sara D. (2016, September 27). How to find evidence-based fixes for schools that fall behind. *Education Week.* Retrieved from http://www.edweek.org/ew/articles/2016/09/28/how-to-find-evidence-based-fixes-for-schools.html

Straub, Debbie, & Peck, Charles A. (1994). What are the outcomes for nondisabled students? *Educational Leadership, 52*(4), 36–40.

Stephens, Diana L., & Lindsey, Randall B. (2011). *Culturally proficient collaboration: Use and misuse of school counselors.* Thousand Oaks, CA: Corwin.

Sullivan, Amanda L. (2011). Disproportionality in special education identification and placement of English language learners. *Exceptional Children, (77)*3, 317–334.

Terrell, Raymond D., & Lindsey, Randall B. (2009). *Culturally proficient leadership: The personal journey begins within.* Thousand Oaks, CA: Corwin.

Test, David W., Browder, Diane M., Karvonen, Meagan, Wood, Wendy, & Algozzine, Bob. (2002). Writing lesson plans for promoting self-determination. *Teaching Exceptional Children, 35*(1), 8–14.

Throneburg, Rebecca, Calvert, Lynn K., Sturm, Jennifer J., Parambourkas, Alexis A., & Paul, Pamela J. (2000). A comparison of service delivery models: Effects on curricular vocabulary in the school setting. *Communication Disorders and Sciences, 9,* 10–20.

Thorpe, Scott. (2000). *How to think like Einstein: Simple ways to break the rules and discover your hidden genius.* New York, NY: Sourcebooks.

Thousand, Jacqueline S., Paolucci-Whitcomb, Phyllis, & Nevin, Ann I. (1996). A rationale for collaborative consultation. In Susan Stainback & William Stanback (Eds.), *Divergent perspectives in special education* (2nd ed., pp. 205–218). Boston, MA: Allyn & Bacon.

Thousand, Jacqueline S., Villa, Richard A., & Nevin, Ann I. (2015). *Differentiating instruction: Planning for universal design and teaching for college and career readiness* (2nd ed.). Thousand Oaks, CA: Corwin.

Tomlinson, Carol Ann. (1999). *The differentiated classroom: Responding to the needs of all learners.* Alexandria, VA: Association for Supervision and Curriculum Development.

Toomey, Fran. (1990) *Learning and individual differences: A cognitive-development model.* Unpublished manuscript, St. Michaels College, Department of Education, Winooski, VT.

Tough, Paul. (2013). *How children succeed: Grit, curiosity and the hidden power of character.* New York, NY: Mariner Books (A division of Houghton Mifflin Harcourt).

Treffinger, David J. (2000). *Practice problems for creative problem solving* (3rd ed.). Waco, TX: Prufrock Press.

Turnbull, Ann, Turnbull, Rutherford H., Erwin, Elizabeth J., Soodak, Leslie C., & Shogren, Karrie A. (2015). *Families, professionals, and exceptionality: Positive outcomes through partnerships and trust* (7th ed.). Boston, MA: Merrill/Prentice Hall.

United States Department of Education. (2014). *New accountability framework raises the bar for state special education programs.* U.S. Department of Education. Retrieved from www.ed.gov/news/press-releases/new-accountability-framework-raises-bar-state-special-education-programs

United States Department of Education. (2015). *37th annual report to Congress on the implementation of the Individuals with Disabilities Education Act.* Washington, DC: Author.

Universal Design for Learning. (2013). What it is, what it looks like, where to learn more. *The Special EDge, 26*(1), 2–3.

Van Bockern, Steven, Brokenleg, Martin, & Brendtro, Larry K. (2000). Reclaiming our youth. In Richard A. Villa & Jacqueline S. thousand (Eds.), *Restructuring for caring and effective education: Piecing the puzzle together* (2nd ed., pp. 56–76).

Van der Klift, Emma, & Kunc, Norman. (2002). Beyond benevolence: Supporting genuine friendship in inclusive schools. In Jacqueline S. Thousand & Richard A. Villa (Eds.), *Creativity and collaborative learning: The practical guide to empowering students, teachers, and families* (2nd ed., pp. 21–28). Baltimore, MD: Paul H. Brookes.

Villa, Richard A., & Thousand, Jacqueline S. (2000). *Restructuring for caring and effective education: Piecing the puzzle together* (2nd ed.). Baltimore, MD: Paul H. Brookes.

Villa, Richard A., & Thousand, Jacqueline S. (2005). *Creating an inclusive school* (2nd ed.). Alexandria, VA: Association for Supervision and Curriculum Development.

Villa, Richard A., & Thousand, Jacqueline S. (2011). *RTI: Co-teaching and differentiated instruction.* Port Chester, NY: National Professional Resources.

Villa, Richard A., & Thousand, Jacqueline S. (2016). *The inclusive education checklist: A self-assessment of best practices.* Naples, FL: National Professional Resources.

Villa, Richard, & Thousand, Jacqueline (2017). *Leading an inclusive school: Access and success for ALL students.* Alexandria, VA: Association for Supervision and Curriculum Development.

Villa, Richard A., Thousand, Jacqueline S., & Nevin, Ann I. (2010). *Collaborating with students in instruction and decision making: The untapped resource: A multimedia kit for professional development.* Thousand Oaks, CA: Corwin.

Villa, Richard A., Thousand, Jacqueline S., & Nevin, Ann I. (2013). *A guide to co-teaching: New lessons and strategies to facilitate student learning* (3rd ed.). Thousand Oaks, CA: Corwin.

Villa, Richard, Thousand, Jacqueline, Paolucci-Whitcomb, Phyllis, & Nevin, Ann (1990). In search of new paradigms for collaborative consultation. *Journal of Educational and Psychological Consultation, 1,* 279–292.

von Oech, Roger. (1986). *A kick in the seat of the pants: Using your explorer, artist, judge, and warrior to be more creative.* New York, NY: Harper & Row.

von Oech, Roger. (1998). *A whack on the side of the head: How you can be more creative.* New York, NY: Warner Books, Inc.

Wang, Margaret, McCart, Amy, & Turnbull, Ann. (2007). Implementing positive behavior support with Chinese American families: Enhancing cultural competence. *Journal of Positive Behavior Interventions, 9*(1), 28–51.

Webb, Noreen M. (1989). Peer interaction and learning in small groups. In Noreen M. Webb (Ed.). *Peer interaction, problem-solving and cognition: Multidisciplinary perspectives* (pp. 21–29). New York: Pergamon Press.

Webb-Johnson, Gwendolyn C. (2002). Strategies for creating multicultural and pluralistic societies: A mind is a wonderful thing to develop. In Jacqueline S. Thousand & Richard A. Villa (Eds.), *Creativity and collaborative learning: The practical guide to empowering students, teachers, and families* (2nd ed., pp. 55–70). Baltimore, MD: Paul H. Brookes.

Wenger, Etienne, McDermott, Richard, & Snyder, William. (2002). *Cultivating communities of practice: A guide to managing knowledge.* Boston, MA: Harvard Business School Press.

Wiggins, Grant. (1992). Foreword. In Richard A. Villa, Jacqueline S. Thousand, William Stainback, & Susan Stainback (Eds.), *Restructuring for a caring and effective education: An administrative guide to creating heterogeneous schools* (pp. xv–xvi). Baltimore, MD: Paul H. Brookes.

Wolter, Deborah. (2016). The opportunity gap in literacy. *Educational Leadership, 74*(3), 30–33.

Index

A SAGE Publishing Company

CORWIN HAS ONE MISSION: to enhance education through intentional professional learning.

We build long-term relationships with our authors, educators, clients, and associations who partner with us to develop and continuously improve the best evidence-based practices that establish and support lifelong learning.

Solutions you want. Experts you trust. Results you need.